Postcolonial
contraventions

MANCHESTER
UNIVERSITY PRESS

For my parents, Gale and Robert Chrisman

Postcolonial contraventions

Cultural readings of race, imperialism and transnationalism

LAURA CHRISMAN

Manchester University Press
Manchester and New York

distributed exclusively in the USA by Palgrave

Published by Manchester University Press
Oxford Road, Manchester M13 9NR, UK
and Room 400, 175 Fifth Avenue, New York, NY 10010, USA
www.manchesteruniversitypress.co.uk

Distributed exclusively in the USA by
Palgrave, 175 Fifth Avenue, New York,
NY 10010, USA

Distributed exclusively in Canada by
UBC Press, University of British Columbia, 2029 West Mall,
Vancouver, BC, Canada V6T 1Z2

British Library Cataloguing-in-Publication Data
A catalogue record for this book is available from the British Library

Library of Congress Cataloging-in-Publication Data applied for

ISBN   0 7190 5827 9   *hardback*
        0 7190 5828 7   *paperback*

First published 2003

11 10 09 08 07 06 05 04 03   10 9 8 7 6 5 4 3 2 1

Typeset by
D R Bungay Associates, Burghfield, Berks

Printed in Great Britain
by Bell & Bain Ltd, Glasgow

Contents

Acknowledgements

Editors Matthew Frost and Kate Fox, and copyeditor John Banks, have been a pleasure to work with. Erica Dillon, Sachi Miyazawa and Sherally Munshi kindly took time from their own studies to make possible the production of this book.

I am grateful to the organisers who gave me the opportunity to try out chapters: Emeka Aniagolu, Keith Ansell-Pearson, Maria Balshaw, Andrew Chitty, Brenda Cooper, Tony Crowley, Attie de Lange, Gail Fincham, Farah Jasmine Griffin, Ken Harrow, Salah Hassan, Larry Landrum, Karen Lazar, Neil Lazarus, Laurent Milesi, Ato Quayson, Judith Squires, Jane Starfield, Patrick Williams and Tukufu Zuberi. Their speaker invitations took me from East Lansing, Michigan, to Soweto, South Africa; my work gained immeasurably from these visits and the critical debate they fostered. Very helpful readings of individual chapters were given by Chris Abuk, Ray Black, Madhu Dubey, Uzo Esonwanne, Rochelle Kapp, Scott McCracken, Benita Parry, Lawrence Phillips, Kelwyn Sole, Jane Starfield, and the late Nick Visser. Without the generous research support of the Nuffield Foundation, the British Academy and the University of Sussex School of African and Asian Studies, this book could not have been begun.

I held a visiting professorship at Brown University during 1999–2000. This considerably assisted the book's development. For making it the best visiting professorship imaginable thanks to Mike Allan, Jim Campbell, Wendy Chun, Marie Clarke, Elliott Colla, Erica Dillon, Mary Ann Doane, Madhu Dubey, Jane Comaroff Gordon, Lewis Gordon, Yogita Goyal, Liza Hebert, Paget Henry, Yi Ping Ho, Jose Itzigsohn, Nancy Jakubowski, Tamar Katz, David Kazanjian, Daniel Kim, Susan McNeil, Sherally Munshi, Phil Rosen, Josie Saldana and Jennifer Walrad.

Ohio State University has given me considerable institutional support as an Associate Professor in the department of African American and African Stuides. Particular thanks to Dean Michael Hogan, Comparative Studies Chair David Horn, AAAS department Chairs Ted McDaniel and John Roberts, and Associate Dean Jackie Royster. For warm collegiality and stimulating exchange I am grateful to John Conteh-Morgan, Abiola Irele, Jill Lane, Rick Livingston, Rebeka Maples, Alamin Mazrui, Isaac Mowoe, Rolland Murray, Nick Nelson, Paulette Pierce, Kate Ramsey, Ahmad Sikainga, Sigrun Svavarsdottir, Jenny Terry, Jim Upton, Julia Watson and Steve Yao.

Stanford Humanities Center awarded me the 2001–2 research fellowship that enabled me to finish the book manuscript. John Bender, Suzie Dunn, Rania Hegazi, and Debra Pounds of the Humanities Center helped to make this a memorable year. Stanford associates Paul Berliner, Gavin Jones, Louise Meintjes, Marc Perlman, Sandra Richards, Richard Roberts, Janice Ross, Mike Saler, Haun Saussy, Jeannie Siegman, Danny and Judy Walkowitz and Aladdin Yaqub supported and generously engaged with my work.

Conversations at various times with Graham Huggan, Simon Lewis, Tina Lupton, Ntongela Masilela, Denise deCaires Narain, Kwadwo Osei-Nyame, Gautam Premnath, Anita Rupprecht, David Schalkwyk, Tim Watson, Lois Wheller and Marcus Wood have fed this book in all sorts of ways. Sussex University students and the interdisciplinary environment of the university itself sharpened my analysis of colonialism and postcolonialism. Jan Brogden and Liz Moore were administrative efficiency personified.

Muff Brady, Joan Brady, Phil Chrisman, Robert Davies, Pele deLappe, Ian and Penny Gibson, the late George Gutekunst, the late Byron Randall, Jon Randall, the late Toby and Lee Rein, and Jimmy Sehon abundantly furnished food, ideas, diversion and so much more. A special thanks goes to my parents Gale and Robert Chrisman. This book has its origins in their unstinting intellectual energy and passion for social justice. To them it is dedicated.

Versions of chapters 1 to 10 have appeared elsewhere in print. I am grateful to the publishers and editors for their kind support in the reprinting of 'Rethinking the Imperial Metropolis of *Heart of Darkness*', *Conrad at the Millennium: Modernism, Postmodernism, Postcolonialism*, edited by Gail Fincham and Attie de Lange. Social Science Monographs/Maria Curie-Sklodowska University/Columbia University Press, 2001, 399–427.

'Gendering Imperial Culture: King Solomon's Mines and Feminist Criticisms', in *Cultural Readings of Imperialism: Edward Said and the Gravity of History*, edited and introduced by Keith Ansell-Pearson, Benita Parry and Judith Squires. Lawrence and Wishart/St Martin's Press, 1997, 290–304.

'Imperial Space, Imperial Place. Theories of Culture and Empire in Fredric Jameson, Edward Said and Gayatri Spivak', *New Formations: A Journal of Culture/Theory/Politics*, number 34, summer 1998, 53–69.

'Journeying to Death: Paul Gilroy's *Black Atlantic*', *Race and Class*, volume 39, number 2, Oct–Dec. 1997, 51–64 and *Crossings*, volume 1, number 2, autumn 1997, 82–96.

'Rethinking Black Atlanticism', *The Black Scholar*, volume 30, number 3/4, winter 2000, 12–17.

'The Transnational Production of Englishness: South Africa in the Postimperial Metropole', *Scrutiny2: Issues in English Studies in South Africa* [Pretoria, South Africa], volume 5, number 2, 2000, 3–12.

'Theorising "Race", Racism and Culture: Some Pitfalls in Idealist Critiques', *Paragraph: A Journal of Modern Critical Theory*, volume 16, number 1, spring 1993, 78–90.

'Questioning Robert Young's Postcolonial Criticism', *Textual Practice*, volume 11, number 1, spring 1997, 38–45. Published by Taylor and Francis: www.tandf.co.uk.

'Appropriate Appropriations? Developing Cultural Studies in South Africa', in *Transgressing Boundaries: New Directions in the Study of Culture in Africa*, edited and introduced by Brenda Cooper and Andrew Steyn. University of Cape Town Press, 1996, 184–95.

'"The Killer That Doesn't Pay Back": Chinua Achebe's Critique of Cosmopolitics', *Proceedings of the Ohio Academy of History 2001 Conference*, edited by Vladimir Steffel, Ohio Academy of History, 2001, 13–19.

Introduction

This book has evolved over nine years. The year 1993 saw the publication of my co-edited *Colonial Discourse and Post-colonial Theory: A Reader*, which was the first anthology of postcolonial cultural studies to appear in print.[1] Since then the field has rapidly expanded into a major academic industry.[2] Diaspora studies, black Atlantic studies, transnational studies, globalisation studies, comparative empire studies have emerged alongside and within the original field. My responses to the field's developments are gathered here. These are a combination of literary, cultural and theoretical discussions, united by a number of critical concerns and by a desire to engage contemporary postcolonial thinkers in productive dialogue.

The goal of my *Post-colonial Theory Reader* was to diversify the field.[3] This goal is continued in this book. I am not among those that call for an absolute rejection of the field on the grounds that it is merely a reflex of late capitalism, the self-aggrandising formation of a few metropolitan academics. My approach has been rather to emphasise the broader contexts of anti-colonial nationalism as antecedents and legitimate elements of the field. And to conceive of the field as the provenance of materialist, historicist critics as much as it is of textualist and culturalist critics. If we look at the publication trajectory of postcolonial studies since 1978, and confine the glance only to metropolitan Anglophone academic publications within cultural studies, we find that materialist contributions have been a significant and persistent element throughout this period.

The year 1989, for example, saw the publication of the textualist *The Empire Writes Back*, but it was also the year of Timothy Brennan's sociological *Salman Rushdie and the Third World*.[4] 1990 saw Robert Young's anti-Marxist *White Mythologies* into print, but it also saw Neil Lazarus's Marxist *Resistance in Postcolonial African Fiction*.[5] Anthologies of essays such as Francis Barker, Peter Hulme and Margaret Iversen's *Colonial Discourse/Postcolonial Theory*, or Padmini Mongia's *Contemporary Postcolonial Theory*, contain as many self-designated materialist as culturalist or textualist contributions.[6] It can furthermore be argued that culturalist hegemony has diminished, and that thinkers such as Robert Young have arguably shifted to registers that are more materialist.[7] It is not only Fanon that, among earlier generations of anti-colonial thinkers, now receives wide metropolitan critical respect and disciplinary inclusion. Individual thinkers such as C.L.R. James have begun to enjoy considerable postcolonial attention.[8] And Elleke Boehmer's *Empire Writing. An Anthology of Colonial Literature 1870-1918* contains a range of anti-colonial voices that includes J.J. Thomas, Sri Aurobindo, Joseph Casely Hayford, Claude McKay, Rabindranath Tagore and Sol Plaatje.[9]

I emphasise these elements and shifts in order to underscore my contention that postcolonial studies has always been a field of divergent orientations, and that Marxist and anti-colonial perspectives have acquired more popular currency than was theirs in the 1980s and early 1990s. But this is not to suggest that there is now no need for a collection of 'contraventions': the critical tendencies that I engage with in this book remain influential, and continue, I fear, to eclipse other kinds of enquiry. I have chosen to include several chapters that deploy a polemical tone. My goal in writing and publishing these was to further academic debate by utilising the conventions of critique. Critique is a long-standing tradition within both Marxism and deconstructionism. Gayatri Spivak's 'Can the Subaltern Speak?' is one example; Benita Parry's 'Problems in Current Theories of Colonial Discourse' is another.[10] These writings work to evaluate another thinker's ideas critically, foregrounding the underlying assumptions and the implications of the reasoning contained, and to suggest (directly or indirectly) alternative ways to conceptualise the issues. There is always a risk that critique will be construed as an ad hominem attack, and indeed several critiques (Aijaz Ahmad on Edward Said, Terry Eagleton on Gayatri Spivak, or Robert Young on Benita Parry, which I discuss in this book) stand guilty of such personal orientation.[11] I have been very stimulated by the works I have chosen to critique here, by Paul Gilroy, Fredric Jameson, David Lloyd, Anne McClintock, Edward Said, and Gayatri Spivak. It is their profound intellectual substance, as much as their canonical power, or their typicality, that has prompted my critical engagement.

In a fascinating analysis of late nineteenth-century imperialism and the Benin bronzes Annie Coombes remarks that

> immediately after Benin forces ambushed and killed the Acting Consul-General Phillips and some of his entourage, the *Illustrated*

London News ... published an article denouncing Benin society as having a 'native population of grovelling superstition and ignorance'. entitled 'A native chief and his followers'.[12]

In other words, African *political* relations with Britain influenced metropolitan accounts of African *cultural* identity. The impact of organised political resistance on imperialism has been a persistent interest of mine. So has the elision of the political within colonial discourse and critical empire studies. I explore this elision in a number of chapters here, and argue for a critical methodology premised on the distinctiveness of the political as a category of identity, activity and analysis. It is not only its distinctiveness that needs further attention, but also its ability to mediate operations of culture, subjectivity and the economy; its complex relationship to imperialist constructions of race, gender, class and nation.[13]

In this book I also address the disparagement of formal oppositional political activity within black diaspora, transnational and nationalist studies. Such disparagement takes a number of forms, but frequently involves the suggestion that these organised mobilisations necessarily work against the interest of subaltern masses and share the repressive values of patriarchal, racist and capitalist bourgeois society. My findings suggest otherwise. I find, for example, that early black South African political nationalism is considerably more variegated than this model can allow for, and contains both liberal-constitutional and radical utopian elements, sexist and pro-feminist strains. I also find that the re-routing of 'legitimate' politics to the spheres of culture and epistemology, or to the practices of suicide and literary production (to name only a few of many such re-routings, is something that postcolonial studies shares with conservative and even reactionary ideologues.

I am far from alone in my findings. A large number of postcolonial scholars, critics and thinkers are currently involved in restoring the emancipatory elements of the political sphere against its detractors. Discussing the national liberationism of Frantz Fanon, for instance, Gautam Premnath avers that Fanon's political programme, and vision, is dialectical rather than linear or vanguardist:

> Rather than glorifying an elite cadre of vanguardist intellectuals, leading the mass of the population to 'catch up' with it along a unilinear developmental path of revolutionary consciousness, Fanon emphasizes the 'mutual current' between leaders and people. Rather

than occulting the pedagogical dimension of intellectual labor, he conceives of a mode of pedagogical leadership premised on the principle of mutual recognition being realized in the new national community, in which the roles of leaders and led are interchangeable. Thus is elaborated an organizational framework in which nationalist leadership and the activity of a nation-people continually bring each other in line – or, more precisely, *in rhythm*.[14]

Discussing other anti-colonial thinkers, Vilashini Cooppan emphasises that:

> like Fanon and like Marti, Du Bois was both intellectual and an activist, both a theoretician and a revolutionary. Such an overlapping of identities, in its troubling of powerful dichotomies and in its boundary-crossing creation of new political formations and new politics, may in fact serve contemporary scholars of postcoloniality both as an investigative object and as a model for our own praxis.[15]

And another kind of political rehabilitation issues from Robin Kelley in his discussion of black diasporic identity-formations:

> Too frequently we think of identities as cultural matters, when in fact some of the most dynamic (transnational) identities are created in the realm of politics, in the way people of African descent sought alliances and political identifications across oceans and national boundaries.[16]

The roots of much postcolonial delegitimation of the political lie in an absolute opposition to the state, and a corollary scepticism towards the liberatory properties of the public sphere and rationality. These are frequently associated with the Enlightenment, taken to be both an historical period and a philosophical disposition. The Enlightenment is then construed as the instrument or origin of racial and colonial domination. I am interested to present other ways, here, of thinking about the relations of racism, colonialism, and the public sphere. A persuasive alternative is suggested in Madhu Dubey's account of contemporary black representation in the USA:

> even in the most difference-sensitive postmodern contexts, black intellectuals are still expected to speak for the entire race. Such demands for racial representation prove difficult to dismantle at the level of discourse because their roots lie in the structural conditions

of African-American access to public culture ... as long as institutional racism curtails wider black access to cultural and political discourse, the part will continue to stand in for the whole, and, in fact, the high visibility of a few token figures will serve to disguise and perpetuate a structure that excludes the many.[17]

It is not public culture that is the source of racial inequality, but institutional racism, which restricts black access to the public sphere and thus creates a metonymic form of black representation. Rather than seeing representation itself as 'always already' inescapably violent, Dubey directs our attention to those coercive structures that control representation. By focusing on public culture as the central agent of racial and colonial domination, postcolonial thinkers do more than overlook the extra-cultural processes that create and perpetuate this domination. They also come close to endorsing an ethos of privatisation. How to contest and expand, rather than abandon, the public sphere is a concern that informs this book.

I have throughout this book argued against static conceptions of 'empire', and placed the emphasis instead on the dynamic processes of imperialism as a project of capitalist expansion and political domination. I am interested in the heterogeneity of its cultural and ideological expressions; the diversity of its geographical articulations. The vast transcontinental range of British imperialism generated significantly different modes of 'othering'. 'Orientalism's ongoing hegemony as an academic template for the entire colonised world suggests that this truism bears reiteration.[18] As I have suggested elsewhere,

> Perhaps it was inevitable that 'The Orient' should have been privileged, given the sheer longevity of European colonial relations with it. But this argues for the highly *unrepresentative* nature of the colonialism that developed there. Nineteenth-century British India, so central to the theoretical work of Spivak and Bhabha, was distinguished by a large, complex administration, necessitating the development of a sizeable 'native' civil service and educational system. Add to that a massive European industry devoted to the codified production of knowledge about the 'other', prompted in part by that 'other's' long-standing written traditions of self-representation, and it is unsurprising that this geo-cultural terrain should correspond so neatly with Foucauldian theoretical priorities of epistemology and governmentality.[19]

Other parts of the colonised world necessitate other analytic priorities and paradigms, as I suggest here.

Imperial and colonial cultural studies are witnessing an exciting expansion of coverage that includes the Americas, North Africa, Oceania and the Pacific.[20] I am concerned, however, that Southern Africa continues to be marginalised within the field, and some of that concern is reflected in this book. Southern Africa was of paramount importance within British 'new imperialism' of the late nineteenth and early twentieth centuries. Postcolonial studies of empire's impact on modernist and realist writing, or imperialism's relationship to socialist and conservative metropolitan cultures, may need radical revision to take account of South Africa's significance. That the Anglo-Boer war occasioned a British national identity crisis has long been recognised by cultural historians. But the war's literary impact upon imperialists such as Rudyard Kipling and Arthur Conan Doyle, or socialists George Bernard Shaw and H.G. Wells, has yet to receive due critical recognition. The aesthetic and ideological effects of the much-publicised Zulu War, the explosion of South African mineral wealth, the empire building of 'colossus' Cecil Rhodes also await future research.

Though I touch on the political and ideological tensions between colonial and metropolitan authorities, and populations, my primary interest in these chapters has been with the British metropolis itself, in its historical imperial and contemporary neo-imperial formations. The recent 'spatial turn' in postcolonial studies has been helpful in broadening the study of the metropole beyond imperial subject-positioning, the production and management of raced, gendered and classed beings (important though such approaches are).[21] The spatial analyses of Edward Said and Fredric Jameson that I focus on here are important enquiries into the cognitive repercussions for metropolitan populations of imperial expansion overseas; they are profoundly insightful into the ways that the reorganisation of space itself had an impact on metropolitan concepts of imperialism. But there are risks that attend these spatial explorations. The conceptualisation of the metropolitan as a spatial unit leads rather easily into the problematic notion that this unit has a unitary consciousness. And, on occasion, this analysis creates an aestheticisation of space that obscures as much as it illuminates the operations of imperial cultures.

That there were many material and figurative spaces within the imperial metropole needs further attention, and so does analysis of the features that different European metropoles shared and did not share.[22] In this light I foreground here the *metropolitan* narrative given by Conrad's *Heart of Darkness*. Critical attention has almost fetishised the spectacular Kurtz, and 'his' Africa, minimising their systemic relations with European capitalist bureaucracy in Europe. It is important to extend criticism by examining how overseas domination is rendered in the textures of ordinary European metropolitan life, labour and leisure in the novella. And equally important is the way metropolitan political power, consumerism and fantasy are seen to control the Company's African employment structures, just as they control Kurtz up to his death. When viewed from this angle, Conrad's critique strongly implicates not only the Belgian but also the British metropole in the atrocities of the Congo. Further scrutiny of Conrad's reification theme additionally involves looking at how market values and reasoning inform idealism itself.

The 1993 publication of Paul Gilroy's *The Black Atlantic* was a landmark for metropolitan postcolonial studies.[23] The book initiated an expressly anti-nationalist form of diasporic cultural studies. This opposed the 'hybrid' formation of black Atlanticism to the 'essentialising' ideology of Afrocentrism, and argued the category of nation to be as unproductive a focus of academic analysis as it was a unit of social liberation. A number of chapters here engage with Gilroy's formulations, and attempt to forge alternative ways to think about the relationship of diaspora and nation. I find the binary opposition model to be conceptually restrictive, and historically inaccurate; we need to think of the dynamic between diasporic and nationalistic cultures as uneven, variable and at times symbiotic.

One of the more valuable contributions of Gilroy's book, within a postcolonial studies context, was the challenge it presented to the critical paradigm of the 'empire writes back to the centre'. Rather than being reduced to a response to imperial metropolitan power, colonised and postcolonial cultures could now be understood as dialogues with other (formerly) colonised and diasporic cultures. These multiple axes have long been recognised, and analysed, within political traditions of Third World internationalism, pan-Africanism, socialism (to name a few), and within disciplines other than literary and cultural studies.[24] But they were most welcome within postcolonial studies.

However, this productive intellectual expansion has been offset by a number of other developments which are also, arguably, by-products of

Gilroy's work. One is a new form of New World or diasporic vanguardism. The opening of African cultures to black Atlantic analysis has generated a critical methodology that positions diasporic African populations as a sovereign class, or icon, of modernity that African populations then uncritically model themselves upon. Such vanguardism at times uncomfortably resembles imperialistic attitudes that structured earlier African-American relations with Africans, as for example in nineteenth-century providentialism, through which as Jim Campbell explains black Americans 'claimed the right, indeed the obligation, to "redeem" Africans, to remake their "benighted" brethren in their own, higher image'.[25]

This vanguardism is open to historical and conceptual contestation. In the case of South Africa, for instance, New World African leaders such as W.E.B. Du Bois, Marcus Garvey and Booker T. Washington wielded considerable influence over South African intellectuals. However, this influence was heavily mediated, modified and interrogated by local and national strains in South African political cultures. My book outlines a non-vanguardist approach, in which anti-colonial (and, by extension, postcolonial) cultures are to be seen as critical interlocutors, not imitators, of black diaspora.

The concept of the black Atlantic is inextricable, in Gilroy's book, from that of modernity. The latter is presented as a largely cultural and philosophical formation, against which black Atlanticism operates as a 'counterculture'. In suggesting that it is modernity that is the exclusive object of black Atlantic critique, Gilroy has made it difficult to consider how black Atlanticism articulates with imperialism and capitalism. My analysis of transnationalism here insists on addressing those elements, and integrating the study of modernisation with that of modernity.

Future work remains to be done on the ways in which commercial concerns and desires inform black Atlantic relations themselves; it is not only the imperialist or capitalist West that is economically coded within black Atlanticism. While Gilroy's model emphasises the anti-commercial, utopian elements of transnational connection, it is worth bearing in mind that early black Atlantic writings valorised commerce. It was promoted

> not only as a pathway to individual and collective autonomy, but a means to rebut prevailing stereotypes about blacks' innate slavishness and inability to survive in a competitive market economy ...

Virtually every back-to-Africa venture, from Paul Cuffe's voyage to Marcus Garvey's ill-fated Black Star Line, included a substantial commercial component.[26]

I am suggesting, then, that cultural study of black transnationalism could benefit from greater attention to the circuits of capital within and against which Africans and diasporic black peoples operated. Contemporary analysis of other diasporic communities and their transnational cultures – including Aihwa Ong's work – has significantly foregrounded these economic structures and diasporic agency within them.[27]

Black Atlantic studies could also give greater attention to alliances that were primarily political rather than racial. As Robin Kelley points out:

neither Africa nor Pan-Africanism are necessarily the source of black transnational political identities; sometimes they live through or are integrally tied to other kinds of international movements – Socialism, Communism, Feminism, Surrealism … Communist and socialist movements … have long been harbingers of black internationalism that explicitly reaches out to all oppressed colonial subjects as well as to white workers.[28]

Peniel Joseph underscores this when he argues for the centrality of Cuba to black American political cultures.[29] He further suggests that 'the story of Afro-Cuban solidarity is only one powerful example of the [black] worldliness that existed during the civil rights era' (p. 123).

In recent years the study of contemporary Englishness has claimed considerable academic attention.[30] The 1980s have become a focal point. It was indeed a significant decade in the production of white and black British post-imperial identities, including as it did the Falklands War; the 'race riots' of 1981 and 1984; the miners' strike; consolidation of the 'new racism'; the 1989 publication of Salman Rushdie's *Satanic Verses* and the subsequent 'Rushdie Affair'. Postcolonial discussion of the decade has, however, focused only on the last item. Both Simon Gikandi's *Maps of Englishness* (1996) and Ian Baucom's *Out of Place: Englishness, Empire, and the Locations of Identity* (1999), for example, culminate in a chapter devoted to Rushdie's novel.[31] The Rushdie Affair, in short, currently risks obscuring other important dynamics of 1980s Englishness, some of which were recognised by Rushdie himself in a 1984 critical essay, 'Outside the Whale'.[32] This drew attention to the operations of white post-imperial nostalgia during the 1980s: specifically, the reinvention of the historical British Raj, or the 'Raj Effect'.

It was not only India that was subjected to this metropolitan nostalgia: in a rather different way, South Africa was too. Its apartheid regime was pushed into acute and terminal crisis during this decade, and became the subject of considerable media interest in the UK. The resulting mass commodification of South Africa contributed to the moral aggrandisement of a white metropolitan consuming subject. My book re-examines one example of this, namely the metropolitan marketing of South African literature. This was strikingly gendered as well as raced, and provided a comforting anti-racist self-image to the prospective white reader. This might appear to corroborate Rosemary Jolly's arguments concerning Western constructions of South African apartheid. Discussing Jacques Derrida's 'identification of South Africa as the most spectacular criminal in a broad array of racist activity', she suggests that the risk is that of rendering 'South Africa … the atavistic other in a neocolonialist gesture that … disguises colonialist imperatives'.[33]

As I have already pointed out, however, Southern Africa has played a prominent, if academically underrecognised, role in British self-imaging, or 'worlding'.[34] And so the operations are simply not a demonic othering, the casting of the country as the racist embodiment of all that 'liberal' Britain is not. Instead they combine British nostalgia for its own early twentieth-century domination in Southern Africa together with a striking disavowal of its own agency in the subsequent racist apartheid dispensation.[35] The example of South Africa suggests that postcolonial studies of contemporary Englishness need to broaden their regional range.

And scholars of diasporic and postcolonial cultures also need to disaggregate 'the West' in their studies of international reception, neo-colonial commodification and institutionalisation.[36] Through notions such as 'World Bank Literature', 'Cosmopolitanism' and 'Postcolonial Exoticism', critics including Amitava Kumar, Tim Brennan and Graham Huggan explore how, in Huggan's words:

> Exoticist spectacle, commodity fetishism and the aesthetics of decontextualisation are all at work … in the production, transmission and consumption of postcolonial literary/cultural texts. They are also at work in the metropolitan marketing of marginal products and in their attempted assimilation to mainstream discourses of cross-cultural representation.[37]

I argue in this book that the national particularities of metropoles, as they exoticise, consume and canonise different cultures of the world, bear further critical exploration. Both the mechanisms for, and functions of, cross-cultural commodification depend upon the history of a particular metropolis and its current relationship to global hegemony. There are significant differences, for example, in the way that Arundhati Roy's 1997 *The God of Small Things* – and the image of the author herself – were commodified within the UK and the USA.[38] If metropoles require differentiation, so do the postcolonial countries over which they exercise power. Huggan's important analysis of general postcolonial exoticism in the Booker Prize industry opens the way for research into the particular functions of different Commonwealth countries within this arena.

The postcolonial dynamics of global electronic media is another area now receiving critical attention.[39] It is not only contemporary mass communication, however, that demand our analysis, as Chinua Achebe points out in his recent *Home and Exile*.[40] His discussion highlights the British institution of the post office in colonial Nigeria. A seemingly benign medium for the creation and furtherment of a global culture, the post office instead was perceived as 'the killer that doesn't pay back' by the community it 'served'. For Achebe there is a direct link between the historical operations of the Post Office and the ideologies of contemporary cosmopolitanism that emanate from various metropoles.

Debates about the meanings of cosmopolitanism have recently intensified and expanded within and alongside postcolonial studies. Homi Bhabha advocates what he terms 'the new cosmopolitanism', which 'has fundamentally changed our sense of the relationship between national tradition or territory, and the attribution of cultural values and social norms'.[41] This, for Bhabha, is a 'vernacular' cosmopolitanism connected with 'survival' (p. 42); he considers himself 'only a conduit for the idea … which has a long tradition of people who really struggled to make it happen in difficult and testing circumstances' (p. 40). Gayatri Spivak construes discourses of cosmopolitanism, and her relationship to them, in a strikingly different way:

> As for the idea of any kind of cosmopolitanism, I almost can't use that word … that is not what I am working in aid of. I don't want some kind of a specular humanist project where you have to construct the other as your … structural image in a cracked mirror in

order to be able to engage that other and to develop that other into
something like yourself because you were the fittest and you survived
and that specular other must now be helped to survive ... I do really
find that to be a part of the ... humanist, universalist backlash ... a
kind of scandal of the US imaginary, the longing for the specular
subject in order to be cosmopolitan.[42]

Achebe's contribution to the debate is enormously suggestive, as I
argue in this book; it asks us to ask more questions about the relation
of imperialism, neo-imperialism, violence, and the project of 'cosmopolitics'.[43]

These chapters have emerged from a number of professional institutional
contexts and occasions. Most of them were produced within Britain, while
I was lecturer in English at the School of African and Asian Studies,
University of Sussex. Since 1999 I have worked as Associate Professor in
the USA, at Brown University's departments of Modern Culture/Media
and English; at The Ohio State University's department of African
American and African Studies. Born in the USA of black, Jewish and white
parentage, brought up initially in San Francisco, then the Highlands of
Scotland, educated at Oxford, my racial and national experiences and
identifications have directly fed my intellectual concerns and writing. So
has my familial political environment, a combination of black nationalism, feminism and Marxism.

I have been fortunate to live in a place and time that allowed me to
pursue easily the disciplinary training that enabled me to become a professional academic, and make a living through ideas. It is by those ideas
that I would like my writing contributions to be judged, and it is the writing, not personal origins, of the thinkers I consider here that is paramount to my analysis. I welcome the debates about location, authority
and the representational politics of speaking for, as and on behalf of
others, that postcolonial studies has generated, and the intellectual and
political insights that have emerged from them. Equally I am concerned
by the authoritarianism that has also, on occasion, emerged from these
debates, as I discuss in my chapter here on Robert Young. I resist, too,
the pessimism that can result from an emphasis on location as determi-
nant of knowledge. All of us who work from within metropolitan academies profit from disempowered 'others'. This does not preclude our also
being able to learn positively from and about those others, and to share

knowledge of those others. Pessimism may deter us from the urgent tasks and responsibilities that our locations create: the task of, as Gayatri Spivak puts it, 'learning to learn from below'.[44] As Aimé Césaire observes, 'there is room for all at the rendez-vous of conquest'.[45]

Notes

1 Patrick Williams and Laura Chrisman (eds.), *Colonial Discourse and Post-colonial Theory: A Reader* (Hemel Hempstead: Harvester Wheatsheaf Press, 1993).

2 John McLeod, *Beginning Postcolonialism* (Manchester: Manchester University Press, 2000), contains useful overviews and bibliographies of the academic field.

3 See Laura Chrisman, 'Inventing Post-colonial Theory: Polemical Observations'. *Pretexts: Studies in Writing and Culture*, 5, 1–2 (1995), pp. 205–12, for an account of the editorial process of preparing the book.

4 Bill Ashcroft, Gareth Griffiths and Helen Tiffin, *The Empire Writes Back: Theory and Practice in Post-colonial Literatures* (London: Methuen, 1989); Timothy Brennan, *Salman Rushdie and the Third World* (London: Macmillan, 1989).

5 Robert J.C. Young, *White Mythologies: Writing History and the West* (London: Routledge 1990); Neil Lazarus, *Resistance in Postcolonial African Fiction* (New Haven: Yale University Press, 1990).

6 Francis Barker, Peter Hulme and Margaret Iversen (eds.), *Colonial Discourse/Postcolonial Theory* (Manchester: Manchester University Press, 1994); Padmini Mongia (ed.), *Contemporary Postcolonial Theory: A Reader* (London: Arnold, 1996).

7 Robert J.C. Young, *Postcolonialism: An Historical Introduction* (Oxford: Blackwell, 2001).

8 Substantial discussions of C.L.R. James's work are contained in Timothy Brennan, *At Home in the World: Cosmopolitanism Now* (Cambridge, MA: Harvard University Press, 1997); Neil Lazarus, *Nationalism and Cultural Practice in the Postcolonial World* (Cambridge: Cambridge University Press, 1999); Edward Said, *Culture and Imperialism* (London: Chatto, 1993); E. San Juan Jr, *Beyond Postcolonial Theory* (New York: St Martin's Press, 1998); and Bill Schwarz, 'Black Metropolis, White England', in Mica Nava and Alan O'Shea (eds.), *Modern Times: Reflections on a Century of English Modernity* (London: Routledge, 1996), pp. 176–207. See also the discussions of Ham Mukasa in Simon Gikandi, *Maps of Englishness: Writing Identity in the Culture of Colonialism* (New York: Columbia University Press, 1996) and of Reverend Samuel Johnson in Ato Quayson, *Strategic Transformations in Nigerian Writing: Orality and History in the work of Reverend Samuel Johnson, Amos Tutuola, Wole Soyinka and Ben Okri* (Bloomington: Indiana University Press, 1997).

9 Elleke Boehmer (ed.), *Empire Writing: An Anthology of Colonial Literature 1870–1918* (Oxford: Oxford University Press, 1998). There is no room for premature optimism however. Many other early anti-colonial writers remain out of print and critically neglected within postcolonial studies. See for example, Edward Wilmot Blyden, *Christianity, Islam and the Negro Race* (London: W.B. Whittingham, 1887); Joseph Casely Hayford, *Ethiopia Unbound: Studies in Race Emancipation* (London: C.M. Phillips, 1911); James Africanus Horton, *West African Countries and Peoples, British and Native: with the Requirements Necessary for Establishing that Self-government Recommended by the Committee of the House of Commons, 1865; and a Vindication of the African Race* (London: W.J. Johnson, 1868); S.M. Molema, *The Bantu Past and Present: An Ethnographical and Historical Study of the Native Races of South Africa* (Edinburgh: W. Green and Son Ltd., 1920); Kwame Nkrumah, *Neo-colonialism: The Last Stage of Imperialism* (London: Heinemann, 1965); Julius Nyerere, *Ujamaa: Essays on Socialism* (Dar es Salaam: Oxford University Press, 1968); George Padmore, *How Britain Rules Africa* (London: Wishart Books, 1936); Leopold Sédar Senghor, *On African Socialism* (London: Pall Mall, 1964).

10 Gayatri C. Spivak, 'Can the Subaltern Speak? Speculations on Widow Sacrifice', in Patrick Williams and Laura Chrisman (eds.), *Colonial Discourse and Postcolonial Theory*, pp. 66–111. Benita Parry, 'Problems in Current Theories of Colonial Discourse', *Oxford Literary Review*, 9, 1–2 (1987), pp. 27–58.

11 Aijaz Ahmad, *In Theory: Classes, Nations, Literatures* (London: Verso, 1992); Terry Eagleton, 'In the Gaudy Supermarket: Review of Gayatri Chakavorty Spivak, *A Critique of Postcolonial Reason*', *London Review of Books*, 21, 10 (1999); Robert J.C. Young, 'Review of Gayatri Spivak's *Outside in the Teaching Machine*', *Textual Practice*, 10, 1 (1996), pp. 228–38.

12 Annie E. Coombes, 'The Recalcitrant Object: Culture Contact and the Question of Hybridity', in Francis Barker, Peter Hulme and Margaret Iversen (eds.), *Colonial Discourse/Postcolonial Theory*, p. 94.

13 For an example of recent literary analysis that explores the impact of political resistance on imperialist fiction see Tim Watson, 'Indian and Irish Unrest in Kipling's *Kim*', in Laura Chrisman and Benita Parry (eds.), *Postcolonial Theory and Criticism* (Cambridge: D.S. Brewer, 2000), pp. 95–114.

14 Gautam Premnath, 'Remembering Fanon, Decolonizing Diaspora', in Laura Chrisman and Benita Parry (eds.), *Postcolonial Theory and Criticism*, p. 66.

15 Vilashini Cooppan, 'W(h)ither Post-colonial Studies? Towards the Transnational Study of Race and Nation', in Laura Chrisman and Benita Parry (eds.), *Postcolonial Theory and Criticism*, pp. 26–7.

16 Robin Kelley, 'How the West was One: On the Uses and Limitations of Diaspora', *The Black Scholar: Journal of Black Studies and Research*, 30, 3–4 (2000), p. 32.

17 Madhu Dubey, 'Postmodernism as Postnationalism? Racial Representation in US Black Cultural Studies', *New Formations: A Journal of Culture/Theory/Politics*, 45 (2001), p. 165.

18 This is now extending to the analysis of neo-colonialism. As an example see Elleke Boehmer, 'Questions of Neo-Orientalism', *Interventions: International Journal of Postcolonial Studies*, 1, 1 (1998), pp. 18–21.

19 Chrisman, 'Inventing Post-colonial Theory', p. 206.

20 See for example Lawrence Phillips, 'The Canker of Empire. Colonialism, Autobiography and the Representation of Illness: Jack London and Robert Louis Stevenson in the Marquesas', in Laura Chrisman and Benita Parry (eds.), *Postcolonial Theory and Criticism*, pp. 115–32; the contributions to Henry Schwarz and Sangeeta Ray (eds.) *A Companion to Postcolonial Studies*, and to Amritjit Singh and Peter Schmidt (eds.), *Postcolonial Theory and the United States: Race, Ethnicity, and Literature* (Jackson: University Press of Mississippi, 2000).

21 Lawrence Phillips, 'Lost in Space: Siting/citing the In-between of Homi K. Bhabha's *The Location of Culture*', *Scrutiny2: Issues in English Studies in Southern Africa* [Pretoria, South Africa], 3, 1 (1998), pp. 16–25, supplies an illuminating analysis of spatiality in the work of Homi Bhabha.

22 The particularities of diasporic London are now receiving a lot of postcolonial cultural analysis. See Gautam Premnath, 'Lonely Londoner: V.S. Naipaul and "The God of the City"', in Pamela Gilbert (ed.), *Imagined Londons* (Albany: State University of New York Press, forthcoming), and Sukhdev Sandhu, 'Pop Goes the Centre: Hanif Kureishi's London', in Laura Chrisman and Benita Parry (eds.), *Postcolonial Theory and Criticism*, pp. 133–54, for interesting discussions.

23 Paul Gilroy, *The Black Atlantic: Modernity and Double Consciousness* (London: Verso, 1993).

24 See, for example, Sidney Lemelle and Robin D.G. Kelley (eds.), *Imagining Home: Class, Culture and Nationalism in the African Diaspora* (London: Verso, 1994) and William E. Nelson, Jr, *Black Atlantic Politics: Dilemmas of Political Empowerment in Boston and Liverpool* (Albany: State University of New York Press, 2000). See also Philippe Wamba, *Kinship: A Family's Journey in Africa and America* (New York: Penguin, 1999).

25 James T. Campbell, 'Redeeming the Race: Martin Delany and the Niger Valley Exploring Party, 1859–60', *New Formations: A Journal of Culture/Theory/Politics*, 45 (2001), p. 128.

26 Ibid.

27 See, for example, Arif Dirlik, 'Bringing History Back In: Of Diasporas, Hybridities, Places, and Histories', *The Review of Education/Pedagogy/Cultural Studies*, 21, 2 (1999), pp. 95–131, and Aihwa Ong, *Flexible Citizenship: The Cultural Logics of Transnationality* (Durham: Duke University Press, 1998).

28 Robin Kelley, 'How the West was One', p. 32.

29 Peniel Joseph, 'Where Blackness is Bright? Cuba, Africa, and Black Liberation During the Age of Civil Rights', *New Formations: A Journal of Culture/Theory/Politics*, 45 (2001), p. 111–24. See also Penny M. Von Eschen, *Race Against Empire: Black Americans and Anticolonialism, 1937–1957* (Ithaca: Cornell University Press, 1997).

30 Literary studies of Englishness developed outside of postcolonial studies; the fields have more recently overlapped. See Robert Colls and Philip Dodd (eds.), *Englishness: Politics and Culture 1880–1930* (London: Croom Helm, 1986); Brian Doyle, *English and Englishness* (London: Routledge, 1989); Antony Easthope, *Englishness and National Culture* (London: Routledge, 1998); David Gervais, *Literary Englands: Versions of 'Englishness' in Modern Writing* (Cambridge: Cambridge University Press, 1993); Judy Giles and Tim Middleton (eds.), *Writing Englishness, 1900–1950: An Introductory Sourcebook on National Identity* (London: Routledge, 1995); and John Lucas, *England and Englishness: Ideas of Nationhood in English Poetry, 1688–1900* (London: Hogarth Press, 1990).

31 Simon Gikandi, *Maps of Englishness,* Ian Baucom, *Out of Place: Englishness, Empire, and the Locations of Identity* (Princeton: Princeton University Press, 1999).

32 Salman Rushdie, 'Outside the Whale', *Imaginary Homelands: Essays and Criticism 1981–1991* (London: Granta, 1991), pp. 87–102.

33 Rosemary Jolly, 'Rehearsals of Liberation: Contemporary Postcolonial Discourse and the New South Africa', in Padmini Mongia (ed.), *Contemporary Postcolonial Theory,* p. 368. Her object of discussion here is Jacques Derrida, 'Racism's Last Word', in Henry Louis Gates, Jr (ed.), *'Race', Writing, and Difference* (Chicago: University of Chicago Press, 1986), pp. 329–38.

34 This point is also made by Jacqueline Rose in 'The English at Their Best', *States of Fantasy* (Oxford: Clarendon Press, 1996), pp. 56–77.

35 For historical accounts of the formative role of the British see Bernard Magubane, *The Making of a Racist State: British Imperialism and the Union of South Africa, 1875–1910* (Trenton: Africa World Press, 1996) and Timothy Keegan, *Colonial South Africa and the Origins of the Racial Order* (London: Leicester University Press, 1996).

36 For discussions of the commodification of black diasporic popular cultures see, for example, Ben Carrington, 'Fear of a Black Athlete: Masculinity, Politics and the Body', *New Formations: A Journal of Culture/Theory/Politics,* 45 (2001), pp. 91–110, and Paul Gilroy, *Against Race: Imagining Political Culture Beyond the Color Line* (Cambridge, MA: Harvard University Press, 2000).

37 Graham Huggan, *The Post-colonial Exotic: Marketing the Margins* (London: Routledge, 2001), p. 20. Timothy Brennan, *At Home in the World: Cosmopolitanism Now,* Amitava Kumar (ed.), *World Bank Literature* (Minneapolis: University of Minnesota Press, forthcoming).

38 See Sherally Munshi, *Cultural Politics and Arundhati Roy,* Senior Honors Thesis, Brown University, 2000.

39 See for example Wendy Chun, 'Scenes of Empowerment: Virtual Racial Diversity and Digital Divides', *New Formations: A Journal of Culture/Theory/Politics,* 45 (2001), pp. 169–88. And see Gayatri C. Spivak, p. 20 of the same issue, in Meyda Yegenoglu and Mahmut Mutman, 'Mapping the Present:

Interview with Gayatri Spivak', *New Formations: A Journal of Culture/Theory/Politics*, 45 (2001).

40 Chinua Achebe, *Home and Exile* (New York: Oxford University Press, 2000).

41 Homi K. Bhabha, 'The Manifesto', *Wasafiri: Caribbean, African, Asian and Associated Literatures in English*, 29 (1999), p. 38.

42 Meyda Yegenoglu and Mahmut Mutman, 'Mapping the Present: Interview with Gayatri Spivak', pp. 16–17.

43 A useful discussion of contemporary globalisation is Crystal Bartolovich, 'Global Capital and Transnationalism', in Henry Schwarz and Sangeeta Ray (eds.), *A Companion to Postcolonial Studies*, pp. 126–62.

44 Meyda Yegenoglu and Mahmut Mutman, 'Mapping the Present', p. 12.

45 Aimé Césaire, *Notebook of a Return to my Native Land* (1956), introduced by Mireille Rosello, translated by Mireille Rosello with Annie Pritchard (Newcastle-upon-Tyne: Bloodaxe, 1995), p. 127.

Part I
Imperialism

1

Tale of the city: the imperial metropolis of *Heart of Darkness*

Many decades ago, in *Discourse on Colonialism*, Aimé Césaire drew attention to the 'boomerang effect' of imperialism. His account suggests that the boomerang operates at two speeds. The fast boomerang returns as soon as it is dispatched: the brutal dehumanisation to which the colonised are subjected is immediately visited upon the coloniser, leading Césaire to the conclusion that 'colonization ... dehumanizes even the most civilized man: that the colonizer, who in order to ease his conscience gets into the habit of seeing the other man as an animal ... tends objectively to transform himself into an animal'.[1] Césaire's evidence for this particular boomerang effect is drawn from French colonial atrocities and provides a gallery of spectacular violence, a fitting home for Kurtz's violations of humanity. Césaire graphically outlines colonial acts of mutilation, decapitation, 'these burned houses, these Gothic invasions, this steaming blood, these cities that evaporate at the edge of the sword' (p. 177).

It is this violent overseas dynamic, with its instantaneous impact upon coloniser and colonised, that has formed the critical practice of colonial discourse analysis.[2] Conrad's Kurtz supplies almost too neat an allegory of this dynamic, whereby the coloniser effects his own animalisation. It is worth recalling that Conrad himself considered Kurtz to fall into the trap of excessive symbolism. Replying to Elsie Hueffer's critique, Conrad in his letter of 3 December 1902 'distinctly admits' to 'the fault of having made Kurtz too symbolic or rather, symbolic at all'.[3] Kurtz has proved so captivating a symbol that the *other* components of the 'imperial boomerang' as Conrad presents them to us in his 1899 *Heart of Darkness*, have been overlooked.

These other components rely, for Césaire, on the slower speed set by transcontinental traffic to and from the metropole. Such boomeranging takes longer, according to Césaire, and started earlier – he contends that

a nation which colonizes … a civilization which justifies colonization … is already a sick civilization, a civilization that is already
morally diseased, that irresistibly, progressing from one consequence
to another … calls for its Hitler, I mean its punishment. (p. 176)

The metropolitan rebound of this imperial boomerang, for Césaire, cul-
minated in fascism, a regime every bit as spectacular as the violence occurring in the colonies.[4]

    This historical trajectory calls for further critical attention – but it is not
my concern here. I want instead to take up an element of the boomerang
that Césaire's formulations hint at but do not develop.[5] The insidious
power of imperial regimes over their 'home' centres developed concur-
rently with the more sensational operations of overseas violence. As *Heart
of Darkness* indicates, within and across metropolitan everyday life, the
economic, political and cultural elements of imperialism reproduced
themselves in ways that were quiet, complex and apparently unspectacular.

    I will outline here some of the ways in which late nineteenth-century
European imperialism inheres in the textures of daily labour and leisure
in Conrad's novella. I will also suggest that the Company's structures and
agents – including Kurtz – need to be reinterpreted through this imperial metropolitan perspective. Ultimately what animates and controls
the Company and Kurtz are urban corporate power, public opinion and
consumption.

    I am proposing this reading of *Heart of Darkness* as a path-clearing
exercise for future critical and theoretical analyses of metropolitan imperialism. This modest activity I justify on the grounds that it is precisely,
and only, through close reading that the full import of the interplay of the
metropolis and imperialism can be traced. Part of this text's subtlety lies
in its depiction of colonialism's casual inscription within the metropole.
The throwaway metaphors and similes, like the casually deployed material objects of leisure, that litter this work, contain within them the seeds
of a comprehensive analysis. The challenge Conrad's novella sets is to de-
casualise imperialism, expose its banality and recentre the metropole as
its primary agent.

(Re)Centring the narrative periphery: metropolitan England

The original narrative scene of the novella is of course the cruising yawl
The Nellie. Frequently overlooked by critics, the boat itself, its crew, their

activities and physical location all contribute mightily to the text's complex thematisation of the imperial metropole.[6] The crew's professional occupations are directly implicated in the financial capitalism of the City of London. But by placing the boat at a physical remove from the 'monstrous city' itself (which stands behind and 26 miles away), Conrad seems equally to suggest and obscure a relationship between the two sites, their respective means and ends of production. It is not easy to reduce the boat and its constituents to a mere and simple allegory of the city itself. Such reduction would indeed belong to the very (economic and narrative) condition that this text is inclined to critique.

It is the first narrator, not Conrad, who proceeds upon a reductive cultural logic that works to dehistoricise the meaning of 'following the sea', fix a single, symbolic status for the Thames and reinforce normative notions of professional subjectivity. This is clear in the narrator's presentation of the Director of Companies, whose role as captain host of the *Nellie* is presented as one he plays with more nautical 'authenticity' and 'typicality' than can be ascribed to the one remaining seaman Marlow himself. According to the narrator, the Director effectively monopolises the whole terrain of maritime 'representativeness': 'On the whole river there was nothing that looked half so nautical'. Furthermore, 'he resembled a pilot, which to a seaman is trustworthiness personified'.[7]

Marlow is the only one among them who is still a professional sailor, but he plays the part less well than the Director of Companies. His deviation from typicality, for the narrator, rests in his physical and subjective wanderlust, and his digressive, opaque methods of yarn telling. The narrator's conception of the essence of sailor centres on habit, stasis and narrative transparency:

> The worst that could be said of him was that he did not represent his class. He was a seaman, but he was a wanderer, too, while most seamen lead, if one may so express it, a sedentary life. Their minds are of the stay-at-home order, and their home is always with them – the ship; and so is their country – the sea. One ship is very much like another, and the sea is always the same. In the immutability of their surroundings the foreign shores, the foreign faces, the changing immensity of life, glide past, veiled not by a sense of mystery but by a slightly disdainful ignorance. (p. 63)

For the narrator, subjectivity is, or should be, a cognate of metropolitan profession. The text, in contrast, questions such essentialisation of professional subjectivity, introducing opacity where the narrator provides transparency. The schematic presentation of the *Nellie* crew – their designation according to capitalised profession, rather than personal name – might invite us to a purely allegorical interpretation, but it seems to me that this is precisely what this text resists. It uses the devices of allegory to invite structural and situational awareness.

There is, clearly, something highly symbolic in the fact that while the professions of Director and Accountant do recur in the functionaries of the Belgian Company, the profession of the Lawyer is conspicuously absent from the Congo operations. The spatial arrangements of the crew's seating also suggest a symbolic charge. The *Nellie's* Lawyer is elderly – and had 'because of his many years and many virtues, the only cushion on deck, and was lying on the only rug' (p. 61). That is, within the metropolitan frame, the forces of law are officially venerated; there is no visible agent of the law outside the metropole.

But the merely allegorical approach to reading metropolitan professionalism is more radically interrogated by the disparities that eventually emerge between the *Nellie's* Director and Accountant and their Company counterparts. As sinister and significant as the mere fact of these roles' repetition may be, the contrast in the performance and setting of the roles is as important. The open responsibility assumed by the *Nellie's* Director, in checking his anchor, is not repeated in the behaviour of Company director, closeted away behind several bureaux and ante rooms, who is presented paradoxically as mere figurehead and font of material power. If the *Nellie's* Director is subject to the dictates of the river tide, the Belgian Company Director is subject to the more subjective, human flows of rumour, feminine influence, 'reputation' and investment in the execution of his office. The *Nellie's* Accountant is engaged in the preliminaries of a game of dominoes. This aligns him with the aleatory properties of any game – and contrasts sharply with the obsessive control of the Company accountant over every aspect of his life, from shirt collars to the books kept in 'apple-pie' order.

This is one of the ways *Heart of Darkness* problematises the notion of human/allegorical representativeness; places symbolic and situational, material modalities in tension; criticises an instrumental and formalist reasoning that renders men mere personifications of their professional functions while at the same time revealing the powerful material impact such instrumentalisation has on subjectivity. This conceptual problematisation extends to the relationship between the processes of metropolitan financial capitalism – the monstrous City – and the space of maritime life and mercantile capitalism – the boat anchored near it in the Thames.

The narrator, again, supplies us with a version of this relationship that seeks to replace 'relationship' with 'identity', to constitute the Thames as a transhistorical emblem of metropolitan England itself. The narrator's eulogy of the Thames has already received sophisticated critical attention from Robert Hampson and Benita Parry, who emphasise the ways in which the triumphalist tone and contents are undercut by his subtle inclusion of sinister, illegitimate and failed elements of the naval project.[8] I am interested in pursuing a different track; I suggest that the very process of this rhetorical twinning of affirmative and negative elements by the narrator empties the Thames of active contradiction, just as it empties it of historicity.

This is a strategy of ideological neutralisation that produces a static not dynamic geography, reads the Thames as a stable referent, defined by nation and service alone. This process also collapses the late nineteenth-century operations of the City, their temporality and specificity, into a dehistoricised space of mercantilism, just as it equates the men who captained ships (Francis Drake, John Franklin) with the ships themselves (the *Golden Hind*, the *Erebus*, the *Terror*):

> The old river in its broad reach rested unruffled at the decline of day, after ages of good service done to the race that peopled its banks, spread out in the tranquil dignity of a waterway leading to the uttermost ends of the earth. We looked at the venerable stream not in the vivid flush of a short day that comes and departs for ever, but in the august light of abiding memories ... The tidal current runs to and fro in its unceasing service, crowded with memories of men and ships it had borne to the rest of home or to the battles of the sea. It had known and served all the men of whom the nation is proud, from Sir Francis Drake to Sir John Franklin, knights all, titled and untitled ... It had borne all the ships whose names are like jewels flashing in the night of time, from the *Golden Hind* returning with her round flanks full of treasure ... to the *Erebus* and *Terror*, bound on other conquests – and that never returned ... They had sailed ... the adventurers and the settlers; kings' ships and the ships of men on 'Change; captains, admirals, the dark 'interlopers' of the Eastern trade, and the commissioned 'generals' of East India fleets. (pp. 62–3)

When Marlow follows this, he opens up the meaning of the Thames that the narrator has attempted to close off from scrutiny and reflection. Marlow's speculations on the colonising experience of ancient Romans in Briton travelling the Thames rescue the Thames from the mythic ahistoricism of the narrator and shift it into radical historicity. Marlow's imaginary Romans are, significantly, also highlighted as members of a metropolitan, nepotistic bureaucracy. This reflects the text's general if overlooked concern with bureaucracy and the way that it conditions maritime employment:

> Imagine the feelings of a commander of a fine – what d'ye call 'em?
> – trireme in the Mediterranean, ordered suddenly to the north; run
> overland across the Gauls in a hurry; put in charge of one of these
> craft the legionaries – a wonderful lot of handy men they must have
> been, too – used to build … And perhaps he was cheered by keep-
> ing his eye on a chance of promotion to the fleet at Ravenna by-and-
> by, or he had good friends in Rome and survived the awful climate.
> Or think of a decent young citizen in a toga – perhaps too much dice,
> you know – coming out here in the train of some prefect, or tax-
> gatherer, or trader even, to mend his fortunes. (pp. 64–5)

The text works consistently against the homologising tendencies of the narrator, just as it works against the narrator's formalist passion for deducing meaning from twinning. While the Roman employment structure prefigures that of the Belgian Company, it does not exactly replicate it, just as the *Nellie*'s Director and Accountant prefigure but do not equal the later manifestations of Directors and Accountants. The Thames and the Congo resemble but are not interchangeable with one another. Instead, the novella insists on relatedness while laying down the challenge for readers to reflect on the nature of the relation.

I have emphasised how, in its thematisation of the metropolis, *Heart of Darkness* devalues the symbolic in favour of the situational, the concrete and particular; interrogates an allegorical view of metropolitan professional subjectivity. But Conrad's text also supplies a critique of the ways in which that metropolitan culture, and economy, is so totally yet casually involved in the process of imperialism. The assault on this imperial inscription begins with the very notion of 'leisure'. The dominoes with which the 'crew' plan to while away their time, for example, are made of *ivory*, though, pointedly, the narrator prefers to designate them by their slang term 'bones'.

The keys of the Intended's piano/sarcophagus are also, one must assume, made of ivory. It is interesting that Conrad chose to make ivory rather than rubber the object of imperial energy in the Congo. While in reality both substances were commercially extracted, the text focuses exclusively on ivory: the advantage is not only to Conrad's colour coding, but also to his theme of metropolitan leisure. The emphasis on ivory reinforces the exploitative decadence of this metropolitan leisure. in a way that the more utilitarian rubber would not.

The men's idea of leisure is to reoccupy a former *work place*, a boat. Bourgeois leisure effectively replicates labour here – which is not only a pointed irony, but also part of a running commentary on the way the structures of imperialism operate. If the processes of maritime expansion facilitate ivory-derived leisure pursuits such as dominoes and piano playing, these processes also exert a powerful control over metropolitan subjectivities. This results in a conception of leisure that is indistinguishable from that of work: self-objectification proves to feature as much in play as in labour.

The domain of imperialism extends as powerfully, and apparently casually, to the arena of unemployment. As does the text's interrogation. The throwaway remarks made by Marlow regarding his period of involuntary unemployment are actually elements of a critical discourse that is sustained throughout the novella. Marlow characterises this period in strikingly imperial language: 'I was loafing about, hindering you fellows in your work, and invading your homes, just as though I had got a heavenly mission to civilise you' (p. 66). This ideologically saturated reference carefully anticipates two of the major themes of his Congo experience. One is European imperialism as an unproductive *waiting game* (my choice of 'game' is deliberate here). Stuck in the Central Station, Marlow waits around for his rivets; the pilgrims wait around for a posting to a station where they can collect ivory; the brickmaker waits around for bricks.

And, of course, Marlow's statement initiates the motif of imperialism as a violent destruction of African settlements and modes of production. But the statement also literally, if elliptically, implicates volatile structures of employment in metropolitan destabilisation. There is a serious undertone to the text's suggestion that unemployed threaten metropolitan 'civil society', passing on to it the social disruption that their unemployment has forced on to them.

In *Heart of Darkness*'s opening account of the British metropolis, we are presented with a double structure, then: the metropole serves as the *cause* of overseas expansionism, and as a loosely microcosmic space in which the dynamics of colonisation are prefigured in a parodic and casual form. Metropolitan 'private', 'social' and 'leisure' space is subject to an inverted 'invasion' by overseas practices of labour and domination, mockingly turned into a virtual masquerade, an imperial simulation which is all the more serious for the apparent lightheartedness of its irony.

Auditing the company: labour, bureaucracy and consumerism

If *Heart of Darkness* thus invites us to re-think the relations between metropolitan 'play' and imperial 'reality', between the pursuits of leisure and the 'serious' 'labour' of overseas colonial enterprise, it also invites us to rethink the relationship between freely given and forced labour, within both the metropole and the colony. The book's most graphic examples of 'unfree', slave labour masquerading as capitalist waged labour occur, of course, in the Company's treatment of African workers – not only those who die in the Grove of Death, but also those who are employed to work on Marlow's boat. The conditions of their labour are shown to be anything but free, trapped as they are on a boat, paid in a useless currency and deprived of the opportunity for basic subsistence. This is compounded by the failure of the boat to stop at 'food stations'.

Marlow's own employment circumstances also destabilise the boundary between free and forced labour. There are similarites between Marlow's metropolitan situation and that of African workers in the Congo. Marlow has been driven to this job in desperation. Though he has been looking long and hard for a posting to a ship, 'the ships wouldn't even look at me' (p. 66). Subtly the text hints that Marlow's plight belongs to a shift from mercantile to imperial capitalism, the narrowing of employment opportunities linked to the advent of the (for Conrad, decadent) Age of Empire with its increase in monopolies and cartels. This is simultaneously a decline to a professional administrative system structured upon multiple mediation and nepotism.

Feminisation runs through this organisational logic. Marlow has to turn to 'the women' of the family to procure his work, just as it is the female secretaries of the Company that are stationed to mediate his institutionalisation. For Marlow, this bureaucracy is nothing less than emasculating. For Conrad too it seems, the degenerate new times is expressed in instrumentalisation and apparent empowerment of women. The mournful secretary of the waiting room has the power to conjure up the

Director from nothing. Conrad's impressionist style heavily pronounced in this scene.[9] In it, the spatial boundaries that clearly distinguish the outer room, with its two receptionist furies, from the waiting room with its sad clerk, are dissolved. The boss – described, significantly, as 'an impression' – instead emerges from the more physically embodied secretary herself.

If feminisation is one aspect of corporatism, reification is another. The Brussels scenes of Marlow's employment provide variations on a theme of commodity fetishism: the objectification of labouring humans accompanied by the animation of objects. The two-dimensional, cartoon Company Director contrasts with the 'heavy writing desk' that, Marlow tells us, 'squatted' in the middle of the room (p. 69). The desk not only occupies more bulk but also is invested with more energy than the Director. In keeping with the logic of commodity fetishism, Conrad's figurative language takes on material properties. The boss's actual handshake with Marlow is indistinct, but the boss's metaphorical grip on millions could not be more concrete:

> He was five feet six, I should judge, and had his grip on the handle-end of ever so many millions. He shook hands, I fancy, murmured vaguely, was satisfied with my French, *bon voyage.*
>
> In about forty-five seconds I found myself again in the waiting-room with the compassionate secretary, who, full of desolation and sympathy, made me sign some document. (p. 70)

The eugenic components of imperial enterprises at 'home' as well as 'abroad' are referenced when the Company doctor measures Marlow's skull and asks him if insanity runs in his family.[10] The socially undesirable, such as the insane, and criminals, are exported abroad as a safety measure, for the health of the nation – and to perpetuate colonial expansionism.

This time round, Empire is clearly farce, as shown in Conrad's allusions to classical culture. Contemporary Brussels becomes a political formation that sustains the cruelty but not the achievements of the ancient Greek and Roman worlds. Take Marlow's figurative self-designation as a Roman gladiator. It is to the 'old knitter of black wool', the secretary, that he remarks '*morituri te salutant*', that is, 'those who are about to die salute you', the gladiators' salutation of their emperor (p. 70). While the receptionist is stationed as farcical proxy for the imperial Caesar, the clerk with whom Marlow drinks becomes a farcical proxy of Plato, someone who reduces the ancient to a form rather than a producer of knowledge. The clerk glorifies the Company but in reply to Marlow's surprise on his 'not going out there' says 'I am not such a fool as I look, quoth Plato to his disciples', a fictitious citation (p. 70).

Marlow's gladiatorial ventriloquism is playful. But the material consequences of his Company hire are hardly less serious than those that faced gladiators: death, in the course of providing entertainment for a desensitised metropolitan population and its emperor. As we see graphically later, on and off the coast of Africa, European employees keep dying off, from disease or attack, about as disposable for the metropolitan administrations that hire them as the African workers themselves.

Marlow's initial Company experiences clearly situate him as an object of metropolitan imperial science, leisure and exploitation. But equally, the text presents Marlow as a free agent, the self-indulgent beneficiary of a nepotistic system. Self-indulgent, because his choice of the Congo derives from a residual juvenile hankering for Africa, reactivated by catching sight of an African map *in a shop window*. Crucially, the image of Africa presents itself to him as a purchasable commodity, one that commands an enchanting aura.[11] The dynamics of this commodity fetishism are quite complex. The Congo is mediated through its representation on the map, which is mediated through the glass window. Marlow transforms the river into a snake that charms him, and he in turn becomes a 'silly little bird' (p. 67). Marlow's own consuming desire is projected on to the object of his gaze; he becomes the imaginary object of consumption. He fetishises both Africa and the image of himself as a consumer.

Marlow's choice is not only that of the desperate unemployed, then, but that of the greedy consumer. The pursuit of his boyhood fantasy is, inevitably, infantilising; Marlow has to compromise his adult autonomy and become in effect the simulated boy of his fantasy, turning to his aunt for assistance in this. And in exchange for this assistance, he has to take on the burden of his aunt's missionary fantasies; this is one of the costs of his self-commodification.

This takes us back to Césaire's thesis of the 'already sick civilisation'. The text invites readers to search out the source of this imperial sickness, but denies them the easy origin of a singular individual or spatial location. Marlow's family, for instance, is implicated in the 'disease' long before Marlow's aunt uses her influence. For their move from England to Belgium, was itself, Marlow explains, motivated by the desire to *capitalise* on the low cost of living there: 'You understand it was a Continental concern, that Trading society; but I have a lot of relations living on the Continent, because it's cheap and not so nasty as it looks, they say' (p. 67). This is a crass expression of English penny-pinching, in which Conrad suggests that contemporary imperialism needs to be understood as having an inter-European as well as an overseas dynamic.

Marlow's family have, in effect, performed a version of 'endo-colonisation' (internal colonisation), which indicates the ease with which some English metropolitans could view mainland Europe as an available colonial site. This novella thus extends the representation of metropolitan imperialism by giving both a continental and a national account. The continental perspective unifies European metropoles: they share capitalist consumption and professional structures of employment. Accordingly, nationalities vanish as soon as Marlow reaches the outer station of the Company. There and in the Central Station subjects are referred to not as members of countries but only according to their professional occupation.

In the 'heart' of the Congo's ivory country, however, singular pan-European identity dissolves because when it comes to colonial capital accumulation, different European countries have unequal access and success. Nationalities recommence as soon as Marlow approaches the interior where Kurtz languishes: allusions are made to Russian, English, French, Dutch representatives. That is, metropolitan identities re-emerge through intra-European competition for resources. Belgium and England are both contributors to the project of overseas acquisition, but they do not benefit in identical ways and do not enter the competition from the same position of material advantage.

That Belgium was relatively poor compared to Britain encourages the likes of Marlow's family to relocate there in a quasi-colonial gesture. It also served, as Eric Hobsbawm remarks, to intensify its own 'need' for colonial expansion:

> the drive for colonies seems to have been proportionately stronger ineconomically less dynamic metropolitan countries, where it served to some extent as a potential compensation for their economic and political inferiority to their rivals ... the new colonialism was a by-product of an era of economic-political rivalry between competing national economies.[12]

What Raymond Williams refers to as 'the miscellaneity of the metropolis', then, informs the novella as much as the European metropole's uniformity.[13]

The metropolis in Africa

I have argued that *Heart of Darkness* sets up the imperial metropolis in both a dominatory and loosely prefigurative narrative relationship with the colony. That Conrad wanted to encourage his metropolitan readers to perceive the relationship as a *complex* one is suggested by his removal of the manuscript account of the colonial hotel, government and tram line.[14] The excised passage is interesting for the way it presents colonial government administration as an unmediated miniature version of metropolitanism, simply transplanted. The final publication makes but passing reference to this part of Marlow's journey: 'It was upward of 30 days before I saw the mouth of the big river. We anchored off the seat of government. But my work would not begin till some 200 miles farther on. So as soon as I could I made a start for a place 30 miles higher up' (p. 75). The manuscript however interrupts the sequence 'we anchored off the seat of government. But my work would not begin' in order to give a detailed account of this governmental seat:

> I had heard enough in Europe about its advanced state of civilisa-
> tion: the papers, nay the very paper vendors in the sepulchral city
> were boasting about the steam tramway and the hotel – especially
> the hotel. I beheld that wonder. It was like a symbol at the gate. It
> stood alone, a grey high cube of iron with two tiers of galleries out-
> side towering above one of those ominous-looking foreshores you
> come upon *at home* in out-of-way places where refuse is thrown out.
> (p. 239; emphasis added)

Marlow becomes yet more explicit, and judgemental, about the links between metropolis and colony when he describes meal times – 'the whole government with the exception of the governor general' descends

> from the hill to be fed by contract … I was astonished at their
> number. An air of weary bewilderment at finding themselves where
> they were sat upon all their faces and in their demeanour they pre-
> tended to take themselves seriously just as the greasy and dingy place
> that *was like one of those infamous eating shops you find near the slums
> of cities*, where everything is suspicious, the linen, the crockery, the
> food, the owner, the patrons, pretended to be a sign of progress; as
> the enormous baobab on the barren top of the hill amongst the gov-
> ernment buildings, soldier's huts, wooden shanties, corrugated iron
> hovels, soared, spread out a maze of denuded boughs as though it

had been a shade giving tree, as ghastly as a skeleton that posturing in showy attitudes would pretend to be, a man.

I was glad to think my work only began two hundred miles away from there. I could not be too far away from that comedy of light at the door of darkness. (pp. 239–40)

By removing this passage, Conrad removes the concrete presence of Belgian government from Africa.[15] The absence of any mediating human officers allows an exclusive focus on the economic power of the Company itself, the relations between its headquarters and its Congo stations, its structures and its agents. Conrad's excision of the government seat is consistent with his minimisation of the Belgian military presence. Each trading station was in reality also a military base; Africans were forced into becoming soldiers who were made to implement barbaric methods of rubber and ivory extraction.[16]

It is significant that Conrad should reduce the military presence to remote posts '300 miles away' from the Company's own trading stations. By constructing the Company here as an economic structure unattached to any national government, Conrad again implicates his British readers in general accountability for African atrocities. The excision of this passage further assists Conrad in highlighting the disastrous nature of infrastructural 'development'. However pathetic they may be, the constructions of the 'hotel' and 'tramway' in this excised passage mitigate Conrad's emphasis on the pure destructiveness of modernisation within this African context.

The removal of human features of government is more than a commentary on the proportions of government to private corporations. It is, I suggest, a commentary on the non-transposability of any version of collective metropolitan life itself. Even in its degraded, parodic, greasy spoon or garbage dump form, the metropole becomes here something that can be viably (if sordidly) reconstituted as a social structure in Africa. The final version provides no stable colonial infrastructure; there is no settlement, only asocial isolated Company office bearers remotely stationed in the interior. Conrad's downsizing is striking. The Marlow of this removed passage is 'astonished at their number', a huge mass of bureaucrats. The substitution of this mass with a series of individual specimens places a spotlight on their internecine competitiveness and their duplicitous relationship with the metropolitan headquarters; the Company's internal organisation can be shown to disintegrate under the atomising violence and accumulative drive that it imposes on Africans.

In probing the meaning of the metropole in this text, it is important to recognise how much both the Company administration and the metropolitan public continue to maintain considerable power over their colonial employees. Kurtz's explanation of the key to metropolitan recognition contains the throwaway insight: 'You show them you have in you something that is really *profitable*, and then there will be no limits to the recognition of your ability,' he would say. 'Of course you must take care of the motives – right motives – always' (p. 138; emphasis added). The metropolitan Company is permanently stationed to receive all the economic profits of its colonial production. Though Kurtz can and does present the Company with an invoice, there is nothing to suggest he ever gets paid:

> This lot of ivory now is really mine. The Company did not pay for it. I collected it myself at a very great personal risk. I am afraid they will try to claim it as theirs though. H'm. It is a difficult case. What do you think I ought to do – resist? Eh? I want no more than justice. (p. 144)

Kurtz's profitability, I am arguing, consists not only in the quantities of ivory he collects, but also in the idealism he peddles. As one of the new 'gang of virtue' he has been brought in over the heads of the Central Station manager and brickmaker precisely because of the political and economic value that this virtuous idealism supplies to the Company. Such idealism purchases not only female public metropolitan support (witness, Marlow's aunt) but also, presumably, investment (from the husbands of the idealistic women). A feminised metropolitan public opinion produces, through society gossip and rumour, the high moral reputation of a Kurtz, or a Marlow that in turn facilitates the nepotistic advancement through the Company of these individuals.

Marlow's account of Kurtz's degeneration may seem to support a binary polarity between the metropolitan and the primitive. But I want to argue the opposite. Kurtz has not 'gone native' to the extent that he rejects a monetary economy and pursues only naked power and/or unspeakable rites for themselves. As much as Kurtz hungers for ivory, he hungers for metropolitan recognition, and status. Some time before Marlow utters his more famous Lie, to Kurtz's Intended, he soothes the delirious Kurtz with the decidedly questionable assertion that 'your success in Europe is assured in any case' (p. 135).

The dying Kurtz can think of nothing but the metropole, in fact, dreaming of a return journey in which kings meet him at railway stations.

Kurtz's images of wealth and fame significantly include 'my ideas' along with 'My Intended', 'my station', 'my career':

> The wastes of his weary brain were haunted by shadowy images now – images of wealth and fame revolving obsequiously round his unextinguishable gift of noble and lofty expression. My Intended, my station, my career, my ideas – these were the subjects for the occasional utterances of elevated sentiments. The shade of the original Kurtz frequented the bedside of the hollow sham ... that soul satiated with primitive emotions, avid of lying fame, of sham distinction, of all the appearances of success and power. (pp. 137–8)

Literary criticism should not (although it frequently does) siphon off the 'ideas' from the materialism they are actually associated with here. And these possessive metropolitan appetites are precisely the primitive emotions that consume Kurtz and claim his rhetorical gift.

All Europe, as we know, has contributed to the making of Kurtz. The contribution is not merely genetic or national, but metropolitan and structural: he has been obliged to turn to a colonial life to amass the wealth and forge the career that will allow him to marry his Intended. In other words, the social forces that drive this impoverished son out of the metropole are the same that make him desire re-entry, to his dying moment.

Rethinking the sepulchral city

I have suggested that, if Conrad's text is critical of the material structures of imperial capitalism, it also criticises their susceptibility to a feminised public opinion based on idealist liberal humanitarianism. It hints at metropolitan irresponsibility in delegating control over production to private corporations which are themselves structured upon delegated overseas control, secretaries and nepotism. The text also displays a rather elitist tendency to detest bourgeois and petty-bourgeois metropolitan subjects less for the barbaric exploitation and domination they sanction but – somewhat like Eliot in *The Waste Land* – for their social conformism, psychological superficiality and existential inauthenticity.[17] This locates the 'deathliness' of metropolitan life as a metaphysical condition, which, in the case of Eliot, can be overcome through collective surrender to a mythic authoritarianism.

I want to suggest, however, that Conrad's attack on mediocrity is never far from the materialist sensitivity I have outlined above. It systematically connects the existential with the economic, the interior with external disciplinary regimes. The 'deathliness' that pervades the 'sepulchral city' is product equally of the living dead – the inhabitants of Brussels – and of the dead Africans killed by the Company in the Congo. The existential snobbery of Eliot is actually embodied in the tenets of Marlow, and as such is subverted by the language of the text itself. Marlow's presentation of metropolitan insularity is challenged by the very figures he selects to illustrate the insularity: the butcher, the policeman and darkness itself. While Marlow suggests that his *Nellie* crew are prevented by their urban institutions from comprehending African 'horrors', the text underscores the structural linkage of those same institutions to the Congo.

These institutions surface when an irritated Marlow defends himself against the charges of absurdity made by his leisure crew: 'This is the worst of trying to tell … Here you all are, each moored with two good addresses, like a hulk with two anchors, a butcher round one corner, a policeman round another, excellent appetites, and temperature normal' (p. 114). They recur soon afterwards, with the new figure of the neighbour added to the urban gallery:

> You can't understand. How could you? – with solid pavement under your feet, surrounded by kind neighbours ready to cheer you or to fall on you, stepping delicately between the butcher and the policeman, in the holy terror of scandal and gallows and lunatic asylums – how can you imagine what particular region of the first ages a man's untrammelled feet may take him into by the way of solitude – utter solitude without a policeman. (p. 115)

Ultimately, suggests this text, there may be nothing more than petty convention to distinguish sanctioned 'butchery' from illicit, or the 'law of the city' from 'the law of the jungle'. 'The butcher' and 'the policeman', like 'the neighbour', are vitally connected to the 'unspeakable' activities performed by Kurtz in the solitude of the 'wilderness'. It is no accident that the leader of the Eldorado Exploring Expedition is described as resembling 'a butcher in a poor neighbourhood' (p. 94). The neighbour whose good opinion and respectability inhibit unlawful violence and reinforce conformity is, ironically, one cause of Kurtz's transgression. The quest for neighbourly reputation and social approval prompts Kurtz's mission overseas, justifies his brutal capital accumulation and remains the ultimate focus of his deathbed aspirations. And despite Marlow's contention that there was nothing 'exactly profitable' in the human heads decorating

Kurtz's residence, the reverse is true: the profit lies in the rule of terror that such heads facilitate. It is a similar rule of terror, Conrad suggests, that dominates the heart of the metropolis: terror of 'scandal ... gallows ... lunatic asylums ...'.

This reading suggests the intensity of the task that awaits postcolonial critical work on metropolitan imperialism.[18] This can be further fed by developments in materialist cultural studies and cultural geography which take 'the every day life of modernity' as their focus, and include the work of Michel de Certeau, David Harvey, Henri Lefebvre, and Edward Soja. By looking in more detail at the ways this text engages issues of reification, bureaucracy and corporatism, we can better situate the metropole itself as Conrad's 'Heart of Darkness'.

Notes

1 Aimé Césaire, 'Discourse on Colonialism', in Patrick Williams and Laura Chrisman (eds.), *Colonial Discourse and Post-colonial Theory: A Reader* (Hemel Hempstead: Harvester Wheatsheaf Press, 1993), p. 177.

2 See for example Mary Louise Pratt, *Imperial Eyes: Travel Writing and Transculturation* (London: Routledge, 1992); Sara Mills, *Discourses of Difference: An Analysis of Women's Travel Writing and Colonialism* (London: Routledge, 1993); V.Y. Mudimbe, *The Invention of Africa: Gnosis, Philosophy, and the Order of Knowledge* (London: James Currey, 1988).

3 Joseph Conrad, 'Letter to Elsie Hueffer, 3 December 1902', in Frederick R. Karl, *The Collected Letters of Joseph Conrad, volume 2, 1898–1902*, ed. and intro. by Frederick R. Karl and Laurence Davies (Cambridge: Cambridge University Press, 1982), p. 461.

4 The connection of European fascism to colonialism was also made by a number of black intellectuals loosely contemporary with Césaire, including W.E.B. Du Bois and Ralph Bunche. See Robin D.G. Kelley's discussion in 'A Poetics of Anticolonialism', *Monthly Review*, 51, 6 (1999), pp. 1–21.

5 Benita Parry has noted the sophistication of Césaire's theorisation of colonialism, its synthesis of Marxism, nationalism and Negritude. See her 'Resistance Theory/Theorising Resistance or Two Cheers for Nativism' in Francis Barker, Peter Hulme and Margaret Iversen (eds.), *Colonial Discourse/Postcolonial Theory* (Manchester: Manchester University Press, 1994), pp. 172–96.

6 Edward Said's discussion of *Heart of Darkness* in *Culture and Imperialism* (London: Chatto, 1994) offers some suggestive remarks on the situational specificity of the *Nellie*; he emphasises the contingency that this introduces to the account of an absolutist imperialism. See pp. 20–35; pp. 198–203.

7 Joseph Conrad, *Heart of Darkness*, edited by D.C.R.A. Goonetilleke (Peterboro, Ontario: Broadview Press, 1995), p. 61.

8 Robert Hampson, 'Conrad and the Idea of Empire', in Gail Fincham and
   Mytle Hooper (eds.), *Under Postcolonial Eyes: Joseph Conrad after Empire*
   (Cape Town: University of Cape Town Press, 1996), pp. 65–77. Benita Parry,
   'Conrad and England', in Raphael Samuel (ed.), *Patriotism: The Making and
   Unmaking of British National Identity. Volume 3: National Fictions* (London:
   Routledge, 1989), pp. 189–98.
9 For an illuminating analysis of the politics of Conrad's impressionism see
   Tamar Katz, '"One of Us": Conrad, Scouting, and Masculinity', in
   Impressionist Subjects: Gender, Interiority, and Modernist Fiction in England
   (Urbana: University of Illinois Press, 2000), pp. 80–137.
10 On eugenics and social Darwinism during this period see Greta Jones, *Social
   Darwinism and English Thought: The Interaction between Biology and Social
   Theory* (Brighton: Harvester Press, 1982). See also Bernard Semmel,
   Imperialism and Social Reform: English Social-imperial Thought 1895–1914
   (London: Allen and Unwin, 1960).
11 See Thomas Richards, *The Commodity Culture of Victorian England:
   Advertising and Spectacle, 1851–1914* (London: Verso, 1991), and in particular his third chapter 'Selling Darkest Africa', pp. 119–67, for important con-
   textual information on the popular commodification of Africa during this
   period.
12 Eric Hobsbawm, *The Age of Empire* (London: Weidenfeld and Nicolson,
   1987), p. 76.
13 Raymond Williams, 'Metropolitan Perceptions and the Emergence of
   Modernism', in Tony Pinkney (ed.), *The Politics of Modernism: Against the
   New Conformists* (London: Verso, 1989), p. 45.
14 See Adam Hochschild's description of the government offices and steam trol-
   ley in the Congo capital Boma, *King Leopold's Ghost: A Story of Greed, Terror,
   and Heroism in Colonial Africa* (Boston and New York: Houghton Mifflin,
   1998), pp. 115–16.
15 Hochschild comments that 'the Congo's governor general had far less power
   than did a British, French, or German colonial governor. More than any other
   colony in Africa, the Congo was administered directly from Europe', p. 115.
16 See Adam Hochschild's chapter 8 'Where There Aren't No Ten Command-
   ments' for further information, pp. 115–39.
17 See Tim James's 'The Other "Other" in *Heart of Darkness*', in Gail Fincham
   and Myrtle Hooper (eds.), *Under Postcolonial Eyes:* pp. 109–19, for an important discussion of the ways in which Conrad's novella is informed by metropolitan representations of the urban working class.
18 For an excellent example of materialist postcolonial analysis of 'everyday life'
   see Keya Ganguly, *States of Exception: Everyday Life and Postcolonial Identity*
   (Minneapolis: University of Minnesota Press, 2001).

2

Gendering imperialism:
Anne McClintock and H. Rider Haggard

Gayatri Spivak's work on nineteenth-century imperialist literature directs feminist analysis to the narrative dynamics of human reproduction and production.[1] She examines the codification of women as racial reproducers, and its relation to the conception of women as imperial producers of human subjectivity itself. Exciting though this direction is, feminist critics also need to further explore how economic production directly informs, and generates, literary themes. Likewise, discussion of reproduction can usefully be extended from Spivak's formulations to include imperial masculinity and its mediation through reproductive ideology.

This is precisely what Anne McClintock's work promises to do. I want to focus here on her celebrated *Imperial Leather* discussion of H. Rider Haggard's popular and influential imperialist Victorian romance *King Solomon's Mines*.[2] This depicts the quest for treasure in southern Africa by three British adventurers, who also restore the 'rightful' heir to the throne of an African kingdom. Several Anglo-American feminist critics, including Sandra Gilbert and Susan Gubar, Elaine Showalter and Rebecca Stott, have favoured Haggard's novels.[3] McClintock differs from these in offering readers a distinctly materialist orientation. McClintock argues that the novel is concerned with

> the reordering of women's sexuality and work in the African homestead and the diversion of black male labor into the mines. The story illuminates not only relations between the imperial metropolis and the colonies but also the refashioning of gender relations in South Africa, as a nascent capitalism penetrated the region and disrupted already contested power relations within the homestead. (p. 233)

She regards *King Solomon's Mines* as deriving from Haggard's 1870s sojourn as a colonial administrator in Natal. The novel, accordingly, reflects Natal's operations against the self-determining Zulu kingdom. Crucial to this non-capitalist Zulu political economy was the productive labour of its women, organised through polygyny. Recognising this, colonialists targeted polygyny and imposed taxes that forced Zulu men into wage labour. By making it impossible for the men to depend upon women's homestead labour, colonialists themselves were able to appropriate the fruits of this labour and effectively supplant Zulu males as patriarchs.

McClintock thereby suggests that *King Solomon's Mines* is an allegory of colonial power; specifically, that the novel allegorises colonial appropriation of African women's reproductive and productive labour. Despite the plausibility of her reading, and its apparently demystificatory power, there is a tendency in McClintock's analysis to reinforce the very categories of power that she claims to be exposing. I want to focus on the way McClintock analyses the dynamics of labour and degeneration, and to explore the political implications of her approach.

Women's bodies and labour

To support her argument about the novel's restructuring of production modes, McClintock cites examples from contemporary colonial discourses. These justify wage labour by denigrating traditional African production, which allegedly stems from pathological male laziness, degeneracy and excessive sensuality. One would expect *King Solomon's Mines* then to reinforce these justifications, and to represent males as idle exploiters of their many labouring wives. But Haggard's fictional Kukuana African society is strikingly free of such representations. Authorial judgement towards this community's production patterns is also absent. Such absences, I want to argue, indicate that Haggard was no simple apologist for Natal colonial expansion. He was, instead, acutely ambivalent about the processes of capitalist modernisation both in the UK and in South Africa.[4] It is such ambivalence that led him to fantasise a precapitalist African society that is, at the close of the novel, guaranteed to remain free from entry into any colonial economy.

If I am not persuaded by McClintock's argument concerning female productive labour within the text, I am also sceptical about her arguments concerning female reproductive labour as an automatic threat to Haggardian imperial culture and sexual order. McClintock presents a version of women's reproductive capability in which women are menacingly powerful regardless of whether they exercise any material control over the

reproductive and productive activities of themselves or others. This precludes recognition of the *positive* role accorded to white maternity within
imperialist ideologies, a recognition upon which Gayatri Spivak's earlier
work was based.[5]

The affirmative imperial function of maternity is suggested by the
journey of the novel's protagonists to the mines. The heroes' path takes
them across a landscape, which goes from a female 'head' (a waterspout)
to her breasts (two massive mountains) and culminates in the vagina or
anus (the treasure cave and exit). McClintock reads this as an allegory of
the 'genesis of racial and sexual order' (p. 241), in which the heroes travel
across a hostile and temporarily castrating female body to the mineral
wealth of the mines and once there perform 'an extraordinary fantasy of
male birthing, culminating in the regeneration of white manhood' (p.
248). One would never know from McClintock's account that Haggard
constructs this feminised landscape as beautiful and on occasion sublime.[6] And that instead of unremitting hostility, the land offers the trav-
ellers maternal sustenance – food and water.

The feminised 'body' of the African land suggests the way that the
sexual sphere is instrumentalised throughout the novel: it becomes, I want
to argue, a means of naturalising and hence legitimating economic imperial accumulation. Acquiring diamonds, Haggard tries to suggest, is as
self-evidently 'natural' as male domination over women, with which he
wants to render it analogous. Sexuality, in other words, functions as a
means of resolving contradictions within the text's political economy.

McClintock argues the evil Gagool to embody the threatening female
power of generation, and bases this on the fact that Gagool is referred to
'by her attendants as the "mother, old mother"', and has the power to sentence people to death, as an *isanusi* (p. 246). This interpretation overlooks
the fact that Gagool does not have a monopoly on Kukuana femininity.
She is constantly juxtaposed with the young, beautiful and nubile Foulata,
in whom the power of female generation is most clearly evident and does
indeed explicitly pose a specific threat to colonialism: the threat of mis-
cegenation. McClintock bases her interpretation on the slenderest of linguistic evidence, the 'mother' word. The fact that Gagool is termed
'mother' is not itself proof of her fundamentally generative coding; the
word is used idiomatically in the text to signify general respect for social
seniority.

There is nothing in the text to associate Gagool with either literal
or symbolic motherhood. On the contrary, I would argue that she is

stationed, as are the other female *isanusis, outside* of femininity, marriageability, and the cycles of reproduction. She is member of a class that publicly controls these feminine activities instead of participating in them. And it is her *departure* from traditionally female 'generative power', including her membership of a politically powerful class, that allows Haggard to align her with the destructive forces of anti-colonialism, coded here as *ressentiment*. In other words, Gagool is not maternal enough, rather than being too maternal, for Haggard. She violates normative femininity and thus takes on demonic qualities.

Degeneration and regeneration

McClintock contends that the novel is 'legitimized by two primary discourses of the time: the discourse on "degeneration" and the discourse on the reinvented "father" of the "family of man"' (p. 234). McClintock's use of 'degeneration' here has little connection with the process of decline from one condition to another. Instead McClintock's 'degeneration' refers to the classification of a group as essentially debased. *Should* an individual white male chance to actively decline, then his deterioration will take him down the evolutionary ladder; he will accordingly begin to resemble those fundamentally degenerate 'others'. This allows her to argue that *King Solomon's Mines* portrays white male regeneration, which they achieve through their ritual relocation as both the paternal evolutionary source and culmination of the human race.

McClintock's account of evolution and degeneration presumes that there is only one position that the classified group can hold within the racial or evolutionary narrative, so that non-white peoples are necessarily degenerate in relation to whites. This presumption is not supported by Haggard's text; the novel does equate degeneracy with blackness, nor does it present white males as the categorical antithesis of degeneration. On the contrary: the writing of Haggard and a number of his late nineteenth-century contemporaries is where these presumptions are *challenged*.[7]

Degeneration is for these thinkers a fear of the debilitation of the imperial British race, occasioned by the development of modern industrial and financial capitalism itself. Modernisation, in other words, is held responsible, and in a number of ways: it enervates the proletariat, it destroys the labouring agrarian classes, it threatens to diminish the ruling classes by making them indolent and hence susceptible to overthrow by more physically powerful races and/or classes. Within this degenerational anxiety, those peoples considered less economically developed may be idealised as repositories of the social, cultural and biological strengths which the modernised UK has lost.[8] British male regeneration then becomes possible through temporary exposure to, and participation in, such peoples' 'primitive' society – especially if such activity involves physical and military exertion. This romantic primitivism, not a conviction of blackness as a totally debased condition, enables Haggard's representation of the neo-Zulu Kukuana people of *King Solomon's Mines*.

Representing Africans

McClintock's perspective on degeneration produces a reading strategy that ignores power differences within racialised and gendered groups. The political, classed mediation of African people disappears. This becomes evident when McClintock constructs King Twala and his adviser Gagool as sole representatives of (Zulu) blackness and femaleness within the text. Thus she argues that

> The Kukuana royal family is itself dangerously degenerate – offering a spectacle of familial disorder run amok. In the features of King Twala's face *one reads the degeneration of the race. He is a black paragon of the putative stigmata of the race, excessively fat, repulsively ugly, flat-nosed, one-eyed.* (pp. 244–5; emphasis added)

It is inaccurate to view Twala as the sole representative of the Kukuana family itself, since the idealised Umbopa/Ignosi is constructed to be as representative, if not more so. In other words, Twala's degeneracy is a function not of his 'race' but of his illegitimate and corrupt kingship. It is his *political*, rather than racial, identity, that is singled out for condemnation here, just as it is Gagool's political rather than her gender identity that is the focus of Haggard's hostility towards her. There is no room in McClintock's formulations for a prominent African such as Umbopa, whose acceptability for Haggard she explains simply by his willingness to recognise white power. This evades the fact that he, like most of the Kukuanas, contradicts the equation of blackness with degeneracy.

Most problematic here is the way McClintock identifies Twala with the people over whom he tyrannises. Colonial and imperial commentators on the Zulu were (when it suited them) inclined to invest heavily in distinguishing between Zulu rulers and people. By construing Zulus in

Haggardian discourse as an undifferentiated mass of hostile degeneracy, personified in the figure of their ruler, McClintock rules out the historical possibility and intellectual study of the ways in which colonial (ideological, political and economic) domination worked through as well as against colonised constituencies. This was achieved by settler and metropolitan alignment with the 'people' against 'oppressive' African rulers.

To equate the corrupt ruler Twala with the people he tyrannises over is to erase the conceptual distinction between dominating and being dominated, which is something that recurs throughout McClintock's book. It is illustrated when McClintock argues that the ideological negativity of Twala's rule derives from his 'unbridled access to women' (p. 245), his 'ritualised control of women' (p. 247) *and* also from the *female* basis of his rule, namely Gagool and the other *isanusis* (p. 246). Paradoxically, the more black men are seen by McClintock to depend upon controlling, profiting from and exploiting women's labour power, the more actual power she attributes to black women. In this account, control *over* women is indistinguishable from control *by* them.

Discourse of the family

McClintock's discussion accentuates figurative paternity: it was the authoritative condition of fatherhood that both animated and legitimated colonial activities. This condition was articulated, she argues, through various images and rituals of power. However in her analysis the status of such images becomes unclear. They fluctuate between *reflecting* and *constituting* that power. At work here is a synecdochic method: locate the word or image of 'the father', 'the family', and you have already identified, and explained, the material power relations that go with these. By naming reproductive woman the image of productive authority, it then becomes unnecessary to detail the processes of production within the literary text or women's place within these processes. To label fathers as the source of the family thus also excuses her from explaining the meanings of 'family' and the power relations within it, as these are automatically implied in the 'founding' term.

This analysis lacks a concrete notion of practices rather than static conditions and images. The focus rests primarily on what texts, like families, look like, not on how they *operate*. The synecdochic perspective makes talismans of the words mother and father, and abstracts them from the context that gives the terms their meaning. Synecdoche, then, leads

McClintock to equate (the representation of) African rulers with the whole society they rule over; it leads her to equate womb/labour power with all forms of power (for women) and simultaneously to equate image power with material power (for men). Haggard's upper-class mother becomes, for McClintock, in many respects indistinguishable from his British domestic women workers and African women rural labourers. All signify generative authority and therefore pose the same threat to an imperial or colonial patriarchy.

Underlying her book as a whole is an idealist feminism (most familiar in the USA) that wants to counterbalance women's material disempowerment by asserting the psychological, reproductive and sexual strength they possess, and to explain patriarchy as a paranoid defensive attempt to deny such power. McClintock's discussion reinforces this through a romantic labourism that affirms work as the empowering expression of social or political agency. It is one thing to argue, as McClintock does beautifully elsewhere in *Imperial Leather*, for the 'power' of nannies to excite sexual desire in, initiate sexual acts with and inflict punishment upon young boys. In this capacity, such figures could clearly provide an example of human agency and thereby contradict femininity's association with passivity and objectification. The domestic labour of these women, in so far as it likewise demonstrated agency rather than idleness, may also have subverted notions of femininity.

But it is disconcerting to watch her slide from this specific, delimited sphere of female 'power' to a social sphere, as for example when she says of Freud that: 'Incapable of ascribing the prime originating power of psycho-sexual development to a working-class woman … he instead represses the nursemaid and displaces her power and his identification with her power, onto identification with the father' (p. 94). McClintock thus overlooks a significant difference between the power embodied in the figures of the father and the nurse. The nurse's power is private, subjective and limited; it has no social currency, whereas the father's power derives from, and is embodied in, his social, political and economic status.

The same attribution of general power crops up McClintock's discussion of the barrister Arthur Munby: 'Perhaps in these encounters Munby could surrender deliriously … to forbidden recognition of the social power of working-class women' (p. 147). In what that 'social' power consists remains unclear, especially when, as McClintock herself proceeds to say, 'the contradiction that Munby faced was his dependence on working-class women whom society stigmatised as subservient' (p. 148). McClintock writes as if social power already inheres within these workers and must simply be named as such for liberation to take place. Celebrating women's psychological power while naming it as social serves to endorse the continuation of the social systems that exploit them. This argument becomes yet more problematic in McClintock's later section's South African material, where we are told, for example, that:

> The power of black women is a colonial secret. White domestic life unfolds itself about this secret, as its dreaded, inner shape. Displaced and denied, its pressure is nonetheless felt everywhere … The invisible strength of black women presses everywhere on white life so that the energy required to deny it takes the shape of neurosis. (p. 271)

Other directions

As my criticisms of McClintock's synecdochic logic might suggest, I am arguing that we need to recover a notion of the whole from which those parts are taken. We need to introduce a working concept of a social-economic and textual totality into which patriarchy feeds and through which it is produced. The analysis of Haggard's novel requires contextualisation that takes account of political-economic developments in both Britain and South Africa. Haggard's ideological formation would then read, not as the product of a cumulative series of apriori metropolitan and colonial threats to patriarchy, but instead as historically contingent, variable and even contradictory.

I contend that Haggard's writing in general – and *King Solomon's Mines* in particular – reveals (even as it attempts to resolve) discontinuities between imperial-metropolitan and settler-colonial interests and ideologies. There emerged in the British invasion of Zululand and the subsequent civil war a number of conflicting interests between politicians and populace based in Britain and those based in Natal.[9] Haggard's non-fictional writings show him to be torn between the two. A typical metropolitan imperial perspective would, in the mid-1880s, invest in the fantasy of an 'imperial', militarily powerful, sovereign Zulu kingdom, whereas a settler-Natal perspective would be interested in the material and ideological conversion of that Zulu into a wage-labouring, indirectly ruled colonial satellite.[10]

King Solomon's Mines reflects this contradiction in both its form and its content. The military actions of the imperial heroes in Kukuanaland correspond to, and reinforce, a colonial concern for establishing control over Zulu monarchy, but these are deliberately divorced from the political and economic relationships to which they would belong in colonial practice. What prevails instead is the *imperial* fantasy of an autonomous Zulu polity, restored with the temporary assistance of British men to its true form after the episode of a tyrannous illegitimate ruler. The same applies with the text's approach to wealth accumulation: what is important is the fact that the beneficiary of the wealth is England, not Natal.

In other words, we need methodologies that can account for, and incorporate, different imperial and colonial agendas. This is particularly important in the analysis of the fantastic genre of romance, which needs to include a notion of literary ideology as following something other than the norms of mimetic realism. The romance genre as pursued by Haggard here is more aligned with imperial-metropolitan than with colonial ideology; Haggard uses African material to satisfy a primarily British readership's imaginary desires, and uses romance as a genre particularly well suited to the symbolic resolution of material contradictions.[11] The particular contradictions which seem most to concern Haggard at the time of *King Solomon's Mines* are those generated by the systematic development of industrial capitalism in the UK, contradictions which by 1885 were beginning to emerge in Southern Africa also.[12] What Haggard finds in the incipient mining industries of South Africa, and in the mythical archaeology of the Great Zimbabwe, are potential analogues for the British modernisation and capital accumulation. What he turns them into is a corrective.

Gender analysis of the novel needs to engage with this modernisation and Haggard's anxieties about it. He fears that urban industrialisation is dangerous to national well-being because of its inhumane production of unfit humans, and therefore to be opposed. He also fears modernisation because of its association with democracy, and its potential destabilisation of 'real' political-economic growth. Haggard's elitist romanticism, then, generates a complex contradiction: 'the people' emerge as both the victim and as the cause of contemporary decline. This gives rise to a fiction in which immense value is invested in the vision of non-reified, non-industrialised humans, Africans whose production and reproduction belong to the workings of nature not culture.

Within such a scheme, as I have already argued, the dynamics of sexual reproduction serve ideologically to naturalise economic production. For Haggard it is axiomatic that sexual difference and reproduction are natural processes, and it is here, through Haggard's twin concerns with capitalist reification and wealth accumulation, that I would begin to analyse the interrelation of reproductive and economic power. Along with the reintroduction of the notion of the totality in feminist postcolonial criticism, I want to argue for the reintroduction of the notion of mediation. The notion of the totality allows us to engage at a macrological level with the structures through which literary subjects are given ideological value. The notion of mediation allows us to engage with the ways in which those values are textually produced. Gagool's case, for example, marks the conjunction of Haggard's sexism and his classism, which found in *isanusis* a class politically antagonistic towards white power. Haggard's political concerns are mediated through the category of gender. Equally, gender ideology is mediated through the politicised category of class.

I am suggesting that for feminist criticism of imperial and colonial culture to develop it needs ironically to go 'backwards'. Back, in the sense that Edward Said in *Culture and Imperialism* has gone back, to the study of the collective properties of imaginative literature as a distinct modality within imperial culture, and away from the analysis of such literature as functionally interchangeable with social science and administrative writings.[13] Back then to notions of totality, mediation and ideology as analytic tools.

Notes

1 Gayatri C. Spivak, 'Three Women's Texts and a Critique of Imperialism', in Henry Louis Gates, Jr (ed.), *'Race', Writing and Difference* (Chicago: University of Chicago Press, 1986), pp. 262–80.

2 Anne McClintock, *Imperial Leather: Race, Gender and Sexuality in the Colonial Contest* (London: Routledge, 1995). For an earlier version see Anne McClintock, 'Maidens, Maps and Mines: *King Solomon's Mines* and the Reinvention of Patriarchy in Colonial South Africa', in Cheryll Walker (ed.), *Women and Gender in Southern Africa to 1945* (London: James Currey, 1990), pp. 97–124. I discuss *Imperial Leather* as a whole in my review essay: Laura Chrisman, 'Soap', *Southern African Review of Books*, 39–40 (1995).

3 Sandra M. Gilbert and Susan Gubar, *No Man's Land. Volume 2: Sexchanges* (New Haven: Yale University Press, 1989); Elaine Showalter, *Sexual Anarchy: Gender and Culture at the Fin de Siecle* (London: Bloomsbury, 1991); Rebecca Stott, 'The Dark Continent: Africa as Female Body in Haggard's Adventure Fiction', *Feminist Review*, 32 (1989), pp. 69–89.

4 See for example Haggard's *Cetywayo and His White Neighbours, Or, Remarks on Recent Events in Zululand, Natal, and the Transvaal* (London: Trubner and

Co., 1882 and 1888); his autobiography *The Days of My Life* (London: Longman, Green and Co., 1926).

5 For historical discussion of white maternity's incorporation into imperialist and eugenic projects, see Anna Davin, 'Imperialism and Motherhood', *History Workshop Journal* 5 (1978), pp. 9–65. For more general historical accounts of white European women in relation to nation and empire see Nupur Chaudhuri and Margaret Strobel (eds.), *Western Women and Imperialism: Complicity and Resistance* (Bloomington: Indiana University Press, 1992); Clare Midgley (ed.), *Gender and Imperialism* (Manchester: Manchester University Press, 1998); Ann Laura Stoler, 'Making Empire Respectable: The Politics of Race and Sexual Morality in Twentieth-century Colonial Cultures', in Anne McClintock, Aamir Mufti and Ella Shohat (eds.), *Dangerous Liaisons: Gender, Nation, and Postcolonial Perspectives* (Minneapolis: University of Minnesota Press, 1997), pp. 344–73; Vron Ware, *Beyond the Pale: White Women, Racism and History* (London: Verso, 1992). Useful literary studies are Deirdre David, *Women, Empire, and Victorian Writing* (Ithaca: Cornell University Press, 1995); Jenny Sharpe, *Allegories of Empire: The Figure of Woman in the Colonial Text* (Minneapolis: University of Minnesota Press, 1993).

6 For a discussion of the sexual dynamics of Haggard's landscape see David Bunn, 'Embodying Africa: Woman and Romance in Colonial Fiction', *English in Africa* [Grahamstown, South Africa], 15, 1 (1988), pp. 1–28.

7 See for example the late nineteenth-century writings on evolution and degeneration of Karl Pearson, *National Life from the Standpoint of Science* (London: Adam and Charles Black, 1901) and James Cantlie, *Degeneration Amongst Londoners* (London: Field & Tuer and The Leadenhall Press, 1885). See also Haggard's own non-fictional musings, found in his writings on the decline of agrarian production, on garden cities and on Great Zimbabwe. These include his *Rural England* (London: Longman, Green and Co., 1902); 'Introductory Address' to T. Adams, *Garden City and Agriculture* (London: Garden City Press, 1905), pp. 1–11; 'Preface' to A. Wilmot, *Monomotapa (Rhodesia): Its Monuments, and its History from the Most Ancient Times to the Present Century* (London: T. Fisher Unwin, 1896), pp. i–xxiv.

8 Gail Low, *White Skins, Black Masks: Representation and Colonialism* (London: Routledge, 1996), contains a useful discussion of this gendered primitivism in relation to Haggard. See also Nicholas Thomas, *Colonialism's Culture: Anthropology, Travel and Government* (Cambridge: Polity Press, 1994); and Marianna Torgovnick, *Gone Primitive: Savage Intellects, Modern Lives* (Chicago: University of Chicago Press, 1990).

9 See Jeff Guy, *The Destruction of the Zulu Kingdom: The Civil War in Zululand, 1879–1884* (London: Longman, 1979).

10 See Laura Chrisman, *Rereading the Imperial Romance: British Imperialism and South African Resistance in Haggard, Schreiner and Plaatje* (Oxford: Clarendon Press, 2000), for an elaboration of the arguments here.

11 See John MacClure, *Late Imperial Romance* (London: Verso, 1994), for a discussion of the imperial romance genre.

12 See Bernard Magubane, *The Making of a Racist State: British Imperialism and the Union of South Africa, 1875–1910* (Trenton: Africa World Press, 1996), for an historical account of this period.
13 For an example of this discourse analysis mode see David Spurr, *The Rhetoric of Empire: Colonial Discourse in Journalism, Travel Writing and Imperial Administration* (Durham: Duke University Press, 1993).

3

Empire's culture in Fredric Jameson, Edward Said and Gayatri Spivak

Aijaz Ahmad's landmark 1992 book *In Theory* argues that materialist and postcolonial cultural studies are fundamentally incompatible projects.[1] Whatever Ahmad may aver, relations between materialism and postcolonialism are more complex than mere incompatibility. For instance, Said's essay on empire in Jane Austen's *Mansfield Park* appears in a recent book titled *Contemporary Marxist Literary Criticism*, where the editor Francis Mulhern defines Said as 'writing in solidarity with Marxism rather than as a declared exponent'.[2] Said's essay originally appeared in a volume of critical essays on Raymond Williams, whose insularly English work on the country and the city is both extended and revised by Said to account for the historical colonial conditions of English self-representation.[3] While Said's historicism establishes his solidarity with leftist cultural criticism, his constructions of space and his (variable) aestheticism do not.

In this chapter I will discuss Said's work alongside that of two influential thinkers who share equally complicated relations with materialist theory: Gayatri Chakravorty Spivak and Fredric Jameson. Spivak, a self-designated 'Marxist-feminist-deconstructionist', is highly regarded as one of the key practitioners of post-colonial theory; Jameson is one of the leading left theorists of culture in the USA. These three thinkers have each produced an impressively large and wide-ranging opus of critical thought. My concern here, however, is exclusively with their respective analyses of nineteenth- and early twentieth-century British imperialism.[4] I want to suggest the strengths and the limitations of their respective theorisations in relation to a materialist postcolonial theoretical practice. This is best achieved, I believe, by an approach that combines immanent critique with a comparative technique whereby the three thinkers are set in dialogue with one another. I will here briefly outline their respective analyses, before proceeding to sections that focus on their conceptualisations of imperial culture and of space.

If Said is prompted to correct and extend the work of Raymond Williams, Spivak is likewise moved to challenge the work of Terry Eagleton for its insularly national account of *Jane Eyre*'s class dynamics. Jameson writes from a different but equally revisionary impulse: to extend Lukácsian aesthetics to include the impact of empire building on metropolitan art, and to amplify Lenin's conceptions of imperialism as the last stage of capitalism. Like Jameson, Said and Spivak are also motivated by expressly contemporary political goals. Spivak offers a strategic intervention against contemporary Anglo-European bourgeois feminism. This animates her discussion of how *Jane Eyre*'s conceptions of European female individualism are predicated on and perpetuate the subordination of non-European women. Said works towards a humanistic politics and a contrapuntal intellectual culture that, for him, will provide progress beyond the contemporary deadlock of imperialism and nationalism.

While all three thinkers perceive imperialism as a matrix of domestic culture and consciousness, their definitions of imperialism itself differ. Said's derive from the notion of geo-political domination. His predominant, Williamsesque concern is with metropolitan 'structures of feeling' and how geographical expansionism influences them.[5] The anti-foundationalist Spivak does not offer an explicit definition of imperialism, but addresses instead its manifestation as 'a territorial and subject-constituting project'. This leads her to analysis of how the 'discursive field of imperialism' can produce 'ideological correlatives for the narrative structuring' in fiction. Whereas Said and Spivak are interested in the pattern of fictional narrative, Jameson is interested in style and language. His discussion of E.M. Forster's *Howards End* discerns a newly spatialised language as compensation for the existential losses incurred by overseas expansion. Jameson like Lenin defines imperialism as the departure from 'the classical stage of national or market capitalism' into an international system of production and consumption.

Jameson argues that this system has a singular impact upon metropolitan-national identity. For Spivak, in contrast, imperialism though ideologically hegemonic is not genderless. Her theorisation of *Jane Eyre* pursues a sexual differentiation of ideology into the registers of 'childbearing' and 'soul making'. Spivak's argument develops through her insights into the divergent forms of Bertha Mason's delegitimation by, respectively, Jane and Rochester. Jane perceives Bertha as more animal than human, thereby aligning Jane all the more emphatically with the sphere of humanity and its reproduction. Rochester, in contrast, perceives Bertha in missionary-colonial terms. He is thereby associated with divinity rather than humanity; his release from his missionary (marital) duties is presented as an injunction issuing from God himself (pp. 266–7). It is the convergence of these female and male imperialist registers that provides the primary animus for the narrative's movement. Their divergence is just as significant at the novel's conclusion, when the 'tangent narrative' of St John Rivers's heroic missionary life in Calcutta emphasises the incommensurability of these two registers. The case of St John Rivers links the dynamic of 'soul making' to the Kantian categorical imperative: when recast as '*make* the heathen into a human so that he can be treated as an end in himself', the imperative becomes accessory to imperialism (p. 267).

Spivak argues clearly and persuasively that the interpellation of imperial subjects is sexually specific. This presents an important challenge to the gender-blindness of both Said and Jameson. Spivak's approach also includes the possibility of effective metropolitan opposition, a possibility that Said and Jameson disallow. That Spivak can conceive of coherent oppositionality is a consequence of her deconstructionist tenets and her primarily philosophical focus on Kantian notions of subject formation. Thus she reads Mary Shelley's *Frankenstein* as an example of oppositional critique. This is articulated in the way it criticises Victor Frankenstein for his substitution of theoretical for practical reason, and his attempt to invent 'a putative human subject out of natural philosophy alone' (p. 275).

Jane Austen's *Mansfield Park*, like Charlotte Brontë's *Jane Eyre*, charts the movement of a woman from social margins to centre. The centre in this case is the country estate of Mansfield Park, which owes its maintenance to the sugar plantations of Antigua. Said does not view the novel's ideology as sexually differentiated; his analysis takes the estate, and the narrative, to operate as a coherent whole, comprised of an ensemble of female and male figures. This is a consequence of his conception of metropolitan culture as spatially fixed and singular. While Jameson sees the metropole as united in its sensory and existential experience, Said sees it as joined by ideology, contending that 'there was scarcely any dissent, any departure, any demurral from them: there was virtual unanimity that subject races should be ruled ... With few exceptions, the women's as well as the working-class movement was pro-empire' (p. 62).

Said's conception of *Mansfield Park* as an ideological unit, affirmative of empire, is also a consequence of his progressive view of social and cultural history. For according to Said, it is only with modernism that narrative structure admits of formal and ideological divisibility, and becomes capable of ironic (not oppositional) awareness of imperialism's political limitations. Said's is the most ambitious and methodologically eclectic of the three works, concerned as it is with the novel's dynamics of spatial movement, its ideological systems of morality and aesthetics, its characters' trajectories and its materialist contextualisation through contemporary Caribbean political and economic processes. At the same time Said pursues an argument about the function of Austen's novel in enabling subsequent material practices of imperialism. This ambitiousness contributes an admirably broad cultural understanding of imperialism. It also creates some tensions, arising in particular from the emphasis on a spatial model of ideology.

Metropolitan culture and imperialism

Spivak, Said and Jameson differ significantly over three key issues: imperialism's date of origin, its relation to aesthetic modernism and its relation to Enlightenment humanistic philosophy. Said tends to date its origin in the eighteenth century, although at times he identifies the seventeenth and even sixteenth centuries as its point of inception. For Jameson, imperialism is a strictly nineteenth-century phenomenon. Both recognise the magnitude of the changes that European cultural, economic and political practices underwent in the late nineteenth century, but while for Said this period merely expresses a new stage of imperialism, for Jameson this marks its beginning. Jameson presupposes that the classical, national stage of capitalism did not involve (let alone depend upon) colonial production and that it was only when formalised (with the 'Scramble for Africa') in the late Victorian era that imperialism made any significant impact on aesthetic culture. To both of these assumptions Said offers effective rebuttal, demonstrating the significance of colonial expansion for metropolitan economic and cultural formations throughout the nineteenth century.

Jameson and Said both consider modernism a compensatory and ultimately collusive reaction to empire. Discussing *Howards End*, Jameson acknowledges Forster's anti-imperial sentiments, but argues that they are undermined by the sensory impact of expansionism on the novelist. Such an impact is for Jameson an inevitable consequence of the economy:

> colonialism means that a significant structural segment of the eco-
> nomic system as a whole is now located elsewhere, beyond the
> metropolis, outside of the daily life and existential experience of the
> home country ... Such spatial disjunction has as its immediate con-
> sequence the inability to grasp the way the system functions as a
> whole ... no scientific deductions on the basis of the internal evi-
> dence of First-World data, can ever be enough to include this rad-
> ical otherness of colonial life, colonial suffering and exploitation, let
> alone the structural connections between that and this, between
> absent space and daily life in the metropolis. (pp. 50–1)

Jameson's phenomenological language stresses the empirical materiality
of the metropolitan senses. This same empiricism structures Jameson's
definitions of modernism as a biological compensation, referring as he
does to 'the work of some new modernist language on our bodies and our
sensorium that is its precondition' (p. 55).

Because both the human body and the geographical nation have physical substance Jameson seems to assume them to be immune from the
processes of subjective mediation: they are not themselves produced by
and experienced as ideologies but they instead serve as the empirical basis
from which subjectivity emerges. The human sense of existence is, it
seems, entirely and directly constituted by the sensations of the physical
body. And since, for Jameson, the nation is the natural limit of the exis-
tential-sensory subject, then whatever occurs outside of that national
space must consequently be unbridgeably 'other' to it. Thus, however dis-
crepant metropolitan people's social, economic, political and intellectual
positions, their existential-cum-physiological experience of imperialism
is identical. In rendering imperialism a fixed fusion of 'objective' eco-
nomic-productive with 'objective' physiological processes, Jameson prob-
lematically naturalises and depoliticises the phenomenon.

In sharp contrast, Said argues that modernism's existential anxiety
was a response in part to the importation of colonial cultural materials,
in part to the knowledge of colonial resistance movements, both of
which threatened metropolitan cultural and political security. He concurs with Jameson that modernism was fuelled by a desire to compen-
sate for a fracturing of self-identity, substituting aesthetic for social
totalities. But whereas Jameson emphasises the sense of loss – modernist
metropolitans as victims of capitalism's splitting – Said emphasises the
sense of domination underlying modernist production; the formal
experimentation

substituting art and its creations for the once-possible synthesis of
the world empires. When you can no longer assume that Britannia
will rule the waves forever, you have to reconceive reality as something that can be held together by you the artist. (p. 229)

Said's formulations can be made to invert Jameson's. The metropole
was flooded during the period of modernism with representations of
imperialism itself as a system and totality, with representations of its contestation by colonised peoples and with examples of colonised cultures
and knowledge-systems. This lowering of spatial boundaries between
colony and metropole in the flows of capital, information and culture was
matched by an increase in the accessibility to metropolitans of colonial
travel, employment and sojourn.[6] From this it becomes possible to argue
that what aroused modernist perceptions of imperialism as constituting
a 'representational dilemma' and an existential loss was the way late nineteenth-century imperialism *broke down* rather than introduced absolute,
spatial boundaries between countries and peoples.

On the connections between Enlightenment humanistic culture and
the material practices of imperialism, Said offers a variety of conceptual
possibilities, while Spivak is noncommittal. Spivak asserts that Kant's categorical imperative 'can be travestied in the service of the state', to 'justify
the imperialist project', resulting as we have already seen in the violence
of the missionary imperative to constitute 'heathens' as human subjects
by rendering them Christians (p. 267). That such a travesty is possible
Spivak attributes to 'the dangerous transformative power of philosophy'
itself; the travesty 'exists within its lineaments as a possible supplement'
(p. 279). Such an explanation is valuable in its non-reductiveness; unlike
a number of post-structuralist thinkers Spivak does not charge
Enlightenment rationality per se with being categorically 'violent'. Indeed,
it is for her possible to conceive of a humanistically progressive
Kantianism. Shelley's *Frankenstein* provides one example through its
fidelity to Kant's schematic division of human faculties into pure reason,
practical reason and judgement.

That philosophy can be travestied is clearly explained by Spivak, but
not why, nor how; she is inattentive to the dynamics of philosophy's mediation by 'the state', and within aesthetic representation. Why Brontë's text
can be read as receptive to imperialism's travesty and why Shelley's can
not, and what it means for an understanding of both culture and the state
that such unevenness of reception can occur, are not questions with which

Spivak is concerned. She avoids reductiveness in her characterisation of Kantian philosophy, only to transfer such reductiveness to the notions of the state (as identical with 'the imperialist project') and aesthetic culture (as indistinguishable from ideology, of which it presents allegorical examples).

Indeed, although Spivak is careful never to define imperialism as such, but instead focuses on its ideological operations and effects, a general definition (and date) emerges anyway. This comes with her postulation of its historical mechanics:

> No perspective *critical* of imperialism can turn the Other into a self, because the project of imperialism has always already historically refracted what might have been the absolutely Other into a domesticated Other that consolidates the imperialist self. (p. 272)

It is difficult to reconcile the notion of the 'always already' with that of 'historical' refraction. The result is a kind of constitutive indeterminacy whereby Spivak's gestures towards historical particularity ambiguously affirm both a contingent materialism and an absolute idealism. European history happens to coincide with the hegemony of imperialism, such that the sum total of European history is inextricable from an imperialist trajectory that continues in overdetermined ways to control the conditions of contemporary cultural and intellectual production. At the same time, it seems, the designation 'imperialism' applies to the conditions of narrative, representation and knowledge production themselves.

Either way, the process of imperialism is viewed as the precondition of a sense of (European or theoretical) narrative Self, and is predicated on a distorting utilisation of the Other. Imperialism then is not only the explicit practice of power. It is also the disavowal of the possession of power through the belief in one's ability to know and represent the Other; to pursue such a narrative representation is necessarily to turn the Other into a version of oneself. This formulation does not admit of any notion of possible or progressive *mediation*. The phenomenon of imperialism/domination derives, in a sense, from the possibility of movement per se: it is 'the dangerous *transformative* power' of Kantian philosophy that enables its instrumentalisation by the state, enables the categorical imperative 'to be mistaken for' (that is, to occupy the place of) the hypothetical imperative.

The preferable political option for Spivak is, it seems, for subjects, like Kantian imperatives, to learn their limits, stay in their naturally

separate places, as taught by Shelley's *Frankenstein*. The spatialised conception of subjectivity as occupying a distinct, fixed and rightful domain,
is marked here; imperialism becomes the by definition expansionist and
dominatory movement across these delineated territories. It is no accident that Spivak should repeatedly refer to imperialism's 'territorial and
subject-constituting projects' in the same breath: the two projects are
seen as flipsides of the same geo-spatial coin. If imperialism expresses a
highly abstracted will-to-power, it is simultaneously identified with the
highly specific ideology, historical period and region selected by Spivak
for her literary discussion. She privileges the ideology of Christian missionary imperialism, the period of early to mid nineteenth century, and
the terrain of India (to a lesser extent the Caribbean). Admittedly she
presents this choice as strategic rather than theoretical. But, in the
absence of any acknowledged alternative regions and periods, these
examples take on the status of theoretical primacy and general allegory.
Thus, the critic can be caught in a double bind: imperialism's theoretical definition as the totality of Western history/knowledge/power is
effectively at one with its definition as mid-Victorian missionary
ideology.[7]

Said's account of the relations between Western aesthetic representation, narrative and empire is strikingly variable. Detailing both their historical and structural dynamics, at one point he argues

> We are not yet at the stage where we can say whether these [cultural]
> structures are preparations for imperial control and conquest, or
> whether they accompany such enterprises, or whether in some reflec-
> tive or careless way they are a result of empire. We are only at a stage
> where we must look at the astonishing frequency of geographical
> articulations in the three Western cultures that most dominated far-
> flung territories. (p. 61)

Said may here emphasise the undecidability of the relationship, but
elsewhere he equally assertively characterises culture as historically
precedent to imperial political practice and enabling of it.[8] And elsewhere he casts these territorial practices as precedent to the cultural
articulations.[9] Still elsewhere, we are told that the two were mutually
fortifying and symbiotic.[10]

Two theoretical perspectives underlie this contradictory diversity.
One is a Foucauldian notion of the cultural and the political practices as
expressive of the same power dynamic:

there is a convergence between the great geographical scope of the empires ... and universalizing cultural discourses. Power makes this convergence possible; ... [W]ith it goes the ability to be in far-flung places, to learn about other people, to codify and disseminate knowledge, to characterize, transport, install, and display instances of other cultures, and above all to rule them. (p. 130)

The second is a Gramscian notion of culture as part of the ideological weaponry of imperialism:

imperialism [is] a process occurring as part of the metropolitan culture, which at times acknowledges, at other times obscures the sustained business of the empire itself. The important point ... is how the national British cultures maintained hegemony over the peripheries. How within them was consent gained and continuously consolidated for the distant rule of native peoples and territories? (p. 59)

Said's Foucauldianism here deploys a predominantly spatial, formal construction of imperial culture, which in jettisoning the conceptual machinery of historical and economic determinations permits culture to be thought of both as antecedent, subsequent to and contemporary with political expansion. Said not infrequently uses spatial figures to convey this: 'the novel steadily ... *opens up a broad expanse* of domestic imperial culture without which Britain's subsequent acquisition of territory would not have been possible' (p. 114). Or:

The British international identity, the scope of British mercantile and trade policy ... provided irresistible models to emulate, *maps to follow,* actions to live up to. Thus representations of what lay beyond insular or metropolitan boundaries came, almost from the start, to *confirm* European power. (p. 127)

The more Gramscian tenets of Said's analysis, in contrast, are concerned with the contents, as opposed to the spatial shape or form, of cultural ideology, and how they come to be instrumentalisable by specific blocs of political agents and authorities. Such an approach seems to support a view of socio-economic imperial power as able both to utilise existing ideological resources in culture and to invent them. [11]

I find it regrettable that the Gramscian elements in Said's thought are subdued throughout *Culture and Imperialism*. Although they might facilitate further theorisation of social agency, and its relationship to imperial economic and political domination, the Gramscian elements operate more rhetorically than conceptually in this work. Were Said to follow through his Gramscianism, he might be led to a more extended account of how ideology operates. He would be able then to explain why it was that ideologies of imperialism were so predominant in metropolitan Britain, or alternatively to perceive these ideologies as rather more contested than he allows.[12]

The conceptions of Gramsci indeed might offer a potential resource for extending the thought of all three thinkers. In Gramsci's notion of 'articulation' one can find ways to escape the absolutism of historical teleology in Said and Jameson, and the equally absolutist basis of Spivak's allegorical methodology. Gramsci's analysis of the relations between state, civil society and ideology might help to explain the mechanisms whereby the state in Spivak's contention distorts Kant's categorical imperative. Gramsci's engagement with the interrelations between politics and economics also suggests ways to avoid Jameson's neglect of politics.[13]

Literature and the aesthetics of space

Jameson and Said share a similar conception of the aesthetic function and meaning of space. This distinguishes them from Spivak, who views spatial representation as dictated by ideology. Jane Eyre prefers to situate herself not within the 'sanctioned architectural space of the ... drawing room' to which the family retires, but instead in the 'small breakfast room' which adjoins it, and avails herself of the contents of the bookcase placed in this room. This illustrates her constitution as a marginalised and private subject. Spatial location, in other words, is determined by the book's ideology of feminist romantic individualism.

In sharp contrast, Jameson and Said view physical space as constitutive of, not constituted by, their novel's ideologies. Jameson, as we have seen, argues that Forster's consciously anti-imperialist sentiments in *Howards End* are belied by his stylistic, sensuous and aesthetic responses to empire's spatial dynamics. Jameson's 'space' initially refers to that which carries physical matter. Thus, he argues that the image of the 'Great North Road ... suggestive of infinity' with which *Howards End* opens condenses philosophical thoughts into 'essentially a spatial representation and a spatial perception', exposing philosophy's dependence on space for its expression. 'Spatial perception' here apparently denotes 'perception of physical matter' rather than a physically derived mode of general perception. Space, that is, here serves as object, not adjective. Jameson proceeds to argue that what marks this episode as proto-modernist is the image's indeterminacy:

> it is undecidable whether the Great North Road is the tenor or the vehicle; whether the roadway is intended ... to concretize the nebulous metaphysical concept, 'infinity', and by a momentary transfer of its visual properties to make that vague but lofty word a more vivid player in the textual game; or whether, on the other hand, it is rather the metaphysical prestige of the more noble Idea that is supposed to resonate back on the banal highway, lending it *noumen* and thereby transforming it into the merest promise of expressivity without having to affirm it as some official 'symbol' ... Modernism is itself this very hesitation; it emerges in this *spatial gap* within Forster's figure. (pp. 54–5)

Space as a figurative term for the 'gap' between phenomenal and noumenal modalities follows space's meaning as phenomenal matter. The next stage in the argument introduces a third notion: 'The solution to this contradiction, which we call "style", is then the substitution of a spatial or perceptual "meaning" ... for the other kind ...' (p. 55). Here 'spatial' shifts to denote 'the initial *ground*' (basis) of meaning. Jameson repeats the semantic indeterminacy he ascribes to modernism, exploiting the ambiguity sanctioned by this abstracted term. 'Space' is designated as that which forms the material object of the modernist gaze, that which constitutes modernism's subjective basis, and that which constitutes the gap between these objective and subjective qualities. 'Space' becomes less a term for a physically material, sensory quality than a mystical term for whatever escapes, or is not reducible to, tangible and rational 'meaning'.

Jameson partially resolves these contradictions through his dialectical methodology. Contending, with Lukács, that aesthetic representation 'is governed by an intention towards totality', he ultimately casts the aesthetically dense, physically substantial yet indeterminate image of the Great North Road as 'a new spatial language' that 'becomes the marker and the substitute of the unrepresentable totality' (p. 58). Thus 'space' is now effectively a word denoting the transcendental totality itself, both a phenomenal *and* a noumenal entity, and so becomes logically both subject and object of modernism. And the totality is imperialism, 'which stretches out the roads to infinity, beyond the bounds and orders of the national state' (p. 57). Jameson's final observation, though, resists dialectical closure:

> if 'infinity' (and 'imperialism') are bad or negative in Forster, its perception, as a bodily and poetic process, is no longer that, but rather a positive achievement and an enlargement of our sensorium: so that the beauty of the new figure seems oddly unrelated to the social and historical judgement which is its content. (p. 58)

Imperialism maintains the modernist body and of the modernist intellect in an allegedly unresolved structural contradiction.

One does not have to share all of Jameson's presuppositions to recognise the brilliance and usefulness of his discussion. In drawing attention to the ways imperialism influenced metropolitan perceptions of domestic landscape, he opens up important new areas for research. He offers important and suggestive insights into the socio-economic matrices and meanings of modernist literary style. Two aspects emerge as particularly suggestive: Jameson's linkage of aesthetic indeterminacy to the operations of imperialism; and his demonstration of the ways in which empire can take on a metaphysical status. That significatory indeterminacy Jameson detects in Forster's Great North Road image, whereby empirical and transcendental, literal and figurative modalities stand in uneasy instrumental relationship with each other, each claiming subject and object status, can obviously be located in a number of contemporary cultural texts. Conrad's *Heart of Darkness*, title and text, plays out a similar semantic indeterminacy, as does Rider Haggard's *She* (who becomes grammatical and ideological subject and object of empire). These texts are, of course, directly engaged with the project of empire; the extension of Jameson's insights to other modernist texts remains to be made.

Said's discussion of *Mansfield Park* does not share Jameson's dialectical methodology. As a consequence, the contradictoriness of his different notions of space stand out, all the more so, ironically, because he characterises Austen's cultural production as expressive of a unified ideology, an ideology in fact *centred on the values of* social, moral and aesthetic cohesion, order and totality. Said's analysis aims at disclosing the dependency of Austen's metropolitan high culture on colonial possessions, more particularly on the slave plantations of the Caribbean. This important demystificatory project however ends up producing its

own kind of mystique, in which the conviction that geographical territory *is* itself an ideology jostles with the counter-notion that spatial relations are pressed into the service of specific ideological, political and
economic imperatives. The conflict, again, emerges from the mismatch
of Said's Foucauldianism and his Gramscianism. For Said's analysis
effectively identifies space or land as an independent source of social
regulation and value-production whilst simultaneously suggesting that
human agents and institutions confer such qualities upon the space in
question.

Thus Said gives a compelling and persuasive account of how Sir
Thomas's social and economic authority both legitimises and is legit-
imised by his possession of colonial space. Commenting on his departure
from the Mansfield Park estate for Antigua, Said explains:

> Whatever was wrong there … Sir Thomas was able to fix, thereby
> maintaining his control over his colonial domain … Austen here syn-
> chronises domestic with international authority, making it plain that
> the values associated with such higher things as ordination, law, and
> propriety must be grounded firmly in actual rule over and posses-
> sion of territory. (p. 104)

Said's discussion of Sir Thomas's authority-constitution slides easily into
a discussion of social value-constitution, concluding that 'to hold and rule
Mansfield Park is to hold and rule an imperial estate in close, not to say
inevitable association with it. What assures the domestic tranquillity and
attractive harmony of one is the productivity and regulated discipline of
the other' (p. 104).

This seems to me to conflate two separate issues, and with it two contending methodologies. That they are in tension is suggested directly by
Said's own analysis of what happens to Mansfield Park 'while Sir Thomas
is away tending his colonial garden' and establishing its 'productivity and
regulated discipline': anarchy and amorality, not 'domestic tranquillity
and attractive harmony', prevail in Mansfield Park (p. 102). Instead of
guaranteeing the Park's aesthetic and social order, the colony can be seen
to threaten it, by removing its requisite authority-figure.

The delinquency of Mansfield Park's wayward inhabitants is understood by Sir Thomas to arise from an inner deficiency, a lack of moral
principle. This inner lack, Said argues, is filled by two outside forces: 'the
wealth derived from a West Indian plantation' and 'a poor provincial relative', Fanny Price, both 'brought in to Mansfield Park and set to work'

(p. 110). Said makes much of this formal movement in space, from the outside to the inside; the movements of Fanny and of wealth not only correspond to one another but also 'require each other' and further, require 'executive disposition' (p. 110). However, Said has already argued a very similar spatial relation between Fanny and Sir Thomas himself:

> To earn the right to Mansfield Park you must first leave home as a kind of indentured servant ... but then you have the promise of future wealth ... Austen sees what Fanny does as a domestic or small-scale movement in space that corresponds to the larger, more openly colonial movements of Sir Thomas, her mentor, the man whose estate she inherits. The two movements depend on each other. (p. 106)

Herein lie a number of problems. Said has been tempted by the very spatiality, and aestheticism, he is concerned to demystify, leading him to attach ideological significance to formal patterns of movements through space. Establishing the existence of these patterns takes precedence over their internal and their external consistency; hence we are presented with two incompatible accounts of Fanny's status, neither of which is problem-free. To posit Fanny's spatial movements as corresponding to those of Sir Thomas is to overlook a crucial difference between them, already revealed in Said's own analysis. Sir Thomas moves about in space because he has power, Fanny moves about (or rather, is moved) in space because she lacks power. Fanny's movement in enables her to attain legitimation and authority, Sir Thomas's movement in and out is, as we have already seen, both constitutive and reflective of his authority. Fanny, Said is suggesting, resembles Sir Thomas in her upright moral qualities, which entitle her to eventual ownership of the estate. Her innate morality, Said argues, derives from her poverty. Morality, he implies, cannot inhere in those like her decadent cousins who do not have to labour for their wealth.

If this is the case, then it becomes difficult to accept the reasoning and the conclusions of Said's second formulation, in which Fanny is likened to the colony's wealth in being an outside force brought into Mansfield Park to supply what is 'wanting within'. If Fanny is aligned, through her spatial activity, with a colonial planter (the owner of production) she cannot at the same time and for the same reason be aligned with the wealth produced and owned by the planter. Said's first formulation, then, juxtaposes Fanny's poverty with her Mansfield Park cousins' wealthy upbringing; wealth is inherent to Mansfield Park and as such antithetical to the acquisition of morality. Said's second formulation reverses both the geographical location and the moral argument attached to wealth; wealth is something brought in from outside and is interdependent with the morality likewise imported through the figure of Fanny.

The inconsistencies here arise, as I have already argued, from Said's desire to accord space a constitutive ideological role. The foregrounding of space and movement through it as intrinsically meaningful allows powerless human subjects to be rendered conceptually interchangeable with powerful human subjects and with economic processes. Where Said's analysis is at its most valuable is in his persuasive demonstration of the conjunction of political and aesthetic ideological values in the Mansfield Park home estate. Fanny learns there the value of large, ordered spaces that express aesthetic harmony and its correlate socio-political propriety. That this aesthetic-political model is an essentially hierarchical one, necessitating an authoritarian administrator, Said makes clear. His argument that this hierarchical model is *transposable to* the estate's over-seas colony is convincing; less so is his suggestion that the functioning of this model in Mansfield Park requires the existence of the colony.

Said and Jameson reveal a striking incuriosity about the social relations imposed upon colonised peoples, an incuriosity which extends to the colonised themselves. For Jameson, it seems, colonised peoples are conceivable only as an extension of the economic system that controls them. This underlies his suggestion that

> The other pole of the relationship, what defines him [the 'Imperial type'] fundamentally and essentially in his 'imperial' function, – the persons of the colonized – remains structurally occluded, and cannot but so remain, necessarily, as a result of the limits of the system. (p. 58)

Consequently, he argues, the colonised can carry no direct purchase on metropolitan aesthetic consciousness but are representable only by proxy, either through symbols of capitalist power or through racialised Europeans. Thus, for instance, he argues of *Howards End* that 'Africa is set in place by the mediation of Charles Wilcox, who works in Uganda for his father's Imperial and West African Rubber Company' (p. 65). Arguing that during this era 'the word imperialism designates, not the relationship of metropolis to colony, but rather the rivalry of the various imperial and metropolitan nation-states among themselves' leads to Jameson's con-tention that the colonised Other is represented in 'high' culture through the demonised representation of another 'imperial nation state' such as

Germany (p. 49). Zola's *La Débâcle* features Germans as 'physically alien and terrifying, barbarous, uncivilized, and still not terribly remote, as stereotypes, from the archaic "wild man of the middle ages"' (p. 49). This rests on assumptions that are empirically questionable, given that some modernist writings do contain direct representations of colonised peoples.[14] Jameson's assumption is politically problematic, too, in its willingness to construct such an elision (of the human-subjective into the economic-objective) as automatically inevitable when it does occur.

For Said, 'slavery, economic depression, and rivalry with France' are grouped together as constituting what was (somewhat vaguely) 'at issue' in the possession of Caribbean colonies. None of these three particular definitions is in fact integral to his ensuing discussion of the meanings of colonial space within the novel. None the less this discussion does posit, even if it does not conclusively demonstrate, that 'right up to the last sentence, Austen affirms and repeats the geographical process of expansion involving trade, production, and consumption that predates, underlies, and guarantee [the novel's] morality' (p. 111).

To add to the sense of analytic disjunction, Said's closing comments in this section contend:

> There is a paradox ... which I have been impressed by but can in no way resolve ... Everything we know about Austen and her values is at odds with the cruelty of slavery. Fanny Price reminds her cousin that after asking Sir Thomas about the slave trade, 'There was such a dead silence' as to suggest that one world could not be connected with the other since there simply is no common language for both. That is true ... In order more accurately to read works like *Mansfield Park*, we have to see them in the main as resisting or avoiding that other setting, which their formal inclusiveness, historical honesty, and prophetic suggestiveness cannot completely hide. (p. 115)

One can detect here, perhaps, Said's identification with Austen: sharing her values of honesty and inclusiveness, he is obliged to include (passing) mention of slavery at the risk of violating his/her values of aesthetic decorum. But what, one is entitled to ask, does the 'trade, production, and consumption' that 'underlies' the novel's morality consist in if not precisely the system of slavery? (p. 115). That Said should thus cursorily mention slavery attests less to the topic's fictional marginality than it does to his lack of desire to engage with the topic. Said's account of slavery's 'silence', then, colludes with that silence.

Said's problematic treatment of slavery is part of a generally problematic presentation of economic processes. The narrative condition of economic wealth is that it be converted by Austen 'to propriety, order, and ... comfort'; for Said, it seems, the human basis of this wealth acquisition in slavery is not readily itself convertible to such aesthetic-political values (p. 108). Only an already abstracted, and rhetorically posited, notion of economic system can undergo the further abstraction of aesthetic conversion. Said's assertions about the way wealth functions in and for the novel thereby become undemonstrable and for that reason problematic.

Instead of arguing an economic aspect to inhere within such narratives, critics might explore the textual mechanisms whereby metropolitan writers such as Austen carefully exclude the economic aspects of their imperial subjects. In addition, critics might utilise a model of cultural representation that permits of more internal ideological contradiction and contestation than Said allows. This would enable a reading of *Mansfield Park* as containing, potentially, both oppositional and affirmative relations to empire. (A strongly oppositional reading issues from Moira Ferguson, whose conclusions are the antithesis of Said's. Ferguson contends an emergent abolitionism at work in the novel, derived from a mediatory concept of textual representation in which Fanny Price is stationed as slave surrogate.) [15]

Both Said and Jameson, I suggest, foreground an aestheticised analysis of colonial space at the analytical expense of space's human occupants. They consequently minimise the historical function of violence in metropolitan culture and empire. Jameson's minimisation of violence meshes with a minimisation of the category of ideology. That he takes the physical senses of metropolitans to stand by definition totally outside of ideology is potentially a rather dangerous formulation, especially since these physical senses are alleged to affirm imperialism: the dangers of ascribing a biologically determined component to political practices need not be spelt out here. To introduce (economic, social and political) violence into Jameson's theorisations is to denaturalise much of what he effectively presents as physiologically natural and structurally inevitable. Thus, for instance, we can examine the *violence* of narratives that can represent colonised peoples only as non-human offshoots of capitalist production. The mechanics whereby metropolitan people equate imperialism with the entirety of human possibility are certainly violent, even if Jameson does not recognise this.

Conclusion

Both the strengths and the weaknesses of Said, Jameson and Spivak here inspire future work on metropolitan, imperial cultures and subjectivities. They clear a path for materialist analysis of the ways in which the metropolis was, like the colonies, a heterogeneous site of hegemonic and counter-hegemonic institutions, movements and subjectivities. Spivak's emphasis on sexual difference of imperial interpellation suggests how future work can explore the function of other kinds of difference in metropolitan ideological formations. Jameson's argument for the constitutive contradictions of Forster – at once rationally, and rhetorically, opposed to empire yet aesthetically affirmative of it – opens a number of theoretical and critical possibilities for future work on political rhetoric, its relations to imperial structures of feeling and aesthetics.

The work of these three attests in very different ways to the fruitfulness of attending to the international, economic, political and philosophical processes which feed imperial culture. Said's macrological approach reveals the complex challenge of accounting for the totality of imperial culture's formations. Spivak and Jameson invite critical exploration of the relative advantages of dialectical and categorical approaches to the analysis of imperial culture. In Jameson we witness a dialectical approach to the production of art – which is held to preserve and sublate its social determinants – conjoined with a resolutely empiricist, categorical formulation of human bodies and economies. These latter provide the material determinants of consciousness in a direct, unmediated manner; they remain for Jameson unconditioned by political and ideological processes. For Spivak, imperial culture directly illustrates philosophical theories of human subject-constitution, themselves corollary to political processes of territory-constitution. If Jameson's notion of imperial subject-constitution excludes the political, Spivak's excludes the economic. The categorical fixity of both constructions precludes apprehension of imperial subjectivity as a dynamic formation, interacting with both political and economic processes.

Finally, Spivak, Jameson and Said all draw attention to the need for materialist postcolonial criticism to engage theoretically with the topic of space and the ways it functions within imperial metropolitan culture. What emerges from their work is the challenge of producing an account that neither aestheticises space nor renders it a synonym for existential aporia but is sensitive both to phenomenological and political processes, to human production of as well as production within space.

Notes

1 Aijaz Ahmad, *In Theory: Classes, Nations, Literatures* (London: Verso, 1992). For materialist critiques of this see Neil Lazarus, 'Postcolonialism and the Dilemmas of Nationalism: Aijaz Ahmad's Critique of Third-Worldism', *Diaspora: A Journal of Transnational Studies*, 2, 3 (1993), pp. 373–400, and Benita Parry's review article of Aijaz Ahmad's *In Theory*, *History Workshop Journal*, 36 (1993), pp. 232–41.

2 Francis Mulhern (ed.), *Contemporary Marxist Literary Criticism* (London: Longman, 1992), p. 97.

3 Terry Eagleton (ed.), *Raymond Williams: Critical Perspectives* (Cambridge: Polity Press, 1989), pp. 150–65.

4 The texts of this article's discussion are Edward Said, *Culture and Imperialism* (London: Chatto, 1993); Gayatri Chakravorty Spivak, 'Three Women's Texts and a Critique of Imperialism', in Henry Louis Gates Jr (ed.), *'Race', Writing and Difference* (Chicago: University of Chicago Press, 1986) pp. 262–80; Fredric Jameson, 'Modernism and Imperialism', in Seamus Deane (ed.), *Nationalism, Colonialism and Literature* (Minneapolis: University of Minnesota Press, 1990), pp. 43–66. Jameson's essay was first published by Field Day Theatre Company (Derry, Northern Ireland) and this edition is titled a 'Field Day Company Book'. A version of Gayatri Spivak's essay can be found in her *Critique of Postcolonial Reason: Toward a History of the Vanishing Present* (Cambridge, MA, and London: Harvard University Press, 1999), pp. 112–40.

5 A useful discussion of Said's book is Bruce Robbins, Mary-Louise Pratt, Jonathan Arac, R. Radhakrishnan, and Edward Said, 'Edward Said's *Culture and Imperialism*: A Symposium', *Social Text*, 40 (1994), pp. 1–38. See also Paul Zeleza's critique: chapter 21 'The Tribulations of Undressing the Emperor', *Manufacturing African Studies and Crises* (Dakar: Codesria, 1997), pp. 478–93.

6 See for example Eric Hobsbawm, *The Age of Empire: 1874–1914* (London: Weidenfeld and Nicolson, 1987); John M. MacKenzie, *Propaganda and Empire: The Manipulation of British Public Opinion, 1880–1960* (Manchester: Manchester University Press), 1984; John M. MacKenzie (ed.), *Imperialism and Popular Culture* (Manchester: Manchester University Press, 1986).

7 For a discussion of Spivak's Indiacentrism and its implications for the analysis of African imperialism see Laura Chrisman, 'The Imperial Unconscious? Representations of Imperial Discourse', *Critical Quarterly*, 32, 3 (1990), pp. 38–58.

8 See for instance Said, *Culture and Imperialism*, p. 10, p. 114, p. 128.

9 See Ibid., p. 119, p. 127.

10 Ibid., p. 40, p. 84.

11 The tensions between Said's Foucauldianism and his Gramscianism are also evident in his *Orientalism*, as observed by Dennis Porter, '*Orientalism* and Its Problems', in Patrick Williams and Laura Chrisman (eds.), *Colonial*

Discourse and Post-colonial Theory: A Reader (Hemel Hempstead: Harvester, 1993), pp. 150–61.

12 See Bernard Porter, *Critics of Empire: British Radical Attitudes to Colonialism in Africa, 1895–1914* (London: Macmillan, 1968).

13 For a suggestive account of Gramsci's uses in the related studies of ethnicity, see Stuart Hall, 'Gramsci's Relevance for the Study of Race and Ethnicity', in David Morley and Kuan-Hsing Chen (eds.), *Stuart Hall: Critical Dialogues in Cultural Studies* (London: Routledge, 1996), pp. 411–40.

14 The most obvious example is Forster's own *A Passage to India*; Jameson's explanation on pp. 65–6 of how this novel conforms to his scheme is unconvincing, based as it is on the dubious contention that Hindus are 'specifically designated as that Other, inaccessible to Western representation'.

15 Moira Ferguson, '*Mansfield Park*: Slavery, Colonialism and Gender', *Oxford Literary Review*, 13 (1991), pp. 118–39.

Part II
Transnationalism and race

4

Journeying to death: Paul Gilroy's
The Black Atlantic

Paul Gilroy's *The Black Atlantic* has received huge international acclaim.[1] Within American studies, anthropology, black studies, Caribbean studies, cultural studies and literary studies the book has been hailed as a major and original contribution. Gilroy takes issue with the national boundaries within which these disciplines operate, arguing that, as the book jacket tells us

> there is a culture that is not specifically African, American, Caribbean, or British, but all of these at once; a black Atlantic culture whose themes and techniques transcend ethnicity and nationality to produce something new and, until now, unremarked.

Political energy animates Gilroy's academic challenge. He sets out to expose the dangers as he sees it of contemporary nationalism: whether academic or popular, implicit or explicit, black or white in focus, Gilroy sees it as socially and politically undesirable. Gilroy's concept of a black Atlantic is then offered as a political and cultural corrective, which argues the cross-national, cross-ethnic basis and dynamics of black diasporic identity and culture.[2]

Gilroy's formulations mesh neatly with the 1990s metropolitan academic climate, which saw the rise in popularity of concepts of fusion, hybridity and syncretism as explanatory tools for the analysis of cultural formation. The 1990s was also a decade in which postmodernist intellectual concerns with language and subjectivity infused both academia and 'new left' politics to create a dominant paradigm of 'culturalism' for the analysis of social relations. This development risked abandoning the tenets and resources of socio-economic analysis. Aesthetics and aestheticism were made to function both as explanation of and solution to social and political processes. For these reasons, Gilroy's book (the aestheticism of which will be discussed later) is a 'sign of the times'. These are also among the reasons it has become so popular.

The 1990s intensification of diverse nationalist movements – ethnicist, secular and fundamentalist – supplies an additional context for the book. Gilroy's characterisation of nationalism tends not to acknowledge such diversity but rather targets a generalised ethnicist nationalism as the only kind of contemporary nationalism, which afflicts both white and black communities in identical ways.[3] Hence another reason for the book's appeal to academics. It licenses an easy armchair condemnation of black politics; it enables academics to feel justified in not taking seriously the challenges posed to their institutional privilege and to hegemonic forms of knowledge-production by black and Third-World nationalisms.

If contesting nationalism is one goal of this book, intervening in debates about modernity is another. Gilroy challenges Marxist, economic and philosophical accounts of the development of modernity as a self-contained European process, based on principles and practices of rationality, economic productivism, Enlightenment egalitarianism and wage labour. Slavery, he argues, was fundamental to modernity; racial terror lies within its heart. Gilroy's concern with the racial terror of slavery chimes with a burgeoning academic interest in the experience of Jews under Nazism (the emergent 'Holocaust studies'), a connection that Gilroy makes explicit in the book.

In contrast to some trends in post modern thought which equate the whole of the Enlightenment project with genocide, Gilroy does not reject modernity altogether but rather accentuates slavery as an unacknowledged part of it. I welcome the way this contests modernity's complacency by its emphasis on the inhuman violence and brutality with which modernity is entwined. However the mere juxtaposition of the concepts 'freedom' with 'coercion', 'reason' with 'terror', does not amount to a reconceptualisation or explanation of the relationship between the two spheres. They remain in frozen, almost mysterious association. Gilroy's formulation arguably caters to current academic predilections for paradox, the sublime and the incomprehensible. The suggestion that certain phenomena 'defy' norms of explanation may encourage analytic passivity; one need not attempt to find more adequate norms.

Of the many important concerns in *The Black Atlantic*, I want to focus on two here: Gilroy's conceptualisation of the relations between nationalism, socialism and black identity; and the characterisation of black expressive culture in relation to slavery and political agency. I am interested in tracing the implications of Gilroy's opposition to nationalism and socialism, and his formulation of a black utopian aesthetic premised on a death-drive.[4]

Gilroy's entire oeuvre rejects what he sees as the inescapably absolutist, vanguardist and essentialist currents of nationalism and socialism.
However the counter-model Gilroy presents, of an outer-national, hybrid
blackness, itself rests on many of the same assumptions. Where Gilroy is
a powerful, materialist deconstructor of other intellectuals and their mys-
tificatory, authoritarian agendas, his own project subscribes to a decidedly mystical ideology and a transcendental notion of blackness that
retains the very ethnicism for which he castigates Afrocentric nationalism. Because his definition of this emancipatory black diasporism repu-
diates the potential resources of nationalism and socialism, and proceeds
by way of positing absolute antinomies between these respective value
systems, Gilroy's formulations become necessarily self-enclosed, hermet-
ically sealed off, resistant to dialogism, dialectical transformation and
cross-fertilisation. 'The Black Atlantic' becomes, despite its immense
potential, an exclusive club liner, populated by 'mandarins' and 'masses'
hand-picked by Gilroy, bound for death.[5]

'*There Ain't No Black in the Union Jack*': the emergence of antinomies

Gilroy's first book, '*There Ain't No Black in the Union Jack*', argues black
British expressive culture to be fundamentally anti-capitalist.[6] This anti-
capitalism, he contends, derives from a wholesale rejection of productivism. The experience of slavery, and its historical memory, has rendered
black peoples, unlike white workers and socialists, resistant to the notion
that productive labour and expansionism of productive capacities are the
medium, or precondition, for human emancipation. Black music, argues
Gilroy, is full of this romantic anti-capitalism, expressed through lyrics
that criticise the alienation of the labour system and which

> celebrate non-work activity and the suspension of the time and dis-
> cipline associated with wage labour … In these cultural traditions,
> work is sharply counterposed not merely to leisure in general but to
> a glorification of autonomous desire which is presented as inherent
> in sexual activity. The black body is reclaimed from the world of
> work and, in Marcuse's phrase celebrated as an 'instrument of pleas-
> ure rather than labour'. (p. 202)

There is much to agree with here. But what I find questionable is the
equation of 'wage labour' with 'labour', so that the critique of capitalist

wage-labour structures is becomes a rejection of productive labour itself, or self-realisation through labour. Gilroy's stark polarisation of work and recreation is also questionable. A more fruitful approach to the analysis of black anti-capitalisms might start with the premise that there is anything *but* an antinomy between work and play in this music. In fact, the labour-intensive process of sexual pleasure that Gilroy presents here is fuelled precisely by the notion that labour has a positive value. Gilroy even discloses such an approach, but seems not to notice, when he argues that 'these tropes are supported by the multi-accentuality and polysemy of black languages. For example, in black American ghetto speech the word work can mean dancing, labour, sexual activity or any nuanced combination of all three' (p. 203). The fact that the word 'work' can denote, equally, 'labour', 'dancing' and 'sexual activity' suggests that, far from an opposition, there is a strong affinity among all the activities. What needs conceptualisation is how and why such a fluid linguistic interchangeability between the spheres can occur. And that requires a methodology that can allow for dialectical and dialogical relationships rather than static oppositions.

If Gilroy's anti-economistic approach precludes dialectical relations between blackness and labour in expressive cultures, it also jettisons the possibility of any economic analysis of black cultures or social movements. Black music, and other recreational activities such as sport, are exactly the media most subject to mass commodification. I recommend, then, that Gilroy's analysis is supplemented by an approach that retains the utility of economic analysis in conceptualising black cultural productions. I advocate too an expansion, not rejection, of class conceptualisation. This needs to be adequate to black experience, neither invalidated by it, as Gilroy alleges, nor invalidating of it.[7]

The same expansion I would urge of the analysis of the nation-state. Gilroy in *'There Ain't No Black'* wants to locate blacks as falling historically outside the received versions of the nation-state by cultural racism and choosing to remain outside by choice, identifying as members of diaspora and local community instead.[8] His intolerance towards all nationalisms reaches new heights in *The Black Atlantic*, where his emphasis falls on a black trans- and anti-national identity as an antidote to the pernicious exclusivisms heralded by black nationalism-as-ethnic-absolutism.

Important though it is, Gilroy's denunciation in *'There Ain't No Black'* of a cosily racialist cultural nationalism, shared by right and left, needs revision and supplementation. His denunciation rests on a fatalism – there ain't no black in the Union Jack and there never can be – which ironically operates to leave such racially exclusive nationalism intact rather than capable of being challenged from within, the more so as he rightly sees right and left as united here. This fatalism however overlooks the historically highly contestable and contested constructions of British nationness and nationalism.[9] In effect, Gilroy's analysis replicates the cultural determinism that he ascribes to cultural nationalists, by presupposing an unchangeable homogeneity of white British national ideology. The more challenging approach would be to work theoretically and politically to foreground the seldom-acknowledged heterogeneity of Britishness through history. And one way to do this is by opening up a comparative mutually illuminating analysis of the languages and practices of British nationalism, colonialism and imperialism. Gilroy, in focusing solely on the interaction of languages of race and nation, forecloses such analysis.

If materialism is useful for explaining and challenging exclusivist types of nationalism, so is the notion of utopia. Gilroy is indeed a big fan of utopianism, but his formulations align utopianism exclusively with outer-national cultural impulses. The utopianism of black music, for him, lies in its expression of a fundamentally migratory identity. And in an anti-capitalism that is, for him, radically opposed to all aspects of the production process. Contemporary Afrocentric black nationalism, however, also has a utopian dimension. This articulates an idealised African heritage to which black Americans rightfully belong, and through which they can in some way transcend socio-economic disadvantage.

Gilroy's critique of this essentialising brand of nationalism is very valuable in its disclosure of Afrocentrism's intellectual fallacies and political shortcomings. Where his critique falls short is in not taking seriously enough the force of the utopianism within it, and recognising its critical, as well as affirmative, relationship to white racist hegemony. Rather than seeing Afrocentrism as a reprehensibly self-inflicted false consciousness, worthy of denunciation, and strangling other possibilities for black political imagination, it might be more productive to find ways to engage with it. And to look at it as a symptom rather than as a cause. My sense is that though some of Afrocentrism can be explained as the product of black petty-bourgeois intellectuals in pursuit of self-aggrandisement – as Gilroy has it – not all of it can be. One would never know from Gilroy's account that Afrocentrism has gained popularity amongst a wide range of black institutions and communities in the context of an ever-worsening socio-economic crisis for black Americans, in which white racial paranoia and hostilities towards black minorities seem to be intensifying.[10] That broader context has to be considered to have some bearing on the phenomenon's popularity; an exclusively immanent critique will not go very far in hastening its demise.

In any case, I do not consider it possible, or desirable, to eliminate all nationalist ideologies, or cancel national entities as objects of analysis. Gilroy's presumption, in his discussion of Afrocentrism as of white British nationalism, is that nationalism can only be ethnically purist and exclusivist and is incapable of pluralisation. This is questionable. To posit nationalism and outer- or trans-nationalism as mutually incompatible political goals, cultural values and analytic perspectives is less productive than to see them as interdependent.

First-World blackness, intellectuals and Europe

Gilroy's conception of the black Atlantic is motivated, in part, by his desire to rebut the fallacies of black nationalism and white English cultural theory. As he argues:

> In opposition to both of these nationalist or ethnically absolute approaches, I want to develop the suggestion that cultural historians could take the Atlantic as one single, complex unit of analysis in their discussions of the modern world and use it to produce an explicitly transnational and intercultural perspective. Apart from the confrontation with English historiography and literary history this entails a challenge to the ways in which black American cultural and political histories have so far been conceived. I want to suggest that much of the precious intellectual legacy claimed by African-American intellectuals as the substance of their particularity is in fact only partly their absolute ethnic property. (p. 15)

What Gilroy then advocates and initiates is a mode of conceptualisation that posits black diasporic identity to be constituted through the triangular relationship of the continents of Africa, Europe and America. He traces the path of this transnational cultural-political formation through an exhilarating series of case studies analysing contemporary black music, the formative sojourns of prominent black intellectuals W.E.B. Du Bois and Richard Wright in Germany and France respectively. Of Du Bois, for example, he argues:

Du Bois's travel experiences raise in the sharpest possible form a question common to the lives of almost all these figures who begin as African-Americans or Caribbean people and are then changed into something else which evades those specific labels and with them all fixed notions of nationality and national identity. Whether their experience of exile is enforced or chosen, temporary or permanent, these intellectuals and activists, writers, speakers, poets, and artists repeatedly articulate a desire to escape the restrictive bonds of ethnicity, national identification, and sometimes even 'race' itself. Some speak … in terms of the rebirth that Europe offered them. Whether they dissolved their African-American sensibility into an explicitly pan-Africanist discourse or political commitment, their relationship to the land of their birth and their ethnic political constituency was absolutely transformed. The specificity of the modern political and cultural formation I want to call the black Atlantic can be defined, on one level, through this desire to transcend both the structures of the nation state and the constraints of ethnicity and national particularity. (p. 19)

Exciting though his readings of black Americans Du Bois and Wright are, and highly insightful into the role that travel and European philosophy played in shaping their personal, political and intellectual identity, as a counter to Afrocentrism they are probably limited. Only from a very specific and academic perspective could the affirmation of black debts to European philosophy be argued to be a counter-model of social emancipation. A better way to counter Afrocentric nationalism might be to emphasise intellectual, political and cultural cross-fertilisation of black America with the Caribbean and Latin America; with proletarian and socialist US cultures; with Third-World liberationist thought. And a way to counter the problematic racial purism of Afrocentrism might be to emphasise and explore the significance of mixed-race intellectuals and their cultural texts.

My other reservation about Gilroy's exclusive focus on Europe as space of liberation for New World blacks is that it overlooks entirely the experience of Europe as historically, and structurally, oppressive for blacks from colonies – so well charted, for instance, in the Senegalese writer and film-maker Sembene Ousmane's *Black Docker*, the novel of a young Senegalese aspiring writer who comes to Marseilles, works as a docker and entrusts his book to a white French woman writer who having promised to help him find a publisher steals the book and has it published to great success under her own name.[11] After accidentally killing the woman, in anger, he experiences the humiliation of being denounced as a liar when he claims the book to be his own, and is imprisoned, sentenced to death.[12]

My reservation is less that Gilroy does not take on black colonialism in what is already a highly ambitious and broad-ranging analysis, but that the way in which he conceptualises the black Atlantic is one which makes totalising claims for itself. The identity and experience of New World slave-descended black people is, by default, seen to contain or represent all modern black experience. Slavery is consistently accorded a primacy which colonialism is not. Slavery becomes the prime shaper of black identity and culture and also takes primacy as the structural or ontological deconstructor of Enlightenment modernity.

Conceptualising slavery

If Gilroy's black Atlantic is concerned with the work of 'high' intellectual black writers, it is also concerned with the mass phenomenon of slavery and its impact on black vernacular culture and sensibility. It is this aspect that I want to focus on here, in some detail, since it is from Gilroy's conceptualisation of slavery that his most controversial, most powerful and also most problematic contributions derive. Gilroy's characterisations of slavery serve two distinct if overlapping aims. The first is to situate slavery and its legacy as constituting in black people a distinct 'counterculture of modernity'; the second is to argue slavery as a condition which forces a reconceptualisation of Enlightenment modernity even as it calls the project into question. I find it fascinating that Gilroy seems split between two very different, and possibly conflicting, representations of slavery's counterculture. The first is essentially holistic, in which slave subjects form a condition that refuses modernity's categorical separation of the spheres of aesthetics, ethics, politics and epistemology. As Gilroy suggests:

> Their progress from the status of slaves to the status of citizens led them to enquire into what the best possible forms of social and political existence might be. The memory of slavery, actively preserved as a living intellectual resource in their expressive political culture, helped them to generate a new set of answers to this enquiry. They had to fight – often through their spirituality – to hold on to the unity of ethics and politics sundered from each other by modernity's

insistence that the true, the good, and the beautiful had distinct origins and belong to different domains of knowledge. First slavery itself and then their memory of it induced many of them to query the foundational moves of modern philosophy and social thought, whether they came from the natural rights theorists ... the idealists who wanted to emancipate politics from morals so that it could become a sphere of strategic action, or the political economists of the bourgeoisie who first formulated the separation of economic activity from both ethics and politics. The brutal excesses of the slave plantation supplied a set of moral and political responses to each of these attempts. (p. 39)

Gilroy explicitly argues that slaves and their descendants are thus set up to occupy the place of humanity's emancipatory subjects in an unabashedly utopian formulation:

This [slave] subculture often appears to be the intuitive expression of some racial essence but is in fact an elementary historical acquisition produced from the viscera of an alternative body of cultural and political expression that considers the world critically from the point of view of its emancipatory transformation. In the future, it will become a place which is capable of satisfying the (redefined) needs of human beings that will emerge once the violence – epistemic and concrete – of racial typology is at an end. Reason is thus reunited with the happiness and freedom of individuals and the reign of justice within the collectivity. (p. 39)

Now, there is much here that I find suggestive. This, notwithstanding Gilroy's contradictory characterisation of slaves' holistic subjectivity as something that they struggled to retain against the pressure of modernity *and* as something bequeathed to them by the very experience of modernity itself. What I find troubling is the next step of his argument, which repeats the polarisation of labour and liberation, labour and art, found in *'There Ain't No Black'*, and already briefly discussed here. Gilroy argues thus:

I have already implied that there is a degree of convergence here with other projects towards a critical theory of society, particularly Marxism. However, where lived crisis and systemic crisis come together, Marxism allocates priority to the latter while the memory

of slavery insists on the priority of the former. Their convergence is
also undercut by the simple fact that in the critical thought of blacks
in the West, social self-creation through labour is not the centre-
piece of emancipatory hopes. For the descendants of slaves, work sig-
nifies only servitude, misery, and subordination. Artistic expression,
expanded beyond recognition from the grudging gifts offered by the
masters as a token substitute for freedom from bondage, there
becomes the means towards both individual self-fashioning and
communal liberation. (pp. 39–40)

I find this problematic for a number of reasons, not least being Gilroy's
assumption that he can pronounce so authoritatively on the meaning that
labour has for these people, a meaning that admits of no positivity what-
soever. I will return to the exclusively negative characterisation of labour
shortly, when I discuss Gilroy's revision of Hegel's master–slave dialectic.
But here I want to focus on the description of the aesthetic activity for
slaves, which is argued to function as their vehicle for individual and collective liberation. For workers, Gilroy implies, labour serves this liberatory function; for slaves, however, it is artistic expression alone that fulfils
such a transfigurative role.

I wonder about this aestheticism. Whereas in *'There Ain't No Black'*
Gilroy did go to some length to argue black expressive culture to be part of
a broader black emancipatory, transfigurative social movement, and
devoted a chapter respectively to the analysis of black music and black
social movements as witnessed in the 1980s black British 'riots', by the time
he writes *The Black Atlantic* he has it seems reached the conclusion that
black art *is* black social movement, not one component but its totality.[13] He
does not altogether outlaw directly political activity by blacks, but accords
it no transfigurative potential, labelling it instead as expressive exclusively
of a politics of bourgeois civic 'fulfilment'. Artistic activity, in contrast, performs what Gilroy terms a 'politics of transfiguration'.[14]

Now what has happened to Gilroy's contention that slave counterculture is distinguishable precisely for its refusal to segregate politics, aesthetics, ethics and knowledge as human categories and operations? From
the challenge posed by this holistic formulation he moves swiftly, and
regrettably, to the less challenging refuge of a traditional aestheticism, in
which, it seems, black art is the only authentic repository of this holism,
the only category which can contain and articulate black countercultural
ethics, politics and knowledge.

Gilroy's refusal to cede political and labouring activity any social transformative capacity is embodied in his account of the master–slave relationship as represented in Frederick Douglass's autobiography. Douglass, a leading nineteenth-century black activist and thinker, had been a slave, and wrote several versions of his autobiography. His first and most famous narrative contains a detailed account of the turning point in his life, when he fights his slave master in a protracted physical struggle. The struggle engenders Douglass's self-respect, masculinity and the respect of his master, who cannot defeat him. Douglass concludes that: 'I was no longer a servile coward, trembling under the frown of a brother worm of the dust, but my long-cowed spirit was roused to an attitude of manly independence. I had reached a point at which I was not afraid to die' (p. 63). Gilroy argues this account to present a radical alternative to Hegel's version of the master–slave dialectic, contending that

> Douglass's tale can be used to reveal a great deal about the difference between the male slave's and the master's views of modern civilisation. In Hegel's allegory, which correctly places slavery at the natal core of modern sociality, we see that one solipsistic combatant in the elemental struggle prefers his conqueror's version of reality to death and submits. He becomes the slave while the other achieves mastery. Douglass's version is quite different. For him, the slave actively prefers the possibility of death to the continuing condition of inhumanity on which plantation slavery depends ...This [is a] turn towards death as a release from terror and bondage and a chance to find substantive freedom ... Douglass's preference for death fits readily with archival material on the practice of slave suicide and needs also to be seen alongside other representations of death as agency that can be found in early African-American fiction. (p. 63)

I am not concerned with the accuracy of Gilroy's interpretation of Hegel, but rather with the way he manipulates Douglass's testimony to pursue his central argument of the death-drive fundamental to slave culture, a drive maintained in what Gilroy argues to be the nihilistic orientation of contemporary black cultures. I want to remark on two things here, before going on to consider the political and intellectual consequences of such a theorisation for the mapping of contemporary black counterculture. The first is that Gilroy seems over-quick to convert a *willingness to risk* death into a positive orientation, a desire for, death. The second is that, even were one to grant the persistence of a death-drive in contemporary and historical black culture, such a desire is articulated, as in the Douglass narrative, within the matrix of a spiritual redemptionism. Douglass throughout his narrative stations himself as a form of Christ, for whom, one supposes, death is not quite the finite condition it is for mortals.[15] Gilroy is so determined to identify death-drive as expressive of a radical nihilism – he bizarrely links Douglass's position to Nietzsche's in its alleged godlessness – that he underestimates here the significance of redemptionism as a condition of Douglass's 'inclination towards death'. For Gilroy, apparently, it matters little whether the death-drive is conditioned by 'apocalyptic or redemptive' sensibilities, as both are the same in their consequences for modernity's rationality, as he argues:

> The discourse of black spirituality which legitimises these moments of violence possesses a utopian truth content that projects beyond the limits of the present. The repeated choice of death rather than bondage articulates a principle of negativity that is opposed to the formal logic and rational calculation characteristic of modern western thinking and expressed in the Hegelian slave's preference for bondage rather than death. (p. 68)

It is extremely important to differentiate between the meanings of a positive and a negative utopianism in black cultures. By the time Gilroy reaches his final chapter, it is clear that his preference is for the negative, drawn from his version of Adornian thought and fused, awkwardly, with a Benjaminian conception of modernity as ontological rupture. In this brand of utopianism, only the principle and representation of negativity, and the rejection of a possible 'afterlife' or future earthly life – only these can gesture towards an 'authentic' emancipatory future condition of being.

The emphasis, that is, falls on nihilism instead of optimism; a nihilism through which its opposite can emerge. To give positive expression to, and literally represent, the forms an emancipated life might take (in heaven or on Earth) is to capitulate to the existing forces of actual domination which exercise control (among other things) over the notion of 'representation' itself. This I find both problematic and inaccurate, in the case of slave cultures. Their explicit emphasis upon utopian notions of spiritual redemption, solace and the imaginings of actual future social transformation is overlooked and undermined by Gilroy's exclusive valorisation of the negative and non-representable.

This emphasis on moribundity as the fundamental, and inescapable, consequence of slavery, along with the refusal to grant legitimacy to modern rationality, is at once politically challenging and disturbing. For all his discussion of modernity and rationality, it is never quite clear to me whether Gilroy is arguing the institution of slavery to be a form of racial terror which is obscene because it *is* rational, systematic, or whether, in contrast, he is arguing for slavery's basis in *irrationality*. The relationship and his argument are mystified and obfuscatory, and all that is clear to me is Gilroy's desire to invite scepticism towards rationality's emancipatory qualities. His own systematic isolation of slavery from any economic context adds to this ambiguity, and his argument at the end of *The Black Atlantic* for the linkage of Jewish Holocaust thinkers (including the Frankfurt School) and their experience with black diasporan experience does nothing in itself to elucidate his position further.

Since the concept of dialectics is refuted by Gilroy's allegorisation of Hegel's allegory, the Frankfurt School's historical-dialectical analysis of the relationship between reason and unreason, and their dialectical linkage of rationality with political economy, is obviously not what Gilroy has in mind when he argues for elective affinities between black and Jewish analysis. Such a dialectical approach, based upon a structural concern with the dynamic, mutually transformative processes of political domination and intellectual production, might be a more productive basis for analysing the connections of slavery, reason and terror than the static, ontological and mystical approach taken by Gilroy.

It is the partiality of Gilroy's death-drive as an account of slavery's counterculture that I want to consider here. Discussing contemporary black culture as derived from the allegedly primal moment of slavery Gilroy argues:

> The turn towards death also points to the ways in which black cultural forms have hosted and even cultivated a dynamic rapport with the presence of death and suffering ... It is integral, for example, to the narratives of loss, exile, and journeying which ... serve a mnemonic function: directing the consciousness of the group back to significant, nodal points in its common history and its social memory ... this music and its broken rhythm of life are important ...The love stories they enclose are a place in which the black vernacular has been able to preserve and cultivate both the distinctive rapport with the presence of death which derives from slavery and in a related ontological state that I want to call the condition of being in pain. (p. 203)

Blues, blues and more blues, seems to be the conclusion. Powerful though this is, and, I find, a convincing gloss on one component of black vernacular culture, it overlooks – actually, precludes – theorisation of other impulses in contemporary black cultures, which arguably derive from more positive, resistant elements in black political history. So intent is Gilroy to emphasise slave suicide and fatalism (see also, for example, his discussion of Margaret Garner in chapter 2) that he neglects other forms of violent and non-violent resistance practised by slaves, such as the regular sabotaging of plantation machinery and the practice of abortion.[16] Both of these practices are themselves complex examples of the performance of a scientific rationality, which is presumably the reason for Gilroy's disinclination to consider them. As technological and calculated practices these do not demonstrate his desired scepticism towards rationality. In deploying knowledge of scientific reasoning, they refute his contention that slave identity is 'opposed to the formal logic and rational calculation characteristic of modern western thinking' (p. 68).

I would however be interested to consider the legacy of industrial sabotage as a component in the black political cultures of graffiti, and more generally to pronounce the iconoclastic, ironic and scatological aesthetics alongside those expressive of pain and death. And since Gilroy emphasises black convergence with Jewish history and experience, how about researching the parallels between black and Jewish *humour* as a response to racial terror, a survival resource and a means of resistance? Black cultures contain an abundance of saturnalian, ludic and trickster elements. As I suggest above, Gilroy may not acknowledge these as significant modalities because they too are rooted in a form of intensified – and often lateral – reasoning.

As a means of conceptualising New World black cultures, Gilroy's model is richly suggestive. But it is also limited by his determination to present antinomies – between socialist and black value systems, between nationalist and internationalist impulses – where it is more useful to consider these as mutually enabling categories. The most serious question concerns Gilroy's presentation of death-drive in black cultures.

Notes

1 Paul Gilroy, *The Black Atlantic: Modernity and Double Consciousness* (London: Verso, 1993).
2 See the critical discussions of the notion of the African diaspora of Robin Kelley, 'How the West Was One: On the Uses and Limitations of Diaspora',

The Black Scholar: Journal of Black Studies and Research, 30, 3–4 (2000), pp. 31–5; Colin Palmer, 'The African Diaspora', *The Black Scholar: Journal of Black Studies and Research*, 30, 3–4 (2000), pp. 56–9; and Richard Roberts, 'The Construction of Cultures in Diaspora: African and African New World Experiences', *South Atlantic Quarterly*, 98, 1–2 (1999). pp. 177–90.

3 A meticulous account of nationalism is Gregory Jusdanis, *The Necessary Nation* (Princeton: Princeton University Press, 2001).

4 Gilroy's formulation of a 'turn towards death' within black subjectivity – discussed later in this chapter – is more ontological than psychoanalytical. He argues it to have its origins in the historically specific, social experience of slavery.

5 For an important critique of *The Black Atlantic* see Neil Lazarus, 'Is a Counterculture of Modernity a Theory of Modernity?', *Diaspora*, 4, 3 (1995), pp. 323–40.

6 Paul Gilroy, *'There Ain't No Black in the Union Jack': The Cultural Politics of Race and Nation* (London: Unwin Hyman, 1987).

7 See Cedric Robinson, *Black Marxism: The Making of the Black Radical Tradition* (1983; Chapel Hill: University of North Carolina Press, 2000), for an example of such an expanded conceptualisation, and see also the journals *The Black Scholar: Journal of Black Studies and Research* and *Race and Class: Journal for Black and Third World Liberation*.

8 Different accounts of contemporary black British diasporic politics and culture can be found in Beverley Bryan, Stella Dadzie and Suzanne Scafe, *The Heart of the Race: Black Women's Lives in Britain* (London: Virago, 1985); Kobena Mercer, *Welcome to the Jungle: New Positions in Black Cultural Studies* (London: Routledge, 1994) pp. 259–85. For historical anthologies of black British writing see Paul Edwards and David Dabydeen (eds.), *Black Writers in Britain 1760–1890* (Edinburgh: Edinburgh University Press, 1993); Caryl Phillips, *Extravagant Strangers* (London: Faber, 1998); Mike Phillips and Trevor Phillips, *Windrush* (London: HarperCollins, 1999); James Procter (ed.), *Writing Black Britain*, 1948–98 (Manchester: Manchester University Press, 2000); Onyekachi Wambu (ed.), *Empire Windrush: Fifty Years of Writing About Black Britain* (London: Gollancz, 1998). For historical and sociological discussions of black communities in Britain see Peter Fryer, *Staying Power: The History of Black People in Britain* (London: Pluto Press, 1984); Winston James and Clive Harris (eds.), *Inside Babylon: The Caribbean Diaspora in Britain* (London: Verso, 1993). For contemporary black British writing see *Wasafiri: Caribbean, African, Asian and Associated Literatures in English*, 29 (1999), special issue 'Taking the Cake: Black Writing in Britain'.

9 See Hugh Cunningham, 'The Language of Patriotism', in Raphael Samuel (ed.), *Patriotism: The Making and Unmaking of British National Identity. Volume 1: History and Politics* (London: Routledge 1989), pp. 57–89, for a contrasting account of the historical variability of English national definitions.

10 In 1993, the year of *The Black Atlantic's* publication, Earl Ofari Hutchinson published 'The Continuing Myth of Black Capitalism', in *The Black Scholar*,

23, 1 (1993), pp. 16–21. He gives some important sociological information: 'more than 70% of the nearly twelve million black workers in America are still concentrated in clerical, services, and the trades. A sizable proportion of blacks are employed as unskilled laborers. The black median income of $19,330 is slightly more than half of the white median income'.

When it comes to net wealth, the gap between blacks and whites is even more glaring. The average for white households is $39,135, for blacks, $3,397 … African Americans own less than 1% of the nation's stock holdings … By 1990, more than 30% of blacks fell below the poverty … While some black firms have prospered, most prospective black entrepreneurs still find the door shut when they seek credit and capital from lending agencies or managerial and technical training from corporations.

Overall, the gross revenues for black business hovers at about 3% of the corporate total' (pp. 17–18). The disparities have grown worse since then.

11 Sembene Ousmane, *Black Docker*, translated by Ros Schwartz (1973; London: Heinemann, 1986).

12 For another fictional exploration of African migration to continental Europe see Ama Ata Aidoo, *Our Sister Killjoy* (London: Longman, 1977) which charts the less-than-positive experience of a young Ghanaian woman sojourning in Germany. See also Caryl Phillips, *The European Tribe* (London: Faber, 1987).

13 For an analysis of these 'riots' see chapter 6 of *'There Ain't No Black'*, 'Conclusion: Urban Social Movements, "Race" and Community', pp. 223–48. See also A. Sivanandan, *A Different Hunger: Writings on Black Resistance* (London: Pluto, 1982) and *Communities of Resistance: Writings on Black Struggles for Socialism* (London: Verso, 1990).

14 See, for example, p. 37 of *The Black Atlantic*, for Gilroy's distinction between what he calls a 'politics of fulfilment' – 'the notion that a future society will be able to realise the social and political promise that present society has left unaccomplished' – and his notion of a 'politics of transfiguration', taken from Seyla Benhabib, which 'exists on a lower frequency where it is played, danced, and acted, as well as sung'. While the 'politics of fulfilment' are, he argues, 'immanent within modernity', the 'politics of transfiguration' 'partially transcend modernity, constructing both an imaginary anti-modern past and a postmodern yet-to-come'.

15 I am grateful to Robert Chrisman whose insight this is.

16 On slave women's reproductive resistance see Barbara Bush-Slimani, 'Hard Labour: Women, Childbirth and Resistance in British Caribbean Slave Societies', *History Workshop: A Journal of Socialist and Feminist Historians*, 36 (1993), pp. 83–99.

5

Black Atlantic nationalism:
Sol Plaatje and W.E.B. Du Bois

The critical era of black Atlanticism began in 1993, with the publication of Paul Gilroy's seminal book *The Black Atlantic*.[1] The book's focus on the cultural, political and economic relations of Africa, Europe and the New World was not original. Such a focus has been the concern of African and African diasporic thinkers from at least Equiano onwards.[2] Rather, what distinguished Gilroy's work was its theoretical and political thrust. This was firmly anti-nationalist. The cultural values and critical perspectives of black nationalism were, Gilroy argued, 'antithetical to the rhizomorphic, fractal structure of the transcultural, international formation of the black Atlantic' (p. 3). He argued nation-centred conceptions of culture to be incompatible with the values of cultural hybridity that had been generated through the black Atlantic, and also viewed the political concerns of nationalism as fundamentally opposed by the transnationalist disposition of black Atlantic politics. Caricaturing nationalism as Afrocentrism, as necessarily ethnically absolutist and generally socially dangerous, Gilroy presented black Atlanticism as its progressive and emancipatory antinomy. Gilroy's black Atlantic formulation was also an attempt to transform paradigms for the analysis of modernity. Insisting on the mutual implication of slavery with modernity, Gilroy argued that black Atlanticism had emerged as ' a distinctive counterculture of modernity' (p. 36) and that 'The distinctive historical experiences of [the African] diaspora's populations have created a unique body of reflections on modernity and its discontents which is an enduring presence in the … struggles of their descendants today' (p. 4).

Gilroy's work had many virtues. These include the release of contemporary African American cultural studies from an insular US exceptionalism, and the presentation of a powerful alternative to Melville Herskovitz's influential notion of African culture as the basis for African diasporic cultural formations. None the less, Gilroy's book has contributed to a mystification of transatlanticism that today threatens to foreclose rather than expand critical studies of black diasporic cultures, African cultures and their relationship. Part of the mystification lies in Gilroy's notion of modernity, of which he gives both a totalising and a narrowly culturalist definition. Speaking of Richard Wright, for instance, Gilroy contends that 'perhaps more than any other writer he showed how modernity was both the period and the region in which black politics grew. His work articulates simultaneously an affirmation and a negation of the western civilisation that formed him' (p. 186). While the 'modernity' word initially promises to incorporate all the complex intellectual, cultural, political and economic strands of Richard Wright's critical project, his contribution is swiftly reduced to an engagement with 'western civilisation'.

We witness a similar slipperiness in the theorisation of Afro-modernity by African American political theorist Michael Hanchard, which draws on Paul Gilroy's work.[3] At times Hanchard defines modernity as 'the discourses of the Enlightenment and processes of modernization by the West, along with those discourses' attendant notions of sovereignty and citizenship' (p. 248). This clear specification of modernity as both philosophical and economic in range disappears when Hanchard comes to define black responses to the phenomenon; then a division arises between capitalism and modernity, with the proletariat being produced through and against capitalism while African peoples are created by and against modernity (p. 246). This move, from a materialist to an idealist construction of modernity, again recurs in South African cultural scholar Ntongela Masilela's recent, Gilroy-inspired, work on imperialism in Africa. He explains:

> The fundamental historical question became: what is it that enabled Europeans to defeat Africans militarily, and subsequently hegemonically impose themselves on us? The only serious response on our part could ... be through the appropriation of that which had enabled Europeans to triumph: modernity. Hence the obsession with Christianity, civilization, and education by the new African intelligentsia.[4]

'Modernity' here appears first to include the material power capitalised technology; but Masilela quickly abandons that component when he defines 'Christianity, civilization and education' as co-extensive with modernity.

Gilroy's legacy consists of more than this ultimately idealist version of black modernity, which works to remove capitalist modernisation from the map and does not credit black thinkers with making anti-capitalist analyses. The anti-nationalist persuasion of Gilroy's book also continues to animate black Atlantic cultural and intellectual research. So does the book's aestheticism – its presentation of art as the best or (at times) the only medium of social and political transformation. I argue here for the importance of rethinking black Atlanticism. Rather than view nationalism, organised political struggle and structural economic analysis as the polar opposites of black Atlanticism, we need to recognise more complexity in their relations; at times, I suggest, black Atlanticism and black nationalism are interdependent practices, not antinomies.

As Gilroy's work has travelled from diasporic to African studies, it has gained a new component: the construction of African Americans as a global vanguard, whose role it is to lead continental Africans into modernity. Gilroy's own work does not argue the utility of diasporic modernity for continental Africans, nor does he suggest that Africans seek to emulate African Americans. But this is exactly the vanguardist spin given to black modernity in Africanist work as diverse as Manthia Diawara's and Ntongela Masilela's.[5]

In fact, Masilela's black Atlantic work sums up all the tendencies that I have been outlining: as I have already suggested, it presents black modernity is essentially a cultural condition, not a political economic and cultural process. Modernity as a condition then becomes easily transposable from America to Africa and strikingly devoid of nationalism, political struggle and Marxism. Describing the early twentieth-century 'New African' movement in South Africa, Masilela argues that:

> The construction of South African modernity by New African intelligentsia who modelled themselves on the New Negro Talented Tenth is inconceivable without the example of American modernity: the New Africans appropriated the historical lessons drawn from the New Negro experience within American modernity to chart and negotiate the newly emergent South African modernity: the Africans learned from African-Americans the process of transforming themselves into agencies in or of modernity. (p. 90)

I find this argument somewhat misleading, not least in its suggestion that New African intelligentsia 'modelled themselves on the New Negro Talented Tenth' (Du Bois's early notion of a leadership class of African

Americans to be drawn from the top ten per cent of the black population).
If we look at the definition of the New African provided by one of its chief
exponents, H.I.E. Dhlomo, in 1945, there is very little trace of talented ten-
thness and still less of the USA: the New African is a

> class [that] consists mostly of organised urban workers who are
> awakening to the issues at stake and to the power of organised intel-
> ligently-led mass action and of progressive thinking African intel-
> lectuals and leaders.
>   The new African knows where he belongs and what belongs to
> him; where he is going and how; what he wants and the methods to
> obtain it. Such incidents as workers' strikes; organised boycotts; mass
> defiance of injustice – these and many more are but straws in the
> wind heralding the awakening of the New African masses. What is
> this New African's attitude? Put briefly and bluntly, he wants a social
> order where every South African will be free to express himself and
> his personality fully, live and breathe freely, and have a part in shap-
> ing the destiny of his country; a social order in which race, colour
> and creed will be a badge neither of privilege nor of discrimination.[6]

As we see, Dhlomo's original definition of the New African rests on
the conception of racialised labour. New Africans are 'organised urban
workers' as much as they are progressive intellectuals, who co-ordinate
militant mass actions to achieve a non-racist society. Note how Dhlomo's
direction remains firmly national: the New Africans seek agency to 'shape
the destiny of his country'. This self-definition of New Africans as nationalist, militant and politically mobilised is unrecognisable in Masilela's
post-Gilroyian definition, which makes the New African an imitator of
black Americans in an act of cultural self-fashioning.

If one challenge is to reconceptualise the national, political and economic dynamics of black Atlanticism, then another challenge is to reconceptualise the reception of black American thought by African
intellectuals. I argue that this reception was considerably more complex,
and critical, than has generally been recognised. Not only did African
intellectuals on occasion question the transplantability of black American
political practice, cultures and thought to their respective African
colonies, they also questioned the adequacy of black American thought
for black America itself. We now need the notion of a critical, interroga-
tive black Atlantic political culture, based on dialogue not emulation. The
peculiar density of this modern critical black Atlanticism is one that

allows African intellectuals both to instrumentalise African America as a fictional space of self-actualisation and to demystify that construction; to position slavery and colonialism as comparable yet incommensurable historical experiences; to delineate a universal racial identity that depends, dialectically, on the notion of political particularity, the struggle and possession of national sovereignty.

That critical black Atlanticism invokes both national difference and racial unity, conjoins cultural affirmation with political critique of African Americans, is clear from as early as 1865, in the writings of black South African clergyman Tiyo Soga. He writes during the historical moment of the American Civil War and before the consolidation and centralisation of white South African colonialism. The past determinacy of New World slavery, contrasted with the present indeterminacy of African colonisation, allows Soga to champion Africans as politically superior both to Europeans and New World diasporic Africans in their retention of national autonomy:

> Africa was of God given to the race of Ham. I find the Negro from the days of the old Assyrians downwards, keeping his 'individuality' and his 'distinctiveness', amid the wreck of empires, and the revolution of ages. I find him keeping his place among the nations, and keeping his home and country.[7]

A great contrast to the African are the slaves 'in the West Indian Islands, in Northern and Southern America, and in the South American colonies of Spain and Portugal', who are, according to Soga, 'opposed by nation after nation and driven from … home' (p. 569).

In the same breath Tiyo Soga can proudly place Africans as politically superior to diaspora black populations yet culturally inferior: he praises the Liberian project for allowing black Americans to return 'unmanacled to the land of his forefathers, taking back with him the civilization and the Christianity of those nations' (p. 569).

By the 1910s, however, the political advantages that Africans could claim over African Americans had largely vanished through European imperialism. In my rethinking of black Atlanticism, I want schematically to present the period between 1865 and 1910 as witnessing the reversal of Tiyo Soga's cultural-political balance. For now political self-determination (in the form of citizenship) has become the theoretical provenance of the African American, through the passage of universal male suffrage, and the majority of continental Africans have lost that right.

And at the same time this period witnesses some nationalist continental Africans starting to question the cultural supremacy of the 'Christianity and civilization' with which Tiyo Soga credits diasporic Africans and Europeans; their diverse cultural productions reveal a highly uneven admixture of Fanon's assimilation, nativist and fighting stages. Thus African relations with African Americans now can simultaneously involve valorisation of black diasporic political possibility and scepticism towards their cultural assimilationism. The shift from nineteenth-century negative to twentieth-century positive perception of African American political status is clear in the comments of African National Congress founder Sol Plaatje when he visited the USA in 1922. What he saw led him to write to a friend:

> It is dazzling to see the extent of freedom, industrial advantage, and costly educational facilities, provided for Negroes in this country by the Union government, the government of the several states, by the municipalities and by the wealthy philanthropists. Those who die and those who remain alive continually pour their millions of money towards the cause of Negro education; and it is touching to see the grasping manner in which Negroes reach out to take advantage of the several educational facilities. And, oh, the women! They are progressive educationally, socially, politically, as well as in church work, they lead the men.
>
> It is very inspiring to get into their midst, but it is also distressing at times and I can hardly suppress a tear when I think of the wretched backwardness between them and our part of the empire … I cannot understand why South Africa should be so Godforsaken, as far as her political and industrial morality is concerned.[8]

Plaatje's perception of African-American achievements here develops from his observation of the national specificity of the USA. Admire African Americans as he does, Plaatje admires even more the objectively superior social, educational and economic opportunities that the USA as a country supplies its black citizens. As he sees it, these material conditions supply the possibility for Negro accomplishment. That he feels inspired by African Americans' example might seem to bear out Masilela's contention that black South African intellectuals were led to imitate African Americans. But the inspiration is quickly offset here by Plaatje's despondent recognition of the incommensurability between the two countries. Without a similar material base, modern African-American activities cannot simply be transposed to South Africa, their achievements imitated within black South Africa. It is the need for a specifically national, and nationally specific, material transformation that Plaatje's account suggests.

The complexity of this critical black Atlanticism that I am arguing for – in general, and in this historical moment of the early twentieth century – becomes clearer if we look at the relationship between Sol Plaatje and W.E.B. Du Bois. Before becoming the ANC's general secretary in 1912, when the organisation was founded, Plaatje worked as a court interpreter and then in the media as founder, editor and journalist of some of the earliest African nationalist newspapers.[9] That there was an intense transnational traffic between Plaatje and Du Bois, which had intellectual, financial, and professional dynamics, is clear. Plaatje, who was eight years younger than Du Bois, starting reading Du Bois's work early on in his newspaper career. Du Bois was responsible for the American publication of Plaatje's book *Native Life in South Africa*, and arranged for Plaatje to participate in the 1921 annual National Association for the Advancement of Colored People convention. These were more than personal connections: there were significant parallels between the official political practices and values of the organisations the two men were active in. The early ANC, the Niagara movement and the NAACP overlapped in their constitutionalist, integrationist version of black nationalism: their formal emphasis fell on the franchise as the means to social justice and opportunity, and the legal protest against racial injustice.[10]

The case for Plaatje's intellectual 'influence' by Du Bois seems to grow when we look at his 1916 masterpiece *Native Life in South Africa*, which is haunted by Du Bois's 1903 *The Souls of Black Folk*.[11] Like *Souls*, *Native Life* is a travelogue in which the writer chronicles the lives of black people under white racism. Both writers use a first-person narrative to explore their own relationship to the black communities they represent. Each book features a chapter given over to the public vilification of a black leader who is criticised for capitulating to white interests: Booker T. Washington in Du Bois's case, Tengo Jabavu in Plaatje's. And each book contains a chapter that charts the passing of the author's infant son.

But here the similarities end. The radical differences are suggested by the contrast between their organising tropes: 'the Veil' of Du Bois, and the '1913 Natives' Land Act' of South Africa. Plaatje belonged to a mission-educated class that had historically perceived the British Empire

as a system of liberal 'equality', epitomised in the colour-blind Cape franchise which allowed men of certain property or income to vote. The 'lib-
erties' of this province sharply contrasted with the Boer republics of the
Transvaal and the Orange Free State, which excluded African people
from the franchise. But in 1910 British and Afrikaner provinces united
to form the nation state of South Africa. This initiated the systematic
assault on Africans which began with the devastating Land Act that
removed land ownership and sharecropping rights from rural Africans,
forced them into 'native reserves' and brutal economic exploitation by
white farmers. This is the context for the composition of *Native Life in
South Africa*, which focuses on the origins and terrible consequences of
that legislation.[12]

Plaatje's book then emerges from an immediate historical event,
whereas Du Bois's *Souls* emerges more broadly from a racial condition.
The objective differences between their national situations create differences of approach. But not all the differences are objective: these nationalists differ profoundly in their ideologies. Plaatje's book, I argue,
performs a deliberate commentary on Du Bois that criticises his open
and his unconscious Talented Tenth elitism. The cohesive if diverse racial
community that Du Bois evokes is not readily available to Plaatje's black
South Africa, any more than is the legal equality theoretically offered by
the US constitution. The Natives' Land Act had exacerbated the inequalities that already fractured the African peoples of South Africa. Some,
like Plaatje, still had the franchise; most were now dispossessed of any
title to the land. These inequalities make it very difficult for Plaatje to
articulate a national black 'imagined community'. They also, I argue,
push Plaatje into a concern with the legitimacy of his own leadership,
something that does not trouble Du Bois. It seems that for Du Bois,
Talented Tenth mobility – his ability to mediate life behind and beyond
the Veil – ratifies his intellectual and political leadership. For Plaatje,
however, this same mobility unsettles his leader's ability to represent his
people.

A close scrutiny of the intertextual relationship between Plaatje and
Du Bois reveals several areas of significant ideological difference, two of
which I want to focus on here. One, as I suggest above, concerns the operations of black leadership, the problems of political representation trig-
gered by the existence of subaltern peoples.[13] The second concerns the
value accorded to aesthetic culture. The differences between Du Bois and
Plaatje need to be taken very seriously; their recognition casts new light

on both of their respective nationalist projects. Such nationalist understanding cannot be produced without this transnational lens. It is only by
putting these texts in comparative framework, and seeing the multiple
ways that Plaatje engages with Du Bois, that the complex contours of their
own specifically national projects emerge.

And in case I am in danger of neglecting the affirmative elements of
Plaatje's black Atlantic connection to Du Bois, I suggest that the very
timing of Plaatje's intertextual involvement expresses a subtle if radical
pan-Africanism. *Native Life* was written in 1916, while Plaatje was part
of an ANC delegation in England, petitioning the British government to
repeal the unjust Natives Land Act. Plaatje, that is, was officiating as a
political representative of the ANC, performing the role of constitutional
liberal nationalist whose political validation and ideology centred on
England. It is at this highly English moment that he chooses to write a
text that engages black America as an object of dialogue, and this in itself
belies the English model of liberalism that the ANC claimed to promote.
Plaatje's text uses Du Bois not only to criticise Du Bois's own nationalist vision, but also as a means of exposing the limits of his own party's
official nationalism. In other words, it is through Du Bois that Plaatje
articulates a critical distance from ANC as well as from Du Bois; Du
Bois's text becomes the means to introduce non self-identity into African
nationalism itself.

This complicated transnational affirmation and critique of nationalist self and other is sharpest in the most openly autobiographical discourse of Plaatje's text, the chapter devoted to the death of his infant son
which is directly lifted from Du Bois's own chapter on the passing of his
first-born. Du Bois never tells us his child's name. This suggests that the
child is to be viewed not as an individual but as an anonymous representative of his race. His name is, effectively, 'Negro and a Negro's son' (p.
170). Since the son is an abstraction for the race, his loss comes to represent the losses experienced by the race as a whole. Du Bois's narrative
accordingly works to consolidate both his authority and his representativeness.[14] The death and burial of Du Bois's son then rely on, and produce, a homology of race, family and nation that is not disturbed by
existing class differences.[15]

In Plaatje's account, the ostentatiously privileged paraphernalia of
his own son's funeral and the version of national symbolism that accompanies it, rhetorically give way to his acute concern with the newly dispossessed Africans, subalterns who stand outside the limits of black

middle-class representation. Plaatje initially appears to endorse the bourgeois nationalist narrative embodied in his son. His son is born in the year of the ANC's birth, 1912: one could not produce a neater allegory of official nationalism. And almost too neatly confirming Benedict Anderson's thesis that print capitalism was crucial to national consciousness, Plaatje the newspaper publisher has named his son after the originator of the medium. As he tells us: 'He first saw the light … on the very day we opened and christened our printing office, so we named him after the great inventor of printing type: he was christened Johann Gutenburg' (p. 142). Thus, Plaatje's son is very much named, while Du Bois's son is not; one is aligned with the print nation, while the other is aligned with the black race.

However, Plaatje's own nationalist equations swiftly implode. There is in fact a nameless dead black child in his narrative, just as there is in Du Bois's, but this child is not his own; it is the child of the Kgobadi family, rendered fugitive through the Natives' Land Act. When the child dies its family has nowhere legally to bury it. Plaatje has informed us that:

> This young wandering family decided to dig a grave under cover of the darkness of that night, when no one was looking, and in that crude manner the child was interred – and interred amid fear and trembling, as well as the throbs of a torturing anguish, in a stolen grave, lest the proprietor of the spot, or any of his servants, should surprise them in the act. (p. 90)

Plaatje's careful chronicle of his son's urban funeral is interrupted by his recollection of this dispossessed family and their illegal burial: 'Our bleeding heart was nowhere in the present procession, which apparently could take care of itself, for we had returned in thought to the July funeral of the veld and its horrid characteristics' (p. 147). This catapults him into 'spirit of revolt' against white racism, culminating in an explosion of apocalyptic rage that borrows from Shakespeare's *King Lear* to curse 'ungrateful man' (pp. 146-7).[16]

Plaatje effectively splits Du Bois's racial symbolism in two. Where Du Bois's own, unnamed child embodies the race, Plaatje instead dramatises the glaring social contradiction between his own, named urban child and the unnamed child of the dispossessed rural family. Plaatje also, implicitly, pushes the symbol of this fugitive family into critical contrast with Du Bois's privileged family. While Du Bois can voluntarily and temporarily migrate, this African family has no such choice; they are forced into permanent relocation. Du Bois takes his dead child up north because, as he explains:

> We could not lay him in the ground there in Georgia, for the earth
> there is strangely red; so we bore him away to the northward, with
> his flowers and his little folded hands. In vain, in vain! – for where,
> O God! beneath thy broad blue sky shall my dark baby rest in peace,
> – where Reverence dwells, and Goodness, and a Freedom that is free?
> (p. 173)

At this point in Du Bois's text, his material freedom to move around the country and select a burial ground is for him less significant than the existential unfreedom suffered by all American black people: what troubles him is figurative not literal slavery. In contrast, Plaatje, all too aware of the legal dispossession ushered in by the Land Act, is more concerned with the literal unfreedom of an impoverished family to conduct a consecrated burial anywhere.

If Plaatje's politics emphasise material over existential dispossession, they also emphasise that the loss of one African life is a loss to all African political community; that all lives carry equal value. This deliberately if subtly criticises the casual elitism that characterises Du Bois's account, for instance when Du Bois rhetorically asks of Death:

> Are there so many workers in the vineyard that the fair promise of
> this little body could lightly be tossed away? The wretched of my race
> that line the alleys of the nation sit fatherless and unmothered; but
> Love sat beside his cradle, and in his ear Wisdom waited to speak.
> (pp. 174–5)

Du Bois wants Death to claim one of the homeless 'wretched of my race' instead of his beloved son. In other words, the loss of a potential talented tenth member appears more lamentable to him than a loss from the ranks of the non-privileged majority. Plaatje's position is diametrically opposed to this: what prompts him to rhetorical rage is not his own son's death but, precisely, that of one of 'the wretched of my race'.

So far I have highlighted how Plaatje's concern with subaltern Africans prompts him to question the legitimacy of his own political representation – he is not representative, therefore he cannot adequately represent. And that this concern emerges from and reinforces a very different, collectivist and relatively egalitarian conception of black identity than the patrician Du Bois possesses at this point in his career. The differences lead Plaatje to produce an indirect critique of Du Bois's Talented Tenth elitism. This critique extends from political representation to aesthetic culture. Du Bois's *Souls* suggests that his entitlement to black leadership rests on his possession of 'high' cultural capital. Thus, for instance, the famous passage: 'I sit with Shakespeare and he winces not. Across the colour line I move arm in arm with Balzac and Dumas, where smiling men and welcoming women glide in gilded halls … So, wed with Truth, I dwell above the Veil' (p. 90). Du Bois unequivocally affirms European culture as an absolute value; its cultivation provides access to a 'Truth' that sets him above the majority of black people who are under the Veil. European culture here consists of a club of great individuals that the black person can join through the mechanics of assimilation. Plaatje interrogates both the individualism and the aestheticism of Du Bois's construction; his positioning of Shakespeare is as a useful collective resource for passing judgement on contemporary racist capitalism. Plaatje does not sit with Shakespeare but, instead, ventriloquises him. This instrumentalisation allows Plaatje to articulate a revolutionary nationalism at odds with the ANC's liberalism and that of the NAACP. The black rage and revenge that Du Bois warns against in *Souls* is exactly what Plaatje uses King Lear to promote.

The intertextual occasion for Plaatje's Learian moment is Du Bois's apostrophe to a personified Death. Du Bois perceives Death as a personal assault:

> O Death! Is not this my life hard enough, – is not that dull land that stretches its sneering web about me cold enough, – is not all the world beyond these four little walls pitiless enough, but that thou must needs enter here, – thou, O Death? About my head the thundering storm beat like a heartless voice, and the crazy forest pulsed with the curses of the weak; but what cared I, within my home beside my wife and baby boy? Was thou so jealous of one little coign of happiness that thou must needs enter there, – thou, O Death? (p. 172)

This is a perception of totalising racist persecution that by invading the domestic space refuses black people the sanctuary of a home and parental fulfilment. The parallel point in Plaatje's discourse is his Shakespearean rhetorical outburst attacking the injustice that, in contrast, casts his people out into the veld. Plaatje chooses the moment when Lear's illusions about his daughters are dissolved; cast out into the heath, he recognises that their will to power makes a mockery of legal contracts or morality. Plaatje/Lear wishes for something to

> Strike flat the thick rotundity o' the world!
> Crack Nature's moulds, all germens spill at once!
> That make ungrateful man!
>
> (p. 147)

Where Du Bois's apostrophe is directed at the abstraction Death, and a correspondingly abstract racism, Plaatje's is directed at very concrete human subjects: the 'ungrateful men' who have profited by expropriating black South African labour and now proceed to dispossess them further by removing their ability to buy and rent land. That Plaatje has black labour in mind, and capitalist exploitation, is clear from the build up to this Learian moment. He writes:

> What have our people done to these colonists, we asked, that is so utterly unforgivable, that this law should be passed as an unavoidable reprisal? Have we not delved in their mines, and are not a quarter of a million of us still labouring for them in the depths of the earth in such circumstances for the most niggardly pittance? Are not thousands of us still offering up our lives and our limbs in order that South Africa should satisfy the white man's greed, delivering 50,000,000 pounds worth of minerals every year? (pp. 146–7)[17]

Plaatje's nationalist discourse here, one might say, bursts out of its civil constitutionalist form – the official ANC approach, which Paul Gilroy would define as the 'politics of fulfilment'.[18] His deathwish against the moulds that 'make ungrateful man' is a revolutionary shift to what Gilroy terms a 'politics of transfiguration': the desire for total destruction of the conditions of possibility of this white South African nation, clearing the space for the creation of a new, autonomous black nation.

I want to return to the allegory contained in the King Lear moment, for I see this as a significant demonstration of Sol Plaatje's complex nationalist logic. I have suggested that he deploys Lear as a figure for the historical African population, rewriting the individual monarch as a collective sovereign that has been betrayed into surrendering its precolonial autonomy to the white society whose growth it has assisted. I have also suggested that Plaatje compounds this by presenting this population as the modern black proletariat, whose own existence does not historically precede white colonialism. In other words, the collective voice that ventriloquises Lear to curse white power consists of both an historical African and a modern black voice.

But this voice carries another, contradictory coding. Earlier I argued that Plaatje calls into question his own and Du Bois's legitimacy as leaders; their very privilege rumbles their capacity to represent subalterns adequately. That was primarily an argument about political representation. The subaltern Kgobadi family exposes the limits of liberal constitutional nationalist leaders to speak for and as black peoples as a whole; they at most can represent their own privileged middle class. I argue that here Plaatje reiterates this through the additional construction of himself as Lear; he is effectively the titular national 'sovereign' here, disqualified from proper rule by his own relative class, aesthetic and educational privilege as well as by the white colonial power that denies his people citizenship. In giving Lear these mutually exclusive significations – that of his own compromised leadership and a modern black South African subaltern majority – Plaatje underscores the barriers to the production of an effective racial national community.

I am arguing that, in sharp contrast to Du Bois, Sol Plaatje is sceptical about the absolute value of European aesthetic culture: he renders that aesthetic culture a tool for political and economic critique, not a goal as it is for Du Bois. To adhere uncritically as Du Bois does here to European aestheticism is furthermore to endorse the unjust structures of economic accumulation that make possible such iconic constructions of art. Plaatje's open invocation of black anti-capitalist rage through the aesthetic device of Shakespeare's king needs to be seen as an assertion of the inextricability of aesthetic, economic and political concerns for black nationalist struggle.

I hope through this textual discussion of Plaatje and Du Bois to have introduced different ways to think about black Atlanticism, as a critical dialogic relationship that questions some of the paradigms for analysis created by Paul Gilroy's book and sustained by a number of Africanists. Against these paradigms, I am arguing that the transatlantic political and cultural flows between black South Africa and African America need an analysis that is alert to the historical variability and complexity of the dynamic. Plaatje's critical engagement with Du Bois refutes any suggestion that Africans were uncritically modelling themselves on African Americans, or that African America supplies a vanguard global class.

Plaatje's example also suggests that the analysis of black Atlanticism should not exclude the nationalist and anti-capitalist components of black Atlantic thinkers. The nationalism of Du Bois and of Plaatje is the condition from which their transnationalism emerges; the two work together, not in opposition.

I am aware however that many of my criticisms of current critical constructions of black Atlanticism arise from particular applications of black Atlanticism within the academic culture of the USA. A very different story is the exploration of black Atlanticism by academics and creative artists within the United Kingdom. Particularly significant is the recent attention given to the memory and meanings of slavery. The black Atlantic connections being made in these explorations have a very different context in which white British amnesia of slavery's historical role in British national development has been kept company by black British tendencies to prioritise the post-1945 historical moment of large-scale immigration. Not just the context but the 'drift' of these British black Atlantic works is very different from the US variants I have criticised. For these works – I am thinking, among others, of recent work by Fred D'Aguiar, Bernardine Evaristo, Caryl Phillips and Marcus Wood – synthesise the material with the subjective dynamics of black Atlanticism, uncover mutual imbrications of the national and the transnational, combine colonialism with slavery, and recognise the historicity of their subjects.[19] In other words, this British work does what I am suggesting the US work does not.

Since I want to end by recognising the situatedness of my own analysis and critique of black Atlanticism, I need to add a further qualification. For within the USA too there is a great deal of black Atlantic academic work being produced that does not follow a Gilroyian path.[20] Since much of this work emerges from the social sciences and history rather than literary and cultural studies, I am beginning to wonder whether black Atlanticism is more susceptible to disciplinary difference than we recognise.

Notes

1 Paul Gilroy, *The Black Atlantic: Modernity and Double Consciousness* (London: Verso, 1993).
2 For examples see Alasdair Pettinger, *Always Elsewhere: Travels of the Black Atlantic* (London: Cassell, 1998); Eric Williams, *Capitalism and Slavery*

(Chapel Hill: University of North Carolina Press, 1944); St Clair Drake, *Black Folk Here and There: An Essay in History and Anthropology* (Los Angeles: Center for Afro-American Studies, University of California, 1990); Ronald Walters, *Pan Africanism in the African Diaspora* (Detroit: Wayne State University Press, 1993); Yekutiel Gershoni, *Africans on African-Americans: The Creation and Uses of an African-American Myth* (New York: New York University Press, 1997).

3 Michael Hanchard, 'Afromodernity: Temporality, Politics, and the African Diaspora', *Public Culture*, 27 (1999), pp. 245–68.

4 Ntongela Masilela, ''The "Black Atlantic" and African Modernity in South Africa', *Research in African Literatures*, 27, 4 (1996), p. 90. For a detailed study of relations between black South African and black American performers of the early twentieth century see Amanda Denise Kemp, *Up from Slavery and Other Narratives: Black South African Performances of the American Negro (1920–1943)*, unpublished Ph.D. dissertation, Northwestern University, 1997. See also Veit Erlmann, *Music, Modernity, and the Global Imagination: South Africa and the West* (New York: Oxford University Press, 1999).

5 Manthia Diawara, *In Search of Africa* (London: Harvard University Press, 1998).

6 Quoted in Tim Couzens, *The New African: A Study of the Life and Work of H.I.E. Dhlomo* (Johannesburg: Ravan, 1985), pp. 33–4.

7 Quoted in David Attwell, 'Intimate Enmity in the Journal of Tiyo Soga', *Critical Inquiry*, 23, 3 (1997), pp. 568–9.

8 Quoted in Brian Willan (ed.), *Sol Plaatje: Selected Writings* (Athens: Ohio University Press, 1996), pp. 287–8.

9 Brian Willan, *Sol Plaatje: South African Nationalist, 1876–1932* (London: Heinemann, 1984), is a superlative biography of Plaatje from which my historical information is taken.

10 See George M. Fredrickson, *Black Liberation: A Comparative History of Black Ideologies in the United States and South Africa* (Oxford: Oxford University Press, 1996) for an account of these movements. For a critical discussion of the early W.E.B. Du Bois as a thinker and leader see Adolph Reed, *W.E.B. Du Bois and American Political Thought: Fabianism and the Color Line* (Oxford: Oxford University Press, 1997). See also David Levering Lewis's prizewinning biography of the early Du Bois, *W.E.B. Du Bois. Biography of a Race, 1868–1919* (New York: Henry Holt, 1993).

11 Solomon T. Plaatje, *Native Life in South Africa Before and Since the European War and the Boer Rebellion*, edited by Brian Willan, foreword by Bessie Head (1916; Athens: Ohio University Press, 1991). W.E.B. Du Bois, *The Souls of Black Folk*, introduced by Donald B. Gibson, and with notes by Monica M. Elbert (1903; New York: Penguin, 1989).

12 Further discussions of Plaatje's *Native Life* include Laura Chrisman, 'Fathering the Black Nation of South Africa: Gender and Generation in Sol Plaatje's *Native Life in South Africa and Mhudi*', *Social Dynamics* [Cape Town, South Africa], 23, 2 (1997), pp. 57–73; J. M. Phelps, 'Sol Plaatje's Mhudi and

Democratic Government', *English Studies in Africa* [Johannesburg, South Africa], 36, 1 (1993), pp. 47–56. See also Toyin Falola, *Nationalism and African Intellectuals* (Rochester: University of Rochester Press, 2001), for an important revisionary account of African nationalism. And see Ken Harrow (ed.), special issue of *Research in African Literatures* on nationalism, 32, 3 (2001).

13 See Kevin K. Gaines, *Uplifting the Race: Black Leadership, Politics, and Culture in the Twentieth Century* (Chapel Hill: University of North Carolina Press, 1996) and Wilson Moses, *The Golden Age of Black Nationalism, 1850–1925* (Oxford: Oxford University Press, 1978) for useful discussions of African American nationalist leadership models during this period.

14 See Hazel Carby's discussion of Du Bois's patriarchal masculinity, 'The Souls of Black Men', *Race Men: The W.E.B. Du Bois Lectures* (Cambridge: Harvard University Press, 1998), pp. 9–41.

15 Paul Gilroy gives a diametrically opposed reading of this episode in his '"Cheer the Weary Traveller": W.E.B. Du Bois, Germany, and the Politics of (Dis)placement', *The Black Atlantic: Modernity and Double Consciousness*, pp. 111–45. See also Alys Eve Weinbaum, 'Reproducing Racial Globality: W.E.B. du Bois and the Sexual Politics of Black Internationalism', *Social Text*, 67, 19, 2 (2001), pp. 15–41, for a stimulating reading of this episode that differs strikingly from my own.

16 Other analyses of *King Lear's* applicability to South Africa are Martin Orkin, 'Cruelty, *King Lear* and the South African Land Act 1913', *Shakespeare Against Apartheid* (Craighall: Ad. Donker, 1978), pp. 130–80; Nick Visser, 'Shakespeare and Hanekom, *King Lear* and Land', *Textual Practice*, 11, 1 (1997), pp. 25–38. On Plaatje and Shakespeare see David Schalkwyk and Lerothodi Lapula, 'Solomon Plaatje, William Shakespeare, and the Translations of Culture', *Pretexts: Literary and Cultural Studies*, 9, 1 (2000), pp. 9–26; Stephen Gray, 'Plaatje's Shakespeare', *English in Africa* [Grahamstown, South Africa], 4, 1 (1977), pp. 1–6. For a wideranging discussion of Shakespeare in South Africa see David Johnson, *Shakespeare and South Africa* (Oxford: Clarendon Press, 1996). See also Martin Orkin, 'The Politics of Editing the Shakespeare Text in South Africa', *Current Writing: Text and Reception in Southern Africa* [Durban, South Africa], 5, 1 (1993), pp. 48–59.

17 See Peter Limb, 'The "Other" Sol Plaatje: Rethinking Plaatje's Attitudes to Empire, Labour and Gender', paper presented at Rand Afrikaans University Sociology Seminar series, July 2001, for an illuminating discussion of Plaatje's pro-labour journalism.

18 Paul Gilroy, *The Black Atlantic*, p. 37.

19 Fred D'Aguiar, *Feeding the Ghosts* (New York: HarperCollins, 1998); Bernardine Evaristo, *Lara* (London: Angela Royal Publishing, 1997); Caryl Phillips, *The Atlantic Sound* (New York: Knopf, 2000); Marcus Wood, *Blind Memory: Visual Representations of Slavery in England and America 1780–1865* (Manchester: Manchester University Press, 2000).

20 See for instance James T. Campbell, *Songs of Zion: The African Methodist Episcopal Church in the United States and South Africa* (Oxford and New York: Oxford University Press, 1995); Stephen D. Gish, *Alfred B. Xuma: African, American, South African* (New York: New York University Press, 2000); J. Lorand Matory, 'Surpassing "Survival": On the Urbanity of "Traditional Religion" in the Afro-Atlantic World', *The Black Scholar: Journal of Black Studies and Research*, 30, 3–4 (2000), pp. 36–43; Philip Zachernuk, *Colonial Subjects: An African Intelligentsia and Atlantic Ideas* (Charlottesville: University Press of Virginia, 2000).

6

Transnational productions of Englishness: South Africa in the post-imperial metropole

'Huge ideological work has to go on every day to produce this mouse that people can recognize as the English.' Thus observes Stuart Hall, one of the foremost practitioners of black cultural studies in Britain.[1] For Hall, the transformation of English national identity began with Margaret Thatcher's 1979 government. The contemporary production of Englishness became, and continues to be, labour-intensive because England had lost the material foundation of that identity: an overseas empire, economic prosperity and global political prestige. To add to England's travails, the old empire has been replaced by the 'Empire Within', generated by flows of black immigration to the British mainland that started in the 1940s and have become increasingly unwelcome to a number of white Britons. As a result, the recently reformulated Englishness – variously referred to as 'the new racism' or 'Thatcherism' – equates national community with the white race.[2] This nationalist discourse eschews the openly racist language of biological superiority and uses instead the more coded language of cultural difference to promote an English nation that is culturally homogeneous and exclusively white.

This account of post-imperial Englishness has become hegemonic in British cultural studies. Its most substantial example remains Paul Gilroy's 1987 landmark *'There Ain't No Black in the Union Jack'*.[3] Literary studies too have adopted this perspective, as is evident in the recent discussions by Simon Gikandi and Ian Baucom of 1980s British literary politics.[4] One of the problems with this approach is that it remains entirely mainland: contemporary Englishness is regarded as arising only in response to diasporic immigration. This perspective excludes the possibility that international elements may be involved in the formation of this national identity. Contra Gilroy *et al.*, I want to suggest that white metropolitan identity develops not only through its black subjects 'at home' but also through those who continue to live abroad, in postcolonial countries that once 'belonged' to the British Empire.

Other scholars have recently recognised the transnational, or (post)colonial, circuits of contemporary Englishness.[5] Their approach construes this national culture as a version of neo-colonialism with the trappings of liberal cosmopolitanism. Graham Huggan's account of the Booker Prize industry, and its invention of a 'postcolonial exotic', exemplifies this intellectual project. Huggan's approach makes the metropolitan literary industry central to the production and circulation of Englishness.[6] His analysis makes clear how its publication, adjudication and consumption of postcolonial literatures allow the English to reinvent their empire. The country is recentred as a sovereign international power; its capital is both cultural and financial. If the dominant features of Englishness, according to Paul Gilroy, are its xenophobia and paranoia, for Huggan it is corrosive paternalism that best describes this national disposition. Looking at its cultural relations with its former colonies, Huggan uncovers the ways that metropolitan Britain arrogates authority over them. Huggan tends however to rely on India to illustrate the neocolonial dynamic between the metropole and postcolony. His discussion of Booker Prize exoticism, for instance, centres on the examples of Salman Rushdie and Arundhati Roy. This leaves unclear how far such a dynamic might describe the relationship of England to other parts of 'its' empire, such as Africa and the Caribbean.

These diasporic and postcolonial perspectives respectively contribute in important ways to the analysis of post-imperial Englishness. However, neither one on its own is adequate to explain how contemporary Englishness has articulated with South Africa. The cultural identity that has emerged through this articulation contains elements both of Gilroy's xenophobia and of Huggan's neo-colonial paternalism. This is partly because of the singular, variable political relationship between the two countries from 1910 South African Union onwards. While remaining a prominent part of the visual architecture of the historic empire – South Africa House borders Trafalgar Square, along with Australia and Canada – for many years South Africa stood neither fully inside nor firmly outside the political imaginary of the British Commonwealth. In many senses, it stood as a disgraced family member, formally excluded in 1961. To add to the complexity, London became a nexus of anti-apartheid activism: it provided the headquarters of the exiled African National Congress. Many South African academics moved to London, taking up residence in the School of Oriental and African Studies, and several of South Africa's progressive intellectuals, including Roger van Zwanenburg and Ros de Lanarolle, left South Africa to set up publishing houses in London.

It is the operation of publishing houses that I am going to address here. I deal with the flurry of metropolitan interest in South Africa that began in the mid-1980s and ended in the early 1990s. I look at how mainstream publishers made South Africa available for popular consumption, and what this tells us about post-imperial Englishness in the metropole. It is important to differentiate the operations of these mainstream publishing houses – Penguin, Bloomsbury, Abacus, The Women's Press and Pandora – from those of radical black and socialist presses such as Zed, Pluto, New Beacon, Karnak House and Bogle L'Ouverture. The latter deal with a small politically committed target readership that by definition stands at a remove from hegemonic English political culture. These are not my primary concern. Neither is a study of the ideology of the publication list of equally specialist literature presses, the Heinemann African Writers Series and Longman. I am interested here in the South African books selected for consecration within what Pierre Bourdieu refers to as 'middle-brow' culture.[7] My analysis proceeds from the knowledge that the majority of black South African texts are consistently ignored by the mainstream houses and published only by specialist presses. Mainstream houses favour white South African material to a disproportionate degree. While I will touch on this process of textual inclusion and exclusion, my focus is on the ideological work these presses perform to commodify those books that they have selected. I examine their mechanisms for appealing to a general white readership.

The readership that these publishers target has a humanitarian concern for the racial injustices of apartheid South Africa. Metropolitan presses were quick to capitalise on the expanded prominence of the South African anti-apartheid struggle in the media. From late 1984, when popular uprising intensified, British television and newspapers across the spectrum devoted frequent and extensive coverage to the police brutalities and militant resistance occurring in the streets of South Africa. It was shortly after this that the flurry of publications began. Mainstream feminist presses were heavily invested in this process. The Women's Press – headed by the South African Ros de Lanarolle – and Pandora were among the most energetic publishers of South African material at this time. Many of the materials they, Penguin and

Bloomsbury published were not originally written for commercial metropolitan purposes. These include political speeches, essays, autobiography, personal letters and academic sociological studies. Several of these
texts were reprints of works by dead authors – including late nineteenth
to early twentieth-century feminist Olive Schreiner, the Ruth First prison
memoirs, Steve Biko's collection of writings. The topical interest in South
African political activists Steve Biko and Ruth First was compounded by
their rendition into film: these publications were timed to coincide with
the release of biopics, Richard Attenborough's *Cry Freedom* and Chris
Menges's *A World Apart.*

I focus here on the cultural labour of blurb writers. Their efforts to
render non-commercial books into cross-over commodities – and, more
generally, to make South Africa resonate with metropolitan white
Englishness – make a significant if generally neglected archive for cultural sociology. It is a crucial irony that the aspects of South Africa that
are most threatening for metropolitan subject constitution are also their
greatest potential selling points: these are the contemporary movement
for political emancipation and the historical relationship between the
two countries. My first section addresses the impact of the contemporary liberation movement; I then go on to explore the historical relationship. The metropolitan commodification of anti-racist political
movement thoroughly bears out Paul Gilroy's suggestion that 'it is easier
to talk about racism than about black emancipation'.[8] The translation
of black emancipation into consumable commodity involves more than
turning black subjects into victims; it also involves the partial redefini-
tion of 'the political' itself away from a social to an epistemological
domain. Political emancipation, I argue, gets rewritten as the salvation
of society through the white female intellectual, and her salvation
through knowledge. The commodification of history, I suggest, rewrites
the past to turn white English South Africa into the primary fatality of
apartheid's 1948 inauguration. A particular form of imperialist nostalgia is deployed to disassociate historical English rule from racist logic,
and to install the empire as the lamented, rightful custodians of black
development into political modernity.

Making anti-racist politics palatable

If public sympathy for violently oppressed black South Africans
prompted these publications, the ideological work needed to persuade

their target public to buy these products was far from simple, since white English responses to black political agency were highly ambivalent by the time South Africa's government declared its first state of emergency in 1985. Triggering English ambivalence were several metropolitan events of the 1980s, among them the so-called race riots of 1981 and 1984.[9] Instead of presenting these as rational responses to racial injustice, the media presented them as senseless, random acts of lawless violence perpetrated by a criminal youth subculture. The resultant post-imperial social vision equated Englishness with commonsensical 'law and order'. Its circular logic identified white subjects as the exclusive bearers of political reason. During and immediately after this same period, South African activists were following the ANC's command to 'make South African ungovernable'. The portrayal by the British media of turbulent black resistance must have created discomfort in a white metropole itself recently destabilised by the energetic protests conducted by its own black population.

The tactics deployed to sell the South African liberation struggle to white English readers consequently seek to depoliticise black authors and centre white women as the most significant agents of anti-racist movement. White women become the bearers of dynamic political authority; black women are made the representatives of a passive and unchanging racial community. The systematic re-orientation of politics away from black subjects began only in 1985, by which time two black women's autobiographies had already been published. These were by the then celebrity Winnie Mandela and the unknown Ellen Kuzwayo.[10] The romantic hagiography of Winnie Mandela's packaging reveals the road that was not to be taken again; thereafter, commodification was to follow Kuzwayo's humbler example. Even this had to be modified, since like Mandela's its taxonomy was openly political: Winnie Mandela's book is listed as 'Biography/Autobiography. World Affairs' and Kuzwayo is listed as 'Autobiography/Politics'. Both books' blurbs also use 'political' as an adjective: 'Winnie Mandela narrates the remarkable story of her life and political development. Courageous and humorous, it is a story as inspiring as that of her husband' and 'In telling her own personal and political story over 70 years, Ellen Kuzwayo speaks for, and with, the women among whom she lives and works'. After 1985, politics was phased out of black classification and description altogether: Steve Biko's *I Write What I Like* is listed most misleadingly under the headings of 'Biography/Autobiography'.[11] White authors such as Nadine Gordimer instead take up the political nomination: her 1989 essays *The Essential Gesture* are classified as 'Literature/Politics'.[12] Depoliticisation also inheres in the publisher's exclusions: after Biko's book came out, there were no further reprints of historic black leaders' autobiographies such as Z.K. Matthews's or Albert Luthuli's. Indeed, with the single – and odd – exception of Bloke Modisane's *Blame Me on History* as a Penguin Modern Classic in 1990, mainstream publishers avoided writing by black men altogether during this period. This moratorium was broken only in 1994, with the publication of Nelson Mandela's *Long Walk to Freedom*.[13]

Part of the depoliticisation process involves desexualisation, so that works written by elderly women who are no longer biologically genera-tive replace those by black women of reproductive age. Penguin's early blurbing for Winnie Mandela sells her as a romantic soul mate, wife and mother of black South Africa; this is replaced by Sindiwe Magona's grand-motherly persona as signalled by her 1991 autobiography title *To My Children's Children*.[14] Profiling black senior women further helps the publishers to displace threatening black male youth from the metropoli-tan cultural imagination. Such youth had been sensationalised as the lead-ers of the 'race riots' of England as well as the *toyi-toying* (dancing in militaristic style) South African opposition.

Not only autobiography was affected by this metropolitan agenda. The determination to present senior black South African women as bear-ers of an authentic racial culture also had an impact on the commodifi-cation of black women's fiction. Publishers downplayed both the creative agency and the personal distinctiveness of these creative writers, prefer-ring instead to present them as documentarists.[15] A quick comparison of three back covers by the same publisher, Pandora, reveals this.

In 1987, Pandora published fiction by two white women: Menan du Plessis's *A State of Fear* and Carol Barash's edition of *An Olive Schreiner Reader*.[16] Their back covers take care to inform the reader about the author and her achievements. We are given a detailed literary biography for Schreiner. And about Menan du Plessis we are told that she 'has received two awards for *A State of Fear*: the Olive Schreiner Prize, 1985, for first novel and the Sanlam Literary Prize, 1986 (shared)'. In 1989 this press published Miriam Tlali's *Soweto Stories*, which significantly was published in South Africa as the rather more fanciful *Footsteps in the Quag*.[17] The British title prefers to suggest an ethnographic rather than a literary project. This back cover supplies no information to the reader

about the author other than that 'Miriam Tlali is South Africa's most significant black woman writer'. The sales technique subordinates black
women's aesthetic individuality to a notion of collective culture; for white
women creative writers it is, on the contrary, their aesthetic distinctiveness that is commercially paramount.

Although Nadine Gordimer's essays are classified as 'Politics', the
methods for marketing white women's writings tended to present the
operations of rationality as an alibi for political activism. I have already
alluded to the ways that England's 1981 and 1984 black protests were
characterised as 'irrational' by dominant media. In effect, these representations racialised rationality as exclusive to white culture. Reason is not
only raced but also sexed in the work of blurb writers: intellectual capacity is made the property of white South African women, whose struggle
to comprehend and transcend apartheid's racism then becomes analogous to (and as valuable as) the struggle to achieve political transformation itself.

Starting in the early 1980s, white British feminism had been soundly
criticised by black British feminists for its 'imperialist' and racist tendencies.[18] These blurbs sell a consoling vision to feminists on the rebound
from this critique: the central representatives of anti-racist knowledge
become white women, whose potential for racism is further mitigated by
their presentation as only partial members of the racist society that has
produced them. This is evident on the back cover of Menan du Plessis's
novel *A State of Fear*, set in a restive Cape Town of 1980:

> Interpreting this turbulence for us is Anna Rossouw, a young white
> teacher at a Coloured high school, who shelters two of her pupils
> from arrest. They are engaged in some kind of political resistance,
> though Anna never quite knows what ... Anna's concern for them is
> central to her attempts to understand herself within the disturbed
> society of which she is part and yet not part.

Anna's political intervention is confined to epistemology; she functions to mediate and interpret knowledge. If South African white women
are only partial members of society, then the same reassuring characterisation applies to white British women as readers. Such metropolitan packaging thus works very hard to play down any hint of structural responsibility
or ideological complicity. Where the book's subject matter itself accentuates this complicity, the blurb goes all out to diminish any potential consumer's discomfort. For instance, Jacklyn Cock's own title *Maids and*

Madams: Domestic Workers under Apartheid situates 'madams' as integral to apartheid and to the book's contents.[19] However, the publisher's back cover blurb on the contrary avoids any implication of white women in the situation:

> At the very heart of apartheid lies a unique relationship, all the more powerful because it belongs in the home. It is the relationship between white employer and black servant – who not only cooks and cleans but also brings up white babies, while her own are left in the township for twelve or twenty-four hours a day.

The black employee is gendered; the white employer is not. The blurb further compensates by emphasising the white author's personal bravery and risk-taking:

> In a series of revealing interviews Jacklyn Cock exposes the truth about the triple oppression of South African domestic workers ... The book was so explosive when it was first published that the author, a lecturer in sociology at the University of the Witwatersrand, Johannesburg, received a stream of abusive phone calls and a dynamite attack on her home.

From this metropolitan commodification, there emerges this distinction: black women tell us their own cultural stories; white women mediate knowledge. They also work with others to produce joint knowledge. Ruth First and Ann Scott's co-written biography of Olive Schreiner is a case in point. Nadine Gordimer's puff praises it for being 'a model of disinterested collaboration and scholarship'.[20] Working with other women, like working on other women, exemplifies their capacity for surpassing a both a racist position and a racial condition.

However this scenario is rarely seamless. The tensions of this ideological work become acute when the white subject, like Ruth First, is herself a high-profile political activist in the ANC and the South African Communist Party, whose intellectual work the blurb writers cannot make to substitute for her activism. This overt political affiliation is out of ideological kilter not only with the cosmopolitan liberal primary readership of Bloomsbury Press, but also with the culturalist turn of the British Communist Party which by the late 1980s, under the influence of Stuart Hall and Martin Jacques, had rejected traditional communist party politics for its economism, workerism, sexism and anachronistic neglect of desire, and shifted towards the postmodern possibilities afforded by the

'New Times' of 'post-Fordism'.[21] All this makes its way into the reissue of Ruth First's 1965 prison memoirs, *117 Days*, to coincide with the film *A World Apart*, which was scripted by Ruth First's daughter Shawn Slovo and deals with First's political persecution from the perspective of injured daughterhood.[22]

The book's blurb opens:

> In 1963 Ruth First, a militant member of both the ANC and the South African Communist Party, was detained under the 'ninety-day' law. There was no warrant, no charge and no trial. This is her account of her months in prison, her solitary confinement, interrogation and instantaneous re-arrest. In 1982 Ruth First was killed by a letter bomb in Maputo, Mozambique.

The blurb then shifts abruptly to the statements that

> In 1988 *A World Apart*, a film written by Ruth First's daughter, Shawn Slovo, herself just a small girl at the time of her mother's imprisonment, is being shown in theatres all over the world, except in South Africa. 1988 is also the year of Nelson Mandela's seventieth birthday.

Nowhere here or on the front cover does the blurb inform the uninitiated that Ruth First is indeed the subject of the film. Here we are told, instead, who scripted the film and where the film is being exhibited. The blurb moves into an apparent *non sequitur* to inform us that 1988 sees Nelson Mandela turn seventy years of age. The blurb is caught between the contradictory demands of First's 'traditional' style of political commitment and a postmodern culturalism that wants to inscribe modern cinematic cultural production and consumption as the locus of political activism. By way of resolution, the blurb links the mother and daughter through a notion of transgenerational female victimhood. The mother's tragedy becomes her daughter's; her childhood at the time of her mother's imprisonment becomes the object of the reader's emotional concern. And this daughter now continues to pay the price for her mother's politics through the loss of her freedom to exhibit, or profit from, her film in South Africa. The jump to Nelson Mandela's birthday stages a competition of emotional value: Ruth First has lost her life, her daughter has lost both a mother and a viewing audience. Mandela, however, has survived to a respectable age. We are not informed that he is still in prison, nor how many years he has spent in prison, and this is significant for a blurb as fixated on dates and numbers as this one.[23]

Historical dissociations: apartheid and imperialist nostalgia

The historical relations of England with South Africa pose a major challenge for blurb writers to negotiate. The challenge lies in tapping the residual sense of imperial kinship while dissociating white English readers from responsibility for South Africa's oppressive social structure. While the apartheid system was formally initiated in 1948, with the electoral victory of the Afrikaner National Party, it is best seen as the culmination of a racist structure that both the metropolitan and colonial English contributed to and profited from. None the less, the fictional narrative of a benign empire of English liberalism being brutally displaced by an evil regime of Afrikaner viciousness in 1948 proved to be a resource that metropolitan publishers could avail themselves of. The operations of English imperialist nostalgia here prove to be quite complex. According to Renato Rosaldo, such nostalgia typically proceeds from the guilty knowledge of the imperialist subject's responsibility for destroying the ahistorical racialised society he proceeds to elegise.[24] The nostalgia peddled by metropolitan publishers instead proceeds on the opposite basis. The lament is not for the loss of black innocence but for that lost possession of imperial power, which itself takes on the aura of a pure and innocent condition. Apartheid is lamented for driving a fatal wedge between the empire and 'its' black subjects. The violence that apartheid has done is primarily to its white English 'victims'; it is their authentic culture, not that of black South Africans, that has been destroyed. And part of that English culture is its dynamic developmentalism. Events of 1948 have removed from the English their racial-cultural mandate to develop the country into liberal political modernity.

An important part of this ideological work, then, is that it seeks to cast black South African subjects as exempt from cultural violence; only English culture has suffered. Black South African culture remains alive, well, and comfortably static, mediated by its grandmothers like Ellen Kuzwayo and Sindiwe Magona. The violence that apartheid racism does to black people is limited to their status as political and historical subjects. Racism becomes a condition whose effects can be isolated. Thus the blurbs for black writing repeatedly present a disjunction: they open by ritually characterising apartheid as an all-powerful evil and then proceed to an account of a resilient black culture that appears to confound such a characterisation since its bears no trace of that evil. For example, of Miriam Tlali's *Soweto Stories* we are first told that 'Her stories sing with the sounds of black South Africa, with the languages of Bantu, Lesotho and Afrikaans as she shows the insidious way that apartheid undermines every aspect of daily life'. The 'insidious undermining of every aspect of daily life' however vanishes from the blurb's ensuing account of the stories, an account that draws upon a discourse of folk comedy to jump from one story's scenario to another without informing us how their narratives develop. The result is the portrait of a township culture characterised by vitality and resilience:

> Velani loves 'Volksie', his Volkswagen more than the 'Struggle'. Aunt Lizzy recalls her days as a Shebeen Queen when they used to hide Alcohol from the police in coffins. M'ma Lithoto sits on a crowded station platform with her niece and bundles of belongings wondering where to go now that she has left her husband. These are Miriam Tlali's people of Soweto – coping with daily life in the city, commuting on segregated trains, avoiding the police.

Apartheid's destructiveness is instead seen to target the imperial project of English political modernity. The latter includes the developmentalist mandate to 'produce' black subjects who are fit for the equality conferred by the modern state and civil society. Such a mandate is evident in the theme of education that runs across these blurbs. Ellen Kuzwayo's rueful nostalgia spells this out: 'Not every grandmother, she remarks wryly, can claim that she had better educational opportunities than her grandchildren.'[25]

The 'educational opportunities' that Kuzwayo invokes predate apartheid and hark back to the good old days of putative English hegemony. Apartheid has deprived the English of their opportunity to educate black people into modernity. Ultimately these blurbs seek to cement black culture in a non-developmental tradition (which the women have been preserving) and, at the same time, to seal white English as the legitimate agent of black edification. Political modernity and cultural traditionalism are made to be mutually reinforcing categories.

Apartheid's metaphysical assault on the missionary educationalist project of imperial Englishness was so powerful that even settler English subjects were themselves co-opted. *Not Either an Experimental Doll: The Separate Worlds of Three South African Women* openly implicates a white English woman in this 'first hand account of the roots of modern Apartheid and the hated Black education system'.[26] Not even Fabian English university professors were able to withstand apartheid's anti-educationalist, anti-developmental logic. The publication explains that

Between 1949 and 1951 three very different South African women
entered into a painful and revealing correspondence, which was to
change their lives. Lily Moya, a young Xhosa girl, desperate to escape
the life dictated to her by a racist state, writes to Mabel Palmer, a 'liberal' British expatriate, working in the 'non European' section of the
University of Natal. Lily hopes that she can gain educational guid-
ance and friendship from Mabel Palmer. Sibusisiwe Makhanya, one
of the first Black social workers in South Africa, tries to act as a medi-
ator between these two women; but what emerges from these letters
is a series of misunderstandings caused by cultural ignorance, racism
and the fear in whites of having any true, free and equal dialogue
with a Black person.

The letters speak for themselves, but Shula Marks has written an
explanatory introduction and epilogue, which tells us of the tragic
ending to this riveting story.

Giving apartheid the inexorable status of national fate effectively miti-
gates the admission of English complicity. Even black agents cannot resist
it, as is confirmed by the failure of Sibusisiwe Makhanya to broker cross-
racial and cross-cultural understanding. Inescapable historical tragedy is
one means of selling this story of English capitulation. But the blurb also
sells the consoling thought that that white metropolitan women – in the
form of Shula Marks – are now free to resume the educationalist mandate
that apartheid took away. The narrative of its historical impossibility in
fact reinforces the contemporary fulfillability of this imperial educational
role: the more inescapable apartheid was then, 'over there', the more
escapable it is now, over 'here'.

I have been arguing that metropolitan publishers used South Africa's
contemporary anti-apartheid movement, and its apartheid past, to con-
secrate a post-imperial English subject. This subject is stationed as the
neo-colonial, intellectual agent of South Africa's social redemption. Such
a scenario assumes that transformative agency is possible, and is the
birthright of white Englishness. However the triumphalist intervention-
ism of this position began to give way in the early 1990s. A new, socially
pessimistic version of metropolitan Englishness emerged to become
hegemonic, fed equally by events in Eastern Europe, the Rushdie Affair,
and the escalation of South African violence that followed the unban-
ning of the ANC in 1990. Together these produced a version of post-
imperial English sovereignty that was characterised not, as before, by its
intellectual authority to lead anti-racist transformation, but instead by

its superior knowledge of the futility of such a project. This is beautifully illustrated in the reception given South African Rian Malan's best-
selling *My Traitor's Heart*.[27] This new post-imperial position selects as
its officiators John le Carré and Salman Rushdie, to authorise the vital
cultural knowledge that political emancipatory, nationalist ideals are
dangerous illusions that either succumb to or disguise racial self-inter-
est.[28] The apparently incongruous coupling of these two post-imperial
authorities bears analysis as the sign of a significant new metropolitan
dispensation. Le Carré's puff lauds Malan's book as 'truth telling at its
most exemplary and courageous'; 'the remorseless exercise of a reporter's
anguished conscience gives us a South Africa we thought we knew all
about: but we knew nothing'. The historical authority that le Carré commands derives from the Cold War, which le Carré rewrote to feature
English intelligence as the privileged voice of the Free World. His specifically English expertise thus is particularly equipped to recognise 'truth'
and 'treachery' when he reads them. This refigures Englishness as arbi-
trational; consecrated by its adjudicatory and 'post-political' role. The
truth that le Carré credits Malan with has been hidden by 'over-opti-
mistic simplification', in other words the totalising ideologies of the
South African liberation struggle.

A fatwah-cursed Salman Rushdie is made the principal bearer of this
'demystificatory' post-imperial position, which now upholds the verdict
of racial determinism. According to Rushdie, Rian Malan's value lies in
how

> Along the way he ran into, and faced up to, the truth that is the
> making of his book – that for all his nigger-loving, leftist views …
> *he was still a Malan*; that he could only write about the atrocity of
> South Africa by admitting the atrocity hidden in his own traitorous
> heart … Here, as in nothing I've read before, is the demonic voice of
> black and Afrikaner South Africa …

The 'demystification' that Rushdie lauds rests on a mystique of racial
essence, in which black and white alike are stuck in primordial hostility.
Rushdie significantly confines the demonic voices to 'black' and
'Afrikaner': English South Africans, are, like white English metropolitan
readers, excused from this scenario. They are thereby confirmed as a
racism-free tribe – though still, of course, a tribe. This English subject can
only shake its head sadly at the 'heart of darkness' that unites South
Africa's more racist tribes.

Conclusion

The analysis I have been pursuing rests on the materialist premise that contemporary cultures need to be analysed through their economic mediations. It is important to look at the contribution that the commod-ification process makes to the meanings of racial and national identity. Looking at the metropolitan culture industry as a productive site of post-imperial Englishness moves us beyond an understanding of national cul-ture as the product only of sanctified intellectuals (a view that informs Gilroy's work). It leads to a greater sense of how the generally anonymous workers of the culture industry, such as the blurb writers, also facilitate the ideological production of national cultures. The irony that I earlier pointed to – that the elements of South Africa that are most threatening for metropolitan subject constitution are also their greatest potential sell-ing points – suggests just how complicated the ideological balancing act is for these workers, to produce a national identity as consumable com-modity.

This approach also takes us beyond the valuable but none the less static approach to the transnational receptions of postcolonial culture, its circulation in 'the West', that has been taken by a number of cultural critics. The discussions of South Africa's transnational reception by Clive Barnett, Sikhumbuzo Mngadi and Rob Nixon – important and excel-lent as they are – share the assumption that the West, or First World, is a singular entity.[29] This implies that South Africa's transnational signif-icance for England and for the USA is identical. But the transformation of South Africa into a prop of post-imperial Englishness is not the same as South Africa's commodification within the USA. The two countries' histories are too dissimilar, and their current relation to global cultural capital too different, for this equation to hold true. Only by breaking down the category of 'the West' into its national constituents can cul-tural criticism generate a methodology fully adequate to the task of anti-colonial opposition.

If in the sphere of transnational studies I am arguing for a greater attentiveness to national specificity, I am also arguing for an analysis of national culture that is not limited to race relations within the boundaries of that nation. My example of South Africa suggests how Englishness is constituted as much by anti-racist uprisings overseas as by anti-racist uprisings within Britain: both intranational and international compo-nents need to be included in future critical work. The challenge remains, to find productive ways to combine 'diasporic' and 'postcolonial' perspectives.

Notes

1 Stuart Hall, 'The Local and the Global: Globalization and Ethnicity', in Anne McClintock, Aamir Mufti and Ella Shohat (eds.), *Dangerous Liaisons: Gender, Nation, and Postcolonial Perspectives* (London: University of Minnesota Press, 1997), p. 178.

2 For sociological and political economic accounts of race in contemporary Britain see Floya Anthias and Nira Yuval-Davis, in association with Harriet Cain, *Racialized Boundaries: Race, Nation, Gender, Colour and Class and the Anti-racist Struggle* (London: Routledge, 1992); Arun Kundani, '"Stumbling on": Race, Class and England', *Race and Class: A Journal for Black and Third World Liberation*, 41, 4 (2000), pp. 1–18; and the special issue of *Race and Class: A Journal for Black and Third World Liberation*, 43, 2 (2001) on 'The Three Faces of British Racism'. See also Gargi Bhattacharyya, 'Wogs South of Calais: Re-thinking Racial Boundaries for Britain in Europe', *Paragraph*, 16, 1 (1993), pp. 23–33.

3 Paul Gilroy, *'There Ain't No Black in the Union Jack': The Cultural Politics of Race and Nation* (London: Unwin Hyman, 1987).

4 Simon Gikandi, *Maps of Englishness: Writing Identity in the Culture of Colonialism* (New York: Columbia University Press, 1996); Ian Baucom, *Out of Place: Englishness, Empire, and the Locations of Identity* (Princeton: Princeton University Press, 1999).

5 See the important studies of Bill Schwarz, '"The Only White Man in There": The Re-racialisation of England, 1956–1968', *Race and Class: A Journal for Black and Third World Liberation*, 38, 1 (1996), pp. 65–78; 'Black Metropolis, White England', in Mica Nava and Alan O'Shea (eds.), *Modern Times: Reflections on a Century of English Modernity* (London: Routledge, 1996), pp. 176–207, and Vron Ware, *Beyond the Pale: White Women, Racism and History* (London: Verso, 1992), which situate the transnational co-ordinates of white Englishness and explore a number of historical periods of its production. See also Phil Cohen and Bill Schwarz (eds.), special issue of *New Formations: A Journal of Culture/Theory/Politics*, 33 (1998), on 'Frontlines/Backyards', for a broad-ranging coverage of contemporary racial politics and culture in England. And see the influential argument of Linda Colley, 'Britishness and Otherness: An Argument', *Journal of British Studies*, 31 (1992), pp. 309–29.

6 Graham Huggan, 'Prizing "Otherness": A Short History of the Booker', *Studies in the Novel*, 29, 3 (1997), pp. 412–33; 'The Postcolonial Exotic: Rushdie's "Booker of Bookers"', *Transition*, 64 (1994), pp. 22–9.

7 Pierre Bourdieu, *The Field of Cultural Production: Essays on Art and Literature*, edited and introduced by R. Johnson (New York: Columbia University Press, 1993).

8 Paul Gilroy, 'Cruciality and the Frog's Perspective', in *Small Acts: Thoughts on the Politics of Black Cultures* (London: Serpent's Tail, 1993), p. 112.

9 I am indebted here to Paul Gilroy's '*There Ain't No Black*'; Cecil Gutzmore, 'Capital, "Black Youth" and Crime', *Race and Class: A Journal for Black and Third World Liberation*, 25, 2 (1983), pp. 13–30; and John Solomos, *Race and Racism in Britain* (New York: St Martin's Press, 1993), on 1980s black British protests and metropolitan responses.

10 Winnie Mandela, *Part of My Soul*, edited by Anne Benjamin and adapted by Mary Benson (Harmondsworth: Penguin, 1985); Ellen Kuzwayo, *Call Me Woman* (London: The Women's Press, 1985).

11 Steve Biko, *I Write What I Like: A Selection of His Writings*, edited by Aelred Stubbs (1978; Harmondsworth: Penguin, 1988).

12 Nadine Gordimer, *The Essential Gesture: Writing, Politics and Places*, edited and introduced by Stephen Clingman (Harmondsworth: Penguin, 1989).

13 Nelson Mandela, *Long Walk to Freedom: The Autobiography of Nelson Mandela* (London: Little, Brown and Company, 1994). Overall, the British book blurbs erase all references to what is specifically black, political and South African about Mandela's experiences, and desexualise him also.

14 Sindiwe Magona, *To My Children's Children: An Autobiography* (London: The Women's Press, 1991).

15 Alternative perspectives on South African women's literature can be found in feminist critical discussion within South Africa. See, for example, the special issue on feminism and writing of *Current Writing: Text and Reception in Southern Africa* [Durban, South Africa], 2, 1 (1990), edited by Margaret Daymond. For debates within South African feminism more generally, see the journal *Agenda: Empowering Women for Gender Equity* [Durban, South Africa].

16 Menan du Plessis, *A State of Fear* (London: Pandora Press, 1987). Carol Barash (ed.), *An Olive Schreiner Reader: Writings on Women and South Africa* (London: Pandora, 1987).

17 Miriam Tlali, *Soweto Stories*, introduced by Lauretta Ngcobo (London: Pandora Press, 1989).

18 The British journals *Feminist Review* and *Spare Rib* carried many of these critical debates during this period. Some of the critiques are collected in Heidi Safia Mirza (ed.), *Black British Feminism: A Reader* (London: Routledge, 1997).

19 Jacklyn Cock, *Maids & Madams: Domestic Workers under Apartheid* (1980; London: The Women's Press, 1989).

20 Ruth First and Ann Scott, *Olive Schreiner: A Biography*. (1980; London: The Women's Press, 1989).

21 See Stuart Hall and Martin Jacques (eds.), *New Times* (London: Lawrence and Wishart, 1990). An important critique of the shift to 'New Times' is A. Sivanandan, 'All that Melts into Air Is Solid: The Hokum of New Times', in *Communities of Resistance: Writings on Black Struggles for Socialism* (London: Verso, 1990), pp. 19–59.

22 Ruth First, *117 Days: An Account of Confinement and Interrogation under the South African Ninety-day Detention Law* (1965; London: Bloomsbury, 1988).

23 The US socialist *Monthly Review Press* provides a strikingly different back cover blurb, in its reprint of *117 Days*. This reads:

The early 1960s were a time of both hope and crisis for progressives in South Africa. The African National Congress had brought blacks and whites together to form a unique nonracial opposition movement; but the ANC was banned in 1960, and harsh new laws were passed to quell the rising tide of dissent.

Ruth First, who along with her husband Joe Slovo was prominent in both the South African Communist Party and the ANC, was at the center of this movement; when the crackdown came she was one of the first to be arrested and jailed without charge under the new Ninety-Day Law. *117 Days* is an account of her months in prison spent fighting back fear, anger, and mental weakness, only to be followed by rearrest at the end of her ninety-day term.

After her release, First continued to battle against the apartheid system from exile until she was killed by a letter bomb in Mozambique in 1982. Her story brings to life a fascinating period in South Africa's history through the experience of one of its most committed activists. A foreword by Albie Sachs, a colleague of Ruth First's, and like her a victim of South African bomb attacks, highlights the tensions in the life of a white middle-class woman in a mass-based black struggle. An afterword by historian Tom Lodge locates these contradictions in the context of the development of the South African resistance movement.

In 1988, *A World Apart*, a film written by First's daughter Shawn Slovo about her experience of her mother's activism and imprisonment, was released to wide acclaim all over the world – except South Africa.

This blurb situates Ruth First's activism and her memoir within a broader political context, and carefully links the film to the text.

24 Renato Rosaldo, 'Imperialist Nostalgia', *Representations*, 26 (1989), pp. 107–21.

25 Ellen Kuzwayo, *Sit Down and Listen: Stories from South Africa* (London: The Women's Press, 1990).

26 Shula Marks (ed.), *Not Either an Experimental Doll: The Separate Worlds of Three South African Women* (London: The Women's Press, 1987).

27 Rian Malan, *My Traitor's Heart: Blood and Bad Dreams: A South African Explores the Madness in His Country, His Tribe and Himself* (London: Vintage, 1990).

28 For an illuminating discussion of Le Carré in this context see Geoff Hemstedt, 'George Smiley and Post-imperial Nostalgia', in Raphael Samuel (ed.). *Patriotism: The Making and Unmaking of British National Identity: Volume III: National Fictions* (London: Routledge, 1989), pp. 233–40.

29 Clive Barnett, 'Constructions of Apartheid in the International Reception of the Novels of J.M. Coetzee', *Journal of Southern African Studies*, 25, 2 (1999), pp. 287–301. Sikhumbuzo Mngadi, 'The Politics of Historical Representation

in the Context of Global Capitalism', in Johannes A. Smit, Johan van Wyk and Jean-Philippe Wade (eds.), *Rethinking South African Literary History* (Durban: Y Press, 1996), pp. 196–208. Rob Nixon, *Homelands, Harlem and Hollywood: South African Culture and the World Beyond* (London: Routledge, 1994). For discussions of US receptions of South African theatre, see Jeanne Colleran, 'South African Theatre in the United States: The Allure of the Familiar and of the Exotic', in Derek Attridge and Rosemary Jolly (eds.), *Writing South Africa: Literature, Apartheid, and Democracy, 1970–1995* (Cambridge: Cambridge University Press, 1998), pp. 221–36; Loren Kruger, 'Apartheid on Display: South Africa Performs for New York', *Diaspora: A Journal of Transnational Studies*, 1, 2 (1991), pp. 191–208.

Part III
Postcolonial theoretical politics

7

Theorising race, racism and culture: David Lloyd's work

My focus here is an important and influential article by postcolonial scholar David Lloyd, 'Race Under Representation', published in the 1991 'Neo-Colonialism' issue of *Oxford Literary Review*.[1] Lloyd sets out to explain 'how the meshing of racial formations can take place between various levels and spheres of social practice, as, for example, between political and cultural spheres or between the individual and the national level' (p. 63). A central argument of his is that 'the terms developed for aesthetic culture in the late 18th century, as constituting the definition of human identity, continue to regulate racial formations through the various sites of contemporary practice' (pp. 63–4). Lloyd situates Kant's formulation of aesthetic culture in the *Critique of Judgement*, and particularly his discussion of concepts of 'common taste' and 'the public sphere', as formative of Western racism.[2] Lloyd states that his 'formal analysis of the ideological Subject' is a necessary complement of 'material histories of the specific transformations that take place through the dialectic between the state and what it perforce negates as a condition of its existence' (p. 87). I want to suggest that Lloyd's formalism proves, on the contrary, antithetical to a materialist approach.

I choose this article for discussion because it seems to condense a number of current dispositions in Western anti-foundationalist critical theory, political critique, and colonial discourse analysis. Lloyd's concern with Enlightenment ideologies is shared by a growing number of postcolonial critics. His work corresponds to the culturalist orientation of the late British journal *Marxism Today*, an orientation also discernible in British 'multiculturalist' and 'antiracist' education policy.[3] Lloyd's interest in Fanonian psychoanalytic formulations also reflect popular strains of colonial discourse analysis.[4] I address only particular aspects of Lloyd's argument: his critique of the public sphere; his accounts of the racialised subject and of anti-colonial subjectivity. Through a series of connected

critical commentaries that engage with the political and critical implications of Lloyd's work, I suggest alternative approaches to the analysis of
racial formation.

The tyranny of the public sphere?

Lloyd's article is based on the conviction that Kant's third critique is 'one
of *the* founding texts of cultural theory' (p. 64; emphasis added).[5] It would
be useful to clarify the status of these founding texts according to their
national and historical specificity. The English, Scottish, German and
French Enlightenments had different cultural and political histories; their
philosophical premises were also, in some regards, different. When (p. 68)
Lloyd refers to 'post-enlightenment liberals such as John Stuart Mill' and
their continuation of Kant's racial thinking, he suggests that Kant's centrality to Victorian England is self-evident.[6] But Kant's pan-European
influence in conceptions of 'race' is a notion that needs further justifica-
tion. So does Lloyd's claim for the primacy of *cultural* theory itself in eigh-
teenth-century conceptualisations of 'human identity'. This claim does
not acknowledge as significant the theorisations produced by *political* and
economic Enlightenment thinkers who include Voltaire, Montesquieu and
Smith. And it also neglects the contributions of Kant's own first two critiques towards a philosophy of the subject, or, rather, implies their irrele-
vance for an understanding of the third critique.[7]

I want to look briefly at the passage from Kant's third critique that
Lloyd quotes to illustrate Kant's conceptions of 'common sense' and the
public sphere. The passage asserts that common sense is

> a critical faculty which in its reflective act takes account (a priori) of
> the mode of representation of every one else, in order, *as it were*, to
> weigh its judgement with the collective reason of mankind, and
> thereby avoid the illusion arising from subjective and personal con-
> ditions ... This is accomplished by weighing the judgement ... with
> the merely possible judgement of others, and by putting ourselves in
> the position of every one else. (p. 65)[8]

For Lloyd, this passage illustrates the epistemic violence implicit in the
notion of 'the public sphere', revealed through its *formalisation* of the
category of the subject. The imposition of form upon heterogeneous
elements is seen as an oppressive act. I would argue that Kant provides
us here with a potentially productive model of liberal morality. This

passage stresses the importance of the subordination of personal desires in the interest of the collective. The injunction to put oneself in the position of others can be considered a helpful safeguard against anti-social individualism. By failing to engage with Kant's anti-individualist argument, Lloyd leaves unclear what relation his own work has to collective values.

It *is* important to examine critically the social and historical contradictions that link the public sphere to racism and other forms of social inequality.[9] We need to interrogate the ways in which this Kantian formulation has been used as a substitute for material transformation. But it is equally important to examine seriously the ways in which oppressed and excluded groups have been *inspired* to formal political and philosophical action by these and kindred notions of the public sphere, political representation and universal subjectivity. Lloyd's later allusions to anti-colonial nationalism suggest that, for him, such organised emancipatory movements merely relocate and repeat the originary violence of the Enlightenment public sphere and its representational 'logic'. Thus he writes: 'Nationalism ... restores continuity to the interrupted narrative of representation by reterritorializing it within the newly conceived nation. Nationalism, in other words, accepts the *verisimilitude* of imperial culture while redefining its purview' (p. 78). Aside from the problematic fatalism of such reasoning, it is also historically questionable.[10] Gregory Jusdanis, for example, argues against the view that 'the nationalist project is complicit with the European Enlightenment', suggesting that

> It is complicit only if we understand by this that it reacted against the Enlightenment. The earliest European nationalism, for instance, fought against the attempt of the French to create a new world order, to extend the principles of the French Revolution across the rest of Europe.[11]

The primacy of the aesthetic in racism?

Lloyd's analysis highlights the developmental ideology of the subject: i.e. the idea that the subject progresses from a condition of immediate sensual gratification to the capacity for identity with others. For Lloyd, racism is structural to this trajectory. As his reasoning is important here, it is necessary to quote a long passage:

it is … the establishment of a peculiar and historically specific social form, the public sphere as defined in aesthetic theory, as the end of humanity, that *defines the logical structure* of racist discourses. *For this reason*, it is possible for an interchangeably ethical, political and aesthetic judgement as to the 'savage races' to saturate post-enlight-enment discourses on race from liberals such as John Stuart Mill or Matthew Arnold to extreme conservatives such as Gobineau, Klemm, Nott or Hunt. The inadequacy of the native to self-government is demonstrated by 'his' lack of aesthetic productions or by 'his' sub-ordination to immediate sensual gratification: the capacity for autonomy is either as yet undeveloped or absent in the savage and requires to be developed or supplied by force. (pp. 68–9; emphases added)

The italicised expressions, as I read them, appear to substitute assertion for argument. They leave unclear how the public sphere can be said to *define* structures of racist discourse. Nor is it clear how the second sentence, regarding the interchangeability of aesthetic, political and ethical judgement, follows on from this arguable definition. And equally unclear is how this interchangeability itself relates to his final sentence, which implies that aesthetic criteria for humanity precede or determine all others. Instead of being simply one of many weapons in the ideological arsenal of racism, the aesthetic here becomes formative.

What does clearly emerge is that, for Lloyd, political conceptions of race, and justifications of racism, *stem* from culture. The allusion to 'aes-thetic production' in his quotation accentuates his omission of the other forms and discourses of production that were so crucial, historically, in fostering racist ideology and practice. Evidence for the lack of humanity of 'natives' was taken, inter alia, from their supposed inferiority as labour-ing subjects. This involved allegations of non-productivity (found for example in colonial 'tropical exuberance' ideologies), and sexual exploita-tiveness (found for instance in colonial criticism of the traditional 'drudg-ery' of African native women in serving their men). And we need also to acknowledge how notions of 'inferior' indigenous structures of gover-nance were enlisted to further racist imperialism. In other words, 'natives' were judged by their political and economic practices as much as by their sensory and aesthetic capabilities; their racial inferiority was deduced from all of these areas of human activity.

Lloyd's contentious conclusion is that *all* racism has its roots in, and is explainable by, the categories of culture. This overlaps with the rather

different context of contemporary anti-racist British ideologies and policies in public sector services. And these, as Paul Gilroy points out, share
an unfortunate overlap with ideologies and policies of contemporary
conservatism:

> The most elementary lessons involved in studying ideas and con-
> sciousness seem to have been forgotten. Racism, like capitalism as a
> whole, rests on the mystification of social relations – the necessary
> illusions that secure the order of public authority ... the definition
> of race exclusively in terms of culture and identity ... ties certain
> strands in antiracism to the position of some of the new right ideo-
> logues. By emphasising this convergence I am not saying that culture
> and identity are unimportant, but challenging the routine reduction
> of race to them alone which obscures the inherently political char-
> acter of the term. The way in which culture is itself understood pro-
> vides the key to grasping the extraordinary convergence between left
> and right, antiracist and avowedly racist over precisely what race and
> racism add up to.[12]

The idea of the subject

Other questions arise when Lloyd moves to consider the practical expression of white racist expansionism in the early nineteenth century. This
discussion foregrounds white European attainment of universal status.
Lloyd asserts that 'his domination is virtually self-legitimating since the
capacity to be everywhere present *becomes an historical manifestation of
the white man's gradual approximation to the universality he everywhere
represents*' (p. 70; emphases added). Because some people in positions of
political power consider themselves the personification of the universal
human subject, the notion of the universal itself is to blame. This notion
is also responsible for the fact of colonialism. Political or racial domination then becomes the inevitable outcome of the idea of the subject.

On the contrary, I want to contend that white European arrogation of
this subject position says something about how power operates, but does
not illuminate inescapable properties of the category of human subject
itself. This behaviour reflects the solipsism of those who control definitions of humanity and are empowered to construct racial and colonised
others as expressions of the merely particular. We need to explore this
process by looking at its material sources, dissemination and institutionalisation. Lloyd almost precludes such explorations by implying that all

that is necessary is to recognise the cause of racism in the idea of 'the Subject' itself. And we need to note how his approach fails to acknowledge how *anti*-liberal notions (social Darwinism, for instance) and *anti*-foundationalist notions (Nietzscheanism, for instance) have also been used to further racism. Such illiberal notions are do not correspond to the abstract universalism that, for Lloyd, is the source of racist thinking.

Anti-colonial critique and metaphor

According to Lloyd, 'it is not in the first instance the antagonistic recognition of difference which constitutes the discourse of racism but the subordination of difference to the demand for identity' (p. 71). He argues that metaphor is the structure of thought responsible for the 'logic' of 'identity' thinking. Metaphor unites two discrete objects under the principle of identity. The process the subject observes in the figure of metaphor – the subordination of difference between two terms – is, for Lloyd, the same process undergone by the subject herself in the act of responding to metaphor. To respond is to be incorporated into its identitarian logic. And this is the same process experienced by the subject in her interpellation by culture and the public sphere.

However, Lloyd's argument repeats what he claims to criticise. If the exchangeability of formerly discrete terms is for Lloyd an effect and cause of racist/identitarian logic, Lloyd's own discourse stands guilty. We get: 'The racism of culture is … an ineradicable effect of its [culture's] fundamental structures' (p. 63), and 'the realization that not only is race a cultural construct but that racism *is* the structure of culture' (p. 83), and 'the culturally *constitutive* function of racism … Racism appears at once as the product and the disabling limit of the cultural formation of that Subject which subtends and gives the possibility of the "public sphere"' (p. 85). The upshot is a seemingly inescapable circle. Aesthetic culture and the public sphere render racism 'always already' both cause and effect of identity. Racism becomes nothing more than a 'metaphor' for the alleged contradictions of 'identity thought' itself.

When Lloyd turns to two anti-colonial critiques of racism – those of the modern Sudanese fiction writer Tayeb Salih and the modern Martiniquan theorist Frantz Fanon – a strange thing happens. 'It is racism itself', Lloyd has said, 'that brings to light the contradictory nature of the powerful and remarkably effective institutional logic of culture' (p. 73). Now, we learn, these anti-colonial critiques do something rather similar.

They expose 'the inherently contradictory metaphoric logic of identity' (p. 83). If racist and anti-racist discourses are so similar in effect, if not in intention, what need for anti-racism? In a sense Lloyd himself turns Salih's novel *Season of Migration to the North* (1969) and Fanon's *Black Skin, White Masks* (1952) into allegories of non-identity, whose chief value lies in their critique of the West. As Lloyd writes:

> the force of novels such as *Season of Migration*, which indeed dram-
> atizes the predicament of the divided subject of colonialism across
> two generations, lies *less in their representation of the damage inflicted
> than in the radical critique of western cultural forms that they draw
> from it.* What comes into question in Salih's novel is that order of
> verisimilitude that I have termed the narrative of representation. (pp.
> 78–9; emphasis added)

Or, as he writes of *Black Skin, White Masks*: 'the enormous task that this work proposes is the transformation of the non-identity of the black man into *the means* to a dismantling of the discourse of racism on several axes' (pp. 82–3). Lloyd thereby turns the texts into instruments. 'Dismantling the discourse of racism' is indeed an important project. But is problematic to present this as the most significant activity that non-Western texts can perform. Ruth Frankenberg and Lata Mani make a similar point about Robert Young's *White Mythologies*:

> Young makes a compelling argument for considering the impact of
> the Algerian War of Independence on French political and philo-
> sophical thought. However, his powerful critique of ethnocentrism
> is undermined by his general tendency to read anti-colonial move-
> ments as primarily engaging the logic of Western philosophy. Thus
> it seems ... that a key object and achievement of the Algerian War
> of Independence was the overthrow of the Hegelian dialectic! ... One
> is tempted to wonder whether we have merely taken a detour to
> return to the position of the Other as resource for rethinking the
> Western Self.[13]

What is to be done about racism?

Lloyd concludes by extending his critique of the racist foundations and effects of culture to the notion of the state, seen as the ultimate expression of the horrors of unificatory 'logic'. His view is an idealist one as he writes himself:

it is the *idea* of the state which regulates the formation of citizen-
subjects fit to participate in what is effectively state culture. For the
state is not merely a contingent ensemble of institutions but is ultimately determined by the desire to unify the public sphere. (p. 87)

The language slides from the *idea* of the state, in the first sentence, to a
reference to the actual state, which is in any case seen to be grounded in
the realm of ideas/desires. Where, one wonders, did 'the desire to unify the
public sphere' come from? And why did it arise?

What does Lloyd see as a solution to the intrinsic epistemic violence
of the immutable state and public sphere? It is worth looking at his diag-
nosis:

> the indices of difference on which racism relies gain their meaning
> from a distribution of values determined by that culture which
> founds the idea of common sense and its space of articulation, the
> public sphere. This implies that there can be no simply cultural solu-
> tion to the problem of racism and that all the measures taken by lib-
> eral cultural institutions in the name of assimilation are at best half
> measures, at worst misrecognized means to the reproduction of a
> singular cultural form which will continue to produce racialized
> residues. For the demand for representation within existent institu-
> tions will be self-defeating as long as it is not accompanied by the
> demand for the transformation of those institutions, since every par-
> tial instance of representation of difference succumbs to the larger
> narrative to representation which absorbs it. (p. 86)

Lloyd is surely accurate when he argues that the solutions to racism can
never be through culture alone. But his argument does not derive from
the recognition that social totalities and racist structures are grounded
in, and controlled by, material processes *other* than cultural ones – such
as flows and dictates of capitalism. Rather than suggesting that the draw-
back to 'cultural solutions' is that racism doesn't exclusively derive from
or exist in the cultural/public sphere, his suggestion is that it is precisely
because racism *does* derive from this sphere that such solutions are
limited.

The non-cultural solutions to racism and aesthetic culture or the
public sphere or the state are, for Lloyd, to be found in a somewhat
abstract violence. And in the subaltern groups which exist entirely beyond
the contamination of any conception, influence or operation of a public

sphere (p. 88). Their value seems to be exclusively formal, as no account of their subjectivities or activities is supplied. The notion of the necessity of violence occurs in Lloyd's discussion of Fanon when Lloyd explains that the:

> impossible predicament [of the racialised individual] issues perforce in madness or resistance as the subjective correlative of the process by which the colonizer's attempt to assimilate produces the national consciousness that revolts. Fanon's subsequent writings accordingly become increasingly concerned with the necessity of violence as the only means to the overthrow of imperial domination. (pp. 85–6)

Fanon's work is candid about the metaphysical basis, and function, of the violence he proposes. At the same time it is grounded in materialist analysis. Lloyd's allusions to violence emerge as more formulaic. The more substantial hope of overcoming racism lies, it seems, in highlighting the self-destructing tendencies of racial subjectivity – what Lloyd describes as 'the insistence of contradiction in racial formations, their inability to totalise the domain of the Subject' (p. 88).

In keeping with the polemic approach of my intervention here, I want to conclude by suggesting that the implications of Lloyd's opposition to the public sphere, and his veneration of a principle of difference, give cause for concern. Whether viewed in British, United States, European, 'developing' or global contexts, the dangers to human well-being of capitalist privatisation, and ethnic chauvinism, are intense. It might be time to stop holding deterministic notions of culture, form, narrative, development and progress as exclusively responsible for racism, and to look more positively at what human subjects *share*. It is also time to look more critically at the languages of 'difference', at the ways they can be used to promote social exclusivism, individualism, and a homogenised view of racialised communities. To quote Paul Gilroy again:

> no single culture is hermetically sealed off from others. There can be no neat and tidy pluralistic separation of racial groups in this country. It is time to dispute with those positions which, when taken to their conclusions, say 'there is no possibility of shared history and no human empathy'. We must beware of the use of ethnicity to wrap a spurious cloak of legitimacy around the speaker who invokes it. Culture, even the culture which defines the groups we know as races, is never fixed, finished or final. (p. 57)

Notes

Thanks to Clara Connolly for useful discussion and criticism.

1 David Lloyd, 'Race under Representation', *Oxford Literary Review*, 13, 1–2 (1991), pp. 62–94. See also David Lloyd, 'Ethnic Cultures, Minority Discourse and the State', in Francis Barker, Peter Hulme and Margaret Iversen (eds.), *Colonial Discourse/Postcolonial Theory* (Manchester: Manchester University Press, 1994), pp. 221–38, which follows similar arguments to his *Oxford Literary Review* article and applies them to the consideration of ethnic cultures within the USA. See Laura Chrisman, 'Local Sentences in the Chapter of the Postcolonial World', *Diaspora: A Journal of Transnational Studies*, 7, 1 (1998), pp. 87–112, for a critical discussion of Lloyd's 'Ethnic Cultures' article.

2 Kant wrote explicitly on race. See, for example, his 'Of the Different Human Races' (1775), *The Idea of Race*, edited by Robert Bernasconi and Tommy L. Lott (Indianapolis: Hackett Publishing Company, Inc, 2000), pp. 8–22. See also E. Chukwudi Eze (ed.), *Race and the Enlightenment: A Reader* (Oxford: Blackwell, 1997).

3 See Timothy Brennan, 'Black Theorists and Left Antagonists', *The Minnesota Review*, 37 (1991), pp. 89–113, for an important discussion of British left culturalism of the 1980s. For a wide-ranging discussion of contemporary British antiracism see the collection of essays *'Race', Culture and Difference*, edited by James Donald and Ali Rattansi (London: Sage Publications, in association with the Open University, 1992).

4 See, for example, the early work of Homi Bhabha 'The Other Question …', *Screen*, 24, 6 (1983), pp. 18–36, and 'Signs Taken for Wonders: Questions of Ambivalence and Authority under a Tree Outside Delhi, May 1817', in Henry Louis Gates, Jr (ed.), *'Race', Writing and Difference* (Chicago: University of Chicago Press, 1986), pp. 108–64.

5 For an excellent account of the historical dynamics and precedents to Kant's third critique see Howard Caygill's 'Post-modernism and Judgement', *Economy and Society*, 17, 1 (February 1988): pp. 1–20. Thanks to David Johnson for drawing my attention to this article.

6 See Paul Gilroy, *Against Race: Imagining Political Culture Beyond the Color Line* (Cambridge, MA: Harvard University Press, 2000), pp. 58–61, for a probing discussion of Kantian constructions of race. See also Gayatri Spivak's discussion of the 'raw man' of Kant's Third Critique, named as the New Hollander or inhabitant of Tierra del Fuego, and her argument that he 'cannot be the subject of speech or judgment in the world of the Critique. The subject as such in Kant is geopolitically differentiated', pp. 26–7 of her *A Critique of Postcolonial Reason: Toward a History of the Vanishing Present* (Cambridge, MA and London: Harvard University Press, 1999). And see Charles W. Mills, *Blackness Visible: Essays on Philosophy and Race* (Ithaca: Cornell University Press, 1998).

7 Perhaps the warning of Stephan Korner is apposite here, that 'the third *Critique* is intimately related to the other two. A reader who tried to study it in isolation would be in great danger of mistaking many of its most significant statements for empty abstractions, and of misunderstanding many others' in *Kant* (Harmondsworth: Penguin, 1990), p. 192.

8 This quotation comes from p. 151 of the James Creed Meredith translation of Kant's *Critique of Judgement* (Oxford: Clarendon Press, 1982), as noted in note 7, p. 89 of Lloyd.

9 For an excellent example of this examination see David Kazanjian, 'Racial Governmentality: Thomas Jefferson and the African Colonization Movement in the United States', *Alternation: Journal of the Centre for the Study of Southern African Literature and Languages* [Durban, South Africa], 5, 1 (1998): pp. 39–84.

10 See Neil Lazarus, 'Disavowing Decolonization: Nationalism, Intellectuals, and the Question of Representation in Postcolonial Theory', *Nationalism and Cultural Practice in the Postcolonial World* (Cambridge: Cambridge University Press, 1999), pp. 68–143, for a detailed discussion of modern nationalist and anti-nationalist theories. Lazarus engages with the deterministic model that Lloyd presents here. See also Elliott Colla, 'The Stuff of Egypt: The Nation, the State and Their Proper Objects', *New Formations: A Journal of Culture/Theory/Politics*, 45 (2001), pp. 72–90, and Salah Hassan, 'Terminus Nation-state: Palestine and the Critique of Nationalism', *New Formations: A Journal of Culture/Theory/Politics,* 45 (2001), pp. 54–71. These articles supply nuanced analysis of shifting relations between the nation and the state as political and cultural formations, and by demonstrating the historical and geographical variability of nationalist politics they supply further alternatives to Lloyd's structural determinism.

11 Gregory Jusdanis, *The Necessary Nation* (Princeton: Princeton University Press, 2001), p. 9.

12 Paul Gilroy, 'The End of Antiracism', in James Donald and Ali Rattansi (eds.), *'Race', Culture and Difference*, p. 57.

13 Ruth Frankenberg and Lata Mani, 'Crosscurrents, Crosstalk: Race, "Postcoloniality" and the Politics of Location', in Padmini Mongia (ed.), *Contemporary Postcolonial Theory: A Reader* (London: Arnold, 1996), p. 355.

8

Robert Young and the ironic authority of postcolonial criticism

When I chanced on postcolonial scholar Robert Young's *Textual Practice* review of Gayatri Chakravorty Spivak's *Outside in the Teaching Machine*, I was startled to find an attack on Benita Parry among its pages.[1] It comes early on, when Young is preparing the ground for a detailed exposition of Spivak's book by comparing Spivak's general critical standing with that of Edward Said and Homi Bhabha (who together create Young's chief constellation of postcolonial theorists). This then is the attack itself, in context:

> Spivak differs from Said and Bhabha, however, in so far as she has not been so widely attacked for alleged obscurity, ungrounded theoreticism, or questionable political agendas. The stance of moral reproof that is customarily wielded against Bhabha or Said is already Spivak's own. And when she is attacked, her responses are sharply to the point: 'When Benita Parry takes us to task for not being able to listen to the natives, or to let the natives speak, she forgets that the three of us, postcolonials, are "native" too'. Spivak's rejoinder *points to the political irony of three Black writers being attacked by an émigré South African critic during the era of apartheid. Her comment prompts the reader to ask what political agenda, what political priorities, drive such offensives.* (pp. 229–30; emphasis added)

Why is it there?

It is interesting that Spivak's defensiveness here should have recourse to the very 'ethnic identitarianism' to which she elsewhere is frequently opposed. Young's preceding paragraph itself bears witness to that opposition:

> It is typical of Spivak that she should spell out the history of the perspective from which she writes: *most 'postcolonial' academics are economic migrants,* either permanent or habitual, *but some play this*

down in an effort to be taken as authentic spokespersons for 'the third world'. Spivak disdains this small-time institutional game, and is always disarmingly up-front about her own provenance. The effect of this in her work is that *she pays attention to texts of the 'third world' not as representative writings of the other with whose voice she seeks to be identified,* but in terms of the problematics of how they are read in the Western academic institution. (p. 229; emphasis added)

Spivak's self-representation as a 'postcolonial native', in response to Parry, is perhaps an example of the 'strategic essentialism' which is part of her theoretical arsenal. Parry's critique does not, in fact, charge 'the three' black writers (Spivak, Bhabha, JanMohamed) with silencing 'the natives'; it is only Spivak's work which is thus represented. Spivak's generalisation of a racial 'we' rests on a misreading, then, one that does not respect the nuances of Parry's argument and analysis. Quite possibly both Parry and Spivak have misread one another.[2] Such misreadings have been productive, to judge by the animated debates which still attach to the question of subalternity.

In any case, my concern here is not with elucidating Spivak's own complex discourses, nor with adding to the debate on subalternity. What concerns me rather is Robert Young's intercession against Parry, the assumptions about power and intellectual authority written into his language use, and the implications of these for postcolonial critical dialogue and analysis. I will pass over the temptation to milk the Youngian 'irony' that it was this same Robert Young who as editor of the *Oxford Literary Review* in 1987 was responsible for the publication of Parry's 'offensive' in the first place.[3] But I will later return to the notion of 'irony', for in Young's use of the word lies a lot of what is problematic about his discursive authority.

Recent metropolitan postcolonial criticism has – thanks in part to Spivak's own work – increasingly moved to a materialist awareness of, and concern with, (institutional, regional, professional, socio-economic) 'locations' in which postcoloniality is produced and circulated. Robert Young's intervention here instead emphasises ethnic or national 'origins' of critics in isolation from, and at the expense of, such 'locations'. Crucial to note here is the inconsistency, the doubleness of Young's standards: he deems ethnicity to be most significant in Spivak's case, but when it comes to Parry switches tack to emphasise the category of nationality. (I wonder what might have resulted had he brought Parry's Jewishness

into the discussion!) That he feels able unselfconsciously and arbitrarily to differentiate and play off his subjects in this way, is, I think, symp-
tomatic of the unquestioned assumptions of authority and power which
animate his discourse here.

I question the intellectual validity and the political utility of deducing
an individual's politics from the mere fact of their birthplace. That Benita
Parry's writing does not do the business of the apartheid state but rather
pursues a recognisably socialist-national liberationist perspective is clear
to this reader, and I encourage other readers to judge for themselves rather
than take Robert Young's textual prejudgements seriously. Since, however,
Young chooses to privilege the experiential rather than the textual sphere
in assessing the politics of Parry's work, I feel coerced into countering his
judgement through enlisting my own personal experience of Parry's extra-
textual activities. Anyone who knows Benita Parry personally knows that
this 'émigré', like many fellow South African socialist Jews, played a militant
active role in the liberation movement before leaving – at a time when
many activists both black and white were leaving for urgent political reasons – to continue her political activism in a far left movement in England.

Of two possibilities, I don't know which I find more troubling. One is
that Robert Young made his insinuations in ignorance of Parry's political
history, in ignorance of South Africa's political history – which ignorance
itself would suggest a certain contemptuous disrespect of the country as
undeserving of research. The other is that he did know of Parry's involvement in anti-government opposition, but considered this irrelevant to the
discussion of her political 'agenda' and 'priorities'. The latter prospect
makes me worry about the definitions of politics, of race, and of the
psyche, being deployed by Young.

On South Africa: I venture to say that not only that country but Western
knowledge-production of it stand at a critical juncture right now. New
material opportunities have emerged for increased British, European and
North American academic intellectual exchange, and enquiry. More striking, perhaps, than the increase in research fellowships is the rise in short-
term visits; South Africa is enjoying a veritable flood of US and UK
dignitaries on lecture tours and conference platforms. Spivak herself,
Fredric Jameson, Terry Eagleton, Ania Loomba, Dipesh Chakrabarty,
Jonathan Dollimore and Alan Sinfield are among the radical critics to have
recently visited the country on such terms. None the less, because 'South
Africa' has acquired, in the West, the fetishistic status of racial allegory, the
danger is that Western-located academics assume, to use a phrase of

Spivak's, a relation of 'sanctioned ignorance' of that country. The kind of presumption evident in Young's commentary – that South Africa is immediately knowable, its non-black intellectuals automatically reducible to politically repressive agendas – itself licenses metropolitan 'neo-colonialist' dynamics of knowledge-production, in which South African intellectuals themselves are considered unworthy of critical engagement.

One has only to contrast Robert Young's summary dismissal of Parry's work and politics with his serious description of, and respectful engagement with, the Marxist anti-postcolonial work of Indian critic Aijaz Ahmad in this same review, to observe the ways in which South Africa and its products may somehow license metropolitan critics to depart from their general intellectual standards of assessment, from their rigorously academic modes of operation.[4]

To return to the matter of Young's unstable discursive modalities: interestingly, his abstract (ethnic/national) determinism here is sometimes accompanied by a more materialist mode, conveyed in his occasional references to geographical and historical specificity. Far from mitigating the effects of determinism, such materialism is deployed to compound it. Benita Parry's 'politics' are undermined not only through pointing to her South African roots but also by attaching to her the label of 'émigré', with its associations of high-class privilege and political reactionariness. She comes under suspicion for being born there *and* for having left.

A situational concern also seems implicit in Young's castigation that Parry's critique was written and published 'during the era of apartheid'. Had Parry's piece been published in a South African journal in violation of the ANC academic boycott – had it, in other words, actually contributed to the apartheid regime – then Young's pronouncement might have more than cheaply gestural import. In any case, no sooner does he evoke this historically specific 'era', and with it an intersubjective emphasis on the social contexts, effects and sources of political meaning, than he shifts to an attack on 'the political priorities driving' Parry. As his use of the word 'drives' reveals, what is of ultimate import to Young in judging, in defining, the 'political' value of a piece of writing is its author's psyche alone. If so much hangs on the psychic matrix, then it is surprising that so little theorisation attends it. As with South Africa the country, so with the psyche: fully knowable spaces (to name is to know), involving the critic in no mediatory labour.

All this amounts to variations on a theme of unacknowledged power-games. If Young's assumptions authorise him to determine a critic's politics from her birthplace, to divine their psyche likewise, they also authorise him to determine for whom ethnicity is the key category and for whom nationality. They allow him to harness materialist terms to idealist and nominalist ends. They allow him to allege political 'irony' of a South African immigrant engaging in critical dialogue with an Indian immigrant. Young's language of 'irony' here seems to rely on, and hence produce, a hierarchy of critical mentalities. If you don't get the irony, it's because you are either not sufficiently sophisticated as a literary critic or you are yourself mired too deep in something nasty that might begin with 'r'. What we are witnessing is a kind of literary elitism passing itself off as 'PC'; and the introduction of fundamentally literary categories as the exclusive basis for analysis of ethnic and political social issues. This to me is an anti-democratic practice that allots the postcolonial franchise to a selected few, removing it from others on the grounds of their ethnic origin.

Most questionable of all, for me, is the way Young opts to remain invisible while graphically scrutinising others. Young's insistent emphases on nationality and ethnicity as determinants in the political identity of Parry and Spivak have no corollary in a national or ethnic self-description. Quick though he is to interrogate Parry there is not a trace of self-questioning. Shades, perhaps, of imperial discourse.[5]

Postscript/supplement

It's not only South Africa as a country, nor South African-born academics that are subject to 'political' postcolonial censure. I too have experienced this, and for the same immediate reasons as Parry, namely, offering a critique of Gayatri Spivak's work for the ways it structurally excludes voices from certain parts of the world from being heard. Several years ago I published an article in *Critical Quarterly*, in which I argued that Spivak's reading of *Jane Eyre*, particularly her contention that the Caribbean Bertha Mason's death-by-fire required to be read in the context of colonial contests over Indian practices of *sati*, reflected an Indiacentrism found elsewhere in her work.[6] I questioned the political effect of granting colonial epistemological primacy to India so that the meanings of such explicitly African and Caribbean figures such as Baudelaire's mistress and Bertha Mason were seen only to derive from Indian matrices. I found this problematic in that it appeared to deny those figures and colonies their own epistemological significance to a

European imperial subject-formation and political project. My concern stemmed from a materialist and Africanist discomfort with the hegemony of Asian models in colonial discourse analysis, its possible effect on the future theorisation of non-Asian materials.

Critical Quarterly subsequently carried a negative description of my piece as the work of a neo-colonialist; in criticising her I performed a gesture analogous to 'the coloniser's displacement of the colonised'.[7] Spivak, my critic suggested, was a 'representative colonised voice'. In his haste to impute a neo-colonialist subject-position to me, Pimomo did not stop to question the large problems attached to conferring colonised 'representativeness', nor did it occur to him, when basing his critique on (among other things) ethnic-identitarian premises, that I too might also have 'colonised' allegiances and concerns. My own experience as the black multiracial daughter of a black Marxist academic, the publisher and editor of the US journal *The Black Scholar*, has been crucial in making sense of my own responses to postcolonial debates. But at the same time, arguments in postcolonial studies surely cannot stand or fall on the basis of each critic's national/racial origins. And any critic who elevates Spivak as an exclusive or foundational example of black colonised subjectivity, and proceeds to measure other critics' politics (and ethnicity) according to whether they share this conviction, is likely to produce a compromisingly authoritarian critical practice.

Notes

Many thanks to Denise deCaires Narain, David Johnson, Neil Lazarus and Vicky Lebeau for helpful discussions and critical feedback.

1 Robert J. C. Young, *Textual Practice*, 10, 1 (1996), pp. 228–38.
2 Spivak has offered a retrospective and clarificatory account of her subaltern argument, which explains that she did not aim to silence 'the natives'. See Donna Landry and Gerald MacLean (eds.), *The Spivak Reader* (London: Routledge, 1996), pp. 287–90. See also Meyda Yegenoglu and Mahmut Mutman, 'Mapping the Present: Interview with Gayatri Spivak', *New Formations: A Journal of Culture/Theory/Politics*, 45 (2001), pp. 9–23, for Spivak's account of how the practice and conceptualisation of subalternity has changed since she wrote and published her original essay. Neil Lazarus provides an insightful contribution to the Spivak/Parry debate: 'Nationalist Consciousness and the Specificity of (Post)colonial Intellectualism', in Francis Barker, Peter Hulme and Margaret Iversen (eds.), *Colonial Discourse/Postcolonial Theory* (Manchester: Manchester University Press, 1994), pp. 197–220.

3 Benita Parry, 'Problems in Current Theories of Colonial Discourse', *Oxford Literary Review*, 9, 1–2 (1987), pp. 27–58.

4 Robert Young's recent *Postcolonialism: An Historical Introduction* (Oxford: Blackwell, 2001) maintains problematic assumptions about South Africa. This passage, from the section on 'South Africa' in the chapter titled 'Africa 1: Anglophone African Socialism', articulates a number: 'Of all groups with Trotskyist links, the Unity Movement was *the most significant … Despite its name*, it became increasingly opposed to the alliance between the S.A.C.P. [South African Communist Party] and the A.N.C., without ever being able to compete with the material as well as political support that the former was able to offer. Subsequent alternative Left forms of political opposition, such as *Biko's Black Consciousness* movement, were all too effectively repressed by the apartheid regime. In the end it was the S.A.C.P. and above all the A.N.C., which, with global international assistance in the form of economic and cultural sanctions, succeeded. It is striking that *though Mandela refused to renounce the armed struggle, his political strategies remained close to those of Gandhi's almost a century earlier*' (p. 232; emphasis added).

   Young's hierarchical and 'great man' discourse leads to the ranking of political movements in terms of 'significance' and 'success'; it characterises Black Consciousness in terms of a single individual. Young's gratuitous nominalism generates a judgemental 'irony' in the fact that the Unity Movement, 'despite its name', opposed the alliance of the SACP and the ANC. And his *Textual Practice* respect for India over South Africa is also evident here, in the construction of the arms-advocate Mandela as a belated exemplar of Gandhian non-violence.

5 For other critical discussions of Robert Young's contributions to postcolonial critique see Aijaz Ahmad, 'The Politics of Literary Postcoloniality', *Race and Class*, 36, 3 (1995), pp. 1–20; Stuart Hall, 'When Was the "Post-colonial"? Thinking at the Limit', in Iain Chambers and Lidia Curti (eds.), *The Post-colonial Question: Common Skies, Divided Histories* (London: Routledge, 1996), pp. 242–60; David Johnson, 'Importing Metropolitan Post-colonials', *Current Writing: Text and Reception in Southern Africa* [Durban, South Africa], 6, 1 (1994), pp. 73–85; Bill Schwarz, 'Conquerors of Truth: Reflections on Postcolonial Theory', in Bill Schwarz (ed.), *The Expansion of England: Race, Ethnicity and Cultural History* (London: Routledge, 1996), pp. 9–31.

6 Laura Chrisman, 'The Imperial Unconscious? Representations of Imperial Discourse', *Critical Quarterly*, 32, 3 (1990), pp. 38–58. A similar point about Indian hegemony has been made by Arif Dirlik in 'The Postcolonial Aura: Third World Criticism in the Age of Global Capitalism', *Critical Inquiry*, 20 (1994), pp. 328–56.

7 Paulus Pimomo, 'The Centre Writes/Strikes Back?', *Critical Quarterly*, 33, 3 (1991), pp. 43–7.

9

Cultural studies
in the new South Africa

How we conceptualise future directions of cultural studies depends on how we have conceptualised the origins and genealogy of that discipline. In the UK, two stories of origins have emerged, the textual and the sociological. The future theorisation and analysis of South African cultural studies may follow either story. The textual version is probably dominant within British academia. It locates three texts, Richard Hoggart's *The Uses of Literacy*, E.P. Thompson's *The Making of the English Working Class* and Raymond Williams's *Culture and Society*, as the progenitors of cultural studies as an academic field. It is interesting that Raymond Williams has himself been one of the most energetic critics of this textualist version. In 'The Future of Cultural Studies', for instance, he argues forcefully that this textualist account is 'only the surface of the real development, and is moreover misleading.'[1] Instead, Williams points to diverse adult education activities in the 1940s as the origins of cultural studies. His sociological account is illuminating even if one prefers to privilege the textual. Those texts were, as Linden Peach has observed,

> written while their authors were working outside the mainstream in higher education: Hoggart was employed as a staff tutor in adult education at Hull University, E.P. Thompson was a staff tutor in the Yorkshire Workers Education Association and Raymond Williams was an Oxford staff tutor in the Sussex W.E.A. and an occasional summer school lecturer in Yorkshire.[2]

As Williams sees it, the core distinguishing characteristic of adult education projects of that period was that

> Academics took out from their institutions university economics, or university English or university philosophy, and the people wanted

> to know what it was. This exchange didn't collapse into some simple
> populism: that these were all silly intellectual questions. Yet these new
> students insisted (1) that the relation of this to their own situation
> and experience had to be discussed, and (2) that there were areas in
> which the discipline itself might be unsatisfactory, and therefore they
> retained as a crucial principle the right to decide their own syllabus.
> (p. 156)

Recognising the intellectual significance of these non-university, non-
textual contexts and origins for cultural studies is not very easy for contemporary professional academics in cultural studies. We often seem
reluctant to address the complexities of the processes of institutionalisation, to perceive and theorise the extent to which our own intellectual
formations are conditioned by our place within this institution. We may
acknowledge that cultural studies historically derive from adult education institutions, and that these local institutions may have determined
the forms of knowledge which once passed as cultural studies, but such
institutional contingencies are rarely regarded as being of theoretical significance. What happens, though, if we follow Williams's suggestion and
analyse how institutionalisation affects our practices?

I will return to issues of institutionalisation. I want now to ask what
these non-textual, non-academic components of cultural studies might
mean for a new South Africa. Among other things, they might send us
to look for African cultural studies as it already exists outside the academy. It might mean that what South African academics 'appropriate'
from the UK are not only aspects of its current theoretical capital but
also insights inspired by the UK's social, educational and cultural history.[3]

I do not want to imply any direct parallel between the history of South
Africa and that of the UK in the twentieth century: on the contrary. (Later
I will address what I see as the dangers of applying theoretical paradigms
developed in the UK, USA and Europe within a new South Africa.) But I
do want to argue that the British historical experience of cultural studies
– and the conflicting ways in which that experience can be interpreted –
are something from which South African academe can learn. Arriving in
South Africa (in 1993), I was struck by the large size of South Africa's com-
munity-led adult education. The size, diversity and energy of community
arts projects and civic organisations also impressed me. There is a lot of
potential for developing an academic cultural studies that is symbiotically

involved with these extra-academic formations, as once was the case in the UK.

One rationale for the new South African development of academic cultural studies is suggested by Williams: the project arises because 'people's questions are not being answered by the existing distribution of the educational curriculum' (p. 160). Cultural theorist Michael Green suggests a compelling goal for such cultural studies:

> for some while Cultural Studies may be of best use, neither as an academic discipline with its own rigours, nor in the revolutions of intellectual/political paradigms (important as these are), but in its consolidation as a public presence. Not an area of new professional 'expertise' with 'answers', but a space openly available for thought and analysis ... Not a vanguard with its own language, but a continuing activity, responsive to short-term pressures and to the longer-term interests of participants.[4]

Cultural studies, indeed, has something particular to offer the rest of the academy here, precisely because of its fluid intellectual boundaries and its newness as a university discipline. More than any other academic field, cultural studies provides the potential for new forms of teaching, learning and knowledge that are local-based and people-led. I would go further and suggest that cultural studies also provides the potential for new forms of cultural production and policy. South African cultural studies could provide an institutional matrix in which the traditional distinctions between academic and aesthetic production, like those between theoretical reflection and policy development, are deliberately interrogated, challenged and transformed.

The importance of policy-making within a cultural studies agenda is something that Australian cultural critics and university departments have frequently addressed, with interesting results. Tony Bennett, for example, provocatively argues against current critical dispositions to view culture as a set of signifying practices and argues instead that

> Culture is more cogently conceived, I want to suggest, when thought of as a historically specific set of institutionally embedded relations of government in which the forms of thought and conduct of extended populations are targeted for transformation – in part via the extension through the social body of the forms, techniques, and regimens of aesthetic and intellectual culture.[5]

From this he argues for a contemporary cultural studies that foregrounds policy and governmental engagement. Because it is both troubling and suggestive, I want to quote his argument in detail:

> It might mean careful and focused work in the service of specific cultural action groups. It might mean intellectual work calculated to make more strategic interventions within the operating procedures and policy agendas of specific cultural institutions. It might mean hard statistical work calculated to make certain problems visible in a manner that will allow them to surface at the level of political debate or to impinge on policy-making processes in ways which facilitate the development of administrative programs capable of addressing them. It might mean providing private corporations with such information. One thing is for sure, however: it will mean talking to and working with what used to be called the Ideological State Apparatuses rather than writing them off from the outset and then, in a self-fulfilling prophecy, criticizing them again when they seem to affirm one's direst functionalist predictions. (p. 32)

I am aware that the above might be sheer anathema for a new South African cultural studies, situated as it is in a new country already saturated by the languages of policy formation. But I take Bennett's final sentence seriously as a call for proactive academic involvement with cultural policy that could effect a positive intervention in the emergence of a democratic culture(s) and government.[6]

Questions of theory:
intellectual paradigms for African cultural studies

I have been outlining the potential of South African cultural studies to break from traditional formulations of academic endeavour. I want to now look at existing academic practices and ask what current theoretical perspectives might assist the South African project.[7] Raymond Williams's discussion of British academic cultural studies largely concerns the implications of the idealist version of the 'linguistic turn' that became dominant in the 1980s. Stuart Hall supplies a succinct definition of the linguistic turn:

> [a conviction of] the crucial importance of language and of the linguistic metaphor to *any* study of culture; the expansion of the notion of text and textuality, both as a source of meaning, and as

that which escapes and postpones meaning; the recognition of the heterogeneity, of the multiplicity, of meanings, of the struggle to close arbitrarily the infinite semiosis beyond meaning; the acknowledgement of textuality and cultural power, of representation itself, as a site of power and regulation; of the symbolic as a source of identity.[8]

I am interested in three aspects of the linguistic turn: the socio-political premises and implications of such theory; the adequacy of this theory as a tool for analysis of contemporary aesthetic practices; the way this theory articulates with professional pressures of self-legitimation.

The most negative explanation positions this cultural theory as the preservation of the status quo. In this vein, Williams condemns postmodern cultural theorists of 1980s Britain for providing 'long-term adjustments to short term situations' by rationalising the ostensible triumph of post-industrial capitalism. He sees this theory as failing in precisely its most crucial role: committed to theorisation of 'the new' developments in cultural production, such theories as were selected for this purpose are 'deficient above all in this key area, of the *nature of cultural formations and thus of ongoing agency and practice*' (emphasis added).[9] The corollary of a theory that constructs 'the text' as the source of critical agency is the exclusion of social agency in the production of these texts. Furthermore, such theoretical textualism does not allow us to account for what is distinctive about new aesthetic expressions. There is no way, that is, of conceptualising the historical meaning of this new culture.

With regards to professional self-legitimation, I want to quote Williams at length, in what may be his most polemical and exasperated mood:

> At just this moment [i.e., the formalisation of cultural studies in/by UK academe], a body of theory came through which rationalized the situation of this formation on its way to becoming bureaucratized and the home of specialist intellectuals ... the theories which came – the revival of formalism, the simpler kinds (including Marxist kinds) of structuralism – tended to regard the practical encounters of people in society as having relatively little effect on its general progress, since the main inherent forces of that society were deep in its structures, and – in the simplest forms – the people who operated them were mere 'agents'. This was precisely the encouragement for

people not to look at their own formation, not to look at this new
and at once encouraging and problematic situation they were in; at
the fact that this kind of education was getting through to new kinds
of people, and yet that it was still inside minority institutions, or that
the institutions exercised the confining bureaucratic pressures of syllabus and examination, which continually pulled these raw questions
back to something manageablewithin their terms. At just that
moment ... there was ... a quite uncritical acceptance of a set of theories which in a sense rationalized that situation, which said that this
was the way the cultural order worked, this was the way in which the
ideology distributed its roles and functions. The whole project was
then radically diverted by these new forms of idealist theory.[10]

(For Williams, structuralism's problematic formalism and pessimism
recur in academic post-structuralism and postmodernism.) What I want
to ask is: how might Williams's account assist our development and
understanding of new cultural studies in South Africa?

This leads me to question the consequences of South African intellectual dependence on idealist metropolitan values and formulations. At
the very moment when the new South Africa is released from isolation,
is ready to reconfigure its cultural, economic and intellectual relations
to Africa and the developing world – why now ratify a neo-colonial axis
of theoretical authority? Why uncritically embrace a methodology that
renounces the possibility of analysing social totality? Now that new
transcontinental history and geography can be developed – why embrace
a theoretical orientation that rejects the contributions of history, a discipline that is surely one of South Africa's greatest intellectual assets?
The axes of overseas theoretical dialogue and stimulation might
profitably multiply to include other 'developing' countries of the
Americas, Africa and Asia. And they might include Australia and Canada,
whose historical similarities as settler colonies may yield theoretical
insight.

I want briefly to transform the question 'what kinds of (post-structuralist) theoretical paradigms could South African cultural studies
deploy?' to something like 'what contributions could South Africa make
to a theoretical (re)formulation of cultural studies as practised in the UK
and the USA?' The linguistic turn itself supplies one answer. Raymond
Williams does not categorically reduce this turn to its idealist expression,
but instead dialectically sees within it the opportunity for materialist
articulation. So he argues that

the 'language paradigm' remains a key point of entry, precisely because it was the modernist escape route from what is otherwise the Formalist trap: that an autonomous text, in the very emphasis on its specificity, is ... a work in a language that is undeniably social ... It is then precisely in this real work on language, including the language of works marked as temporarily independent and autonomous, that modern cultural theory can be centred: a systematic and dynamic *social language*, as distinct from the 'language paradigm'. [11]

I want to suggest that South African cultural critics and theorists are exceptionally well placed to develop this kind of 'real work', a cultural studies grounded in the sociality of language. Knowledgeable as South Africans necessarily are of the complexity and potency of language formations, they – you – could use that knowledge to produce textual, theoretical and sociological analyses from which European and US academies might learn.

Cultural studies and social analysis

I turn, finally, to issues of social and political analysis: what role could a South African cultural studies play in such analyses? What relations obtain between cultural, political and economic power in the new South Africa? What insights from cultural studies and theory could assist in the understanding – and transformation – of these relations? In particular, I want to look at ways in which the Gramsci-inflected political analyses may help or hinder South African discussions. Can paradigms appropriated from what may loosely be termed the 'subjective turn' in political theory (parallel to the 'linguistic turn' in cultural theory) assist in developing a new public sphere, a new civil society, a new understanding of the state in South Africa?

All I can do here is to toss up a few polemical observations. It would not be useful, appropriate or possible to enter into a full critical discussion of the pros and cons of the British postmodern socialist theory exemplified by recent work by Stuart Hall, by the sadly defunct Communist Party journal *Marxism Today* and its influential analyses of post-Fordist 'New Times'.[12] Instead I will focus my observations on a recent article by Grant Farred that draws upon the above theoretical currents to advance an argument about the role of cultural and social difference in a new South African polity.

Farred's article takes up a number of notions central to British socialist cultural theory: the rejection of economistic Marxism; the notion that culture is an important factor in shaping social relations; the suspicion of the state; the belief in the preservation of cultural difference and identity against the unifying tendencies of government; the advocacy of coalitionist political mobilisations that are local, contingent and predicated on cultural affinity. Where Farred differs is in the context and the political impetus of his argument. He writes (this is before the 1994 election) as a socialist who is concerned that the ANC – as opposition and future government – is silencing the voices and the priorities of working-class and socialist movements. His concern is to find a way for progressive and marginalised constituencies to create a politics that challenges the ANC's monopoly.[13]

There is a lot to agree with in Farred's argument. But I find problematic both the fatalism and the ambiguity of his presentation; his article suggests both a pragmatic and an idealist perspective. Farred focuses a lot on Inkatha-gate (the correct funding of the Inkatha party by De Klerk's government), the Third Force (correct operations organised to destabilise liberation movements) and, more generally, the ways in which apartheid fostered and then exploited cultural differences among peoples. He focuses equally on the cultural differences generated through a variety of anti-apartheid struggles, in the labour movement and the women's movement in particular. This leads him to contend that

> The distinctiveness of Inkatha, the women's struggle, the trade union and community activists, suggests that black South Africa cannot be naturalised into an undivided cultural entity … it will be extremely difficult for the movement to efface not only the distinct cultural identities that apartheid has foisted upon black South Africans, but also those identities that have been achieved through struggle with the apartheid state and within the black community.

This then leads to his argument that 'cultural divisions can actually be used by women's groups, leftists within the ANC, other left black political organisations, community activists, and trade unionists to give voice to political and ideological differences' (p. 223). It would seem crucial to differentiate 'difference': to establish a theoretical political discourse that does not lump together those differences created by apartheid with those created through struggle against apartheid. But this differentiation is what Farred's analysis cannot pursue. The notions of 'culture' and of 'difference' with which Farred is working do not readily allow for such a differentiation.

I am not altogether sure how his article defines culture. At times it denotes ethnicity, at other times it denotes political and/or ideological identities, and at other times culture is a general word for the conscious-ness that accompanies a certain relation to economic production. This multiplicity of meanings is the intellectual heritage of a postmodern Gramscianism. The reasons Farred cannot creatively differentiate between difference as imposed and as produced through struggle are, again, to do with the fact that the original context in which difference was conceptualised was that in which a free-market hegemony rather than coercion was the method of government. It is also arguable that the val-orisation of difference within its original Western European context was, as Raymond Williams suggests, politically problematic, reflecting a criti-cal inability to do more than fatalistically accept, rationalise and adapt to the logics of the market.

Such fatalism is clearly indicated when Farred suggests that

> The articulation of their differences will enable these [the above] groups to distinguish and distance themselves from the blossoming partnership between the A.N.C. and ... the N.P. ... Such a critical platform can also be used to create a space for leftist politics within the ranks of black South Africa, a space which is desperately needed so that debates about difference can be initiated before therhetoric of 'unity' preempts any such critiques. *At this point, the insistence upon difference – cultural, political, and ideological – may be all that stands between the masses of exploited black South Africans and the tri-umvirate ... of a newly embourgeoised and entrepreneurial black middle class, the white upper and middle classes, and multinational capitalism.* (p. 224; emphasis added)

The pessimism lies in the conceptualisation of the emergent government. The ANC, by virtue of its very ascendancy to state power, is unable to avoid ideological convergence with the outgoing pro-apartheid Nationalist Party. As with his construction of cultural difference, however, Farred's construction of the ANC is ambiguous. He argues that through its own historical agency the party has gained political hegemony, and now elects to operate centripetally in order to exclude difference. Farred also seems to suggest that the ANC has been placed in its hegemonic posi-tion by the operations of (home and outside) governments and media, and that its exclusions of difference are not so much voluntary as the result of outside determination. In other words, he blurs the distinction between an ANC identity created through resistance to the state, and that invented by the state.

Within this somewhat deterministic trajectory, in which the state is seen as necessarily antagonistic to the differences it has worked to create, all that is left to those oppositional constituencies of difference is to bond together provisionally in what Farred calls a 'politics of affinity'. They are to articulate difference within what appears to be a discursive, ideological and cultural rather than formally political space. Farred is committed to a socialist redistribution of wealth, but his arguments do indicate how the politics of affinity, and the preservation of differences, are to achieve such redistribution. The languages of difference as evolved and practised in the British left were connected to flows of consumption than production and distribution, and so cannot provide an indication of how this redistribution might work in the new South Africa.

If I am unclear as to how cultural forces are to translate into political and economic ones here, I am also unsure whether this is necessary or altogether desirable. To insist that cultural difference is a material fact of post-apartheid South Africa is one thing, but to suggest that this is the *only* political resource left to underprivileged groups is a different matter. The South African left and labour movements (in comparison with Western Europe) still have, it seems to me, the potential for active representation in government power and economic policy. If such potential is threatened by the dominance of the ANC, why must the *only* response be the renunciation of formal ties with the ANC and the development of a counter-hegemonic bloc, derived from cultural differences, and situated somewhere in civil society? This may be a very important project to develop, but it need not and cannot be the only one. Ultimately, Farred's social analysis reveals both the promise and the insufficiency of contemporary Gramscian thought for the new South African situation. This is what I hope the new project of cultural studies in South Africa can work beyond.

Notes

1 Raymond Williams, 'The Future of Cultural Studies', *The Politics of Modernism: Against the New Conformists*, edited and introduced by Tony Pinkney (London: Verso, 1989), p. 155.

2 Linden Peach, 'Yorkshire and the Origins of Cultural Politics', *Red Letters: A Review of Cultural Politics*, 27 (1990), p. 6.

3 The title of the 1993 conference at which the talk on which this chapter was based was given was 'Appropriations: New Directions in African Cultural Studies?'. For useful discussions of the issues involved in applying British cultural studies outside of the UK see Jon Stratton and Ien Ang, 'On the Impossibility of a Global Cultural Studies: "British" Cultural Studies in an "International" Frame', in David Morley and Kuan-Hsing Chen (eds.), *Stuart Hall: Critical Dialogues in Cultural Studies* (London: Routledge, 1996), pp. 361–91; Kuan-Hsing Chen, 'Cultural Studies and the Politics of Internationalization: An Interview with Stuart Hall', in ibid., pp. 392–408. See also South African reflections by P. Eric Louw, 'Rethinking Cultural Studies to Meet the Challenge of the "Information Age" in South Africa', *Social Dynamics* [Cape Town, South Africa], 21, 1 (1995), pp. 71–8; Keyan G. Tomaselli, 'Reading Stuart Hall in Southern Africa', in Paul Gilroy, Lawrence Grossberg and Angela McRobbie (eds.), *Without Guarantees: In Honour of Stuart Hall* (London: Verso, 2000), pp. 375–87 and Keyan G. Tomaselli, 'Cultural Studies and Renaissance in Africa: Recovering Praxis', *Scrutiny2: Issues in English Studies in Southern Africa* [Pretoria, South Africa], 4, 2 (1999), pp. 43–8.

4 Michael Green, '"Cultural Studies!", Said the Magistrate', *News from Nowhere: Journal of Cultural Materialism*, 8 (1990), p. 36.

5 Tony Bennett, 'Putting Policy into Cultural Studies', in Lawrence Grossberg, Cary Nelson and Paula Treichler (eds.), *Cultural Studies* (London: Routledge, 1992), p. 26.

6 For an interesting discussion of writing centres (based on US models) within South African universities, and their contribution to the democratisation of higher education, see Pam Nichols, 'A Snowball in Africa with a Chance of Flourishing: Writing Centres as Shifters of Power in a South African University', *Current Writing: Text and Reception in Southern Africa* [Durban, South Africa], 10, 2 (1998), pp. 84–95. See also Kelwyn Sole, 'Democratising Culture and Literature in a "New South Africa": Organisation and Theory', *Current Writing: Text and Reception in Southern Africa*, 6, 2 (1994), pp. 1–37; Tony Parr, 'Saving Literature', *Scrutiny2: Issues in English Studies in Southern Africa*, 1, 1–2 (1996), pp. 70–7, and Margaret Daymond, 'Contexts for "Literature": On "Literary" and "Cultural" Studies in an English Department Syllabus', *Scrutiny2: Issues in English Studies in Southern Africa*, 1, 1–2 (1996), pp. 78–88.

7 See Kelwyn Sole, 'South Africa Passes the Posts', *Alternation: Journal of the Centre for the Study of Southern African Literature and Languages* [Durban, South Africa], 4, 1 (1997), pp. 116–51, for a critical discussion of contemporary theoretical strands in South African humanities.

8 Stuart Hall, 'Cultural Studies and its Theoretical Legacies', in Lawrence Grossberg, Cary Nelson and Paula Treichler (eds.), *Cultural Studies*, p. 283.

9 Raymond Williams, 'The Uses of Cultural Theory', *The Politics of Modernism: Against the New Conformists*, p. 171.

10 Raymond Williams, 'The Future of Cultural Studies', p. 157.
11 Raymond Williams, 'The Uses of Cultural Theory', p. 174.
12 For a sympathetic retrospective discussion of New Times see Angela McRobbie, 'Looking Back at New Times and its Critics', in David Morley and Kuan-Hsing Chen (eds.), *Stuart Hall: Critical Dialogues in Cultural Studies*, pp. 238–61. For a critical discussion see Neil Lazarus, 'Doubting the New World Order: Marxism Postmodernist Social Theory', *Differences: A Journal of Feminist Cultural Studies*, 3, 3 (1991), pp. 94–138.
13 Grant Farred, 'Unity and Difference in Black South Africa', *Social Text*, 31–2 (1992), pp. 217–34.

10

'The Killer That Doesn't Pay Back':
Chinua Achebe's critique of cosmopolitics

'Cosmopolitics' is a neologism of recent invention. A response to the pro-
liferation of ethnic-based nationalisms, and to the post-Fordist restructuring of global capitalism, 'cosmopolitics' is what a number of liberal
thinkers now advocate: a freely created, cosmopolitan cultural identity
based on notions of 'global' citizenship.[1] This worldly sensibility may
express itself through voluntary exile from one's homeland; it may con-
strue the act of travel itself as a socially emancipatory project: good for
the worldly soul, good for the soul of the world. Perhaps one of cosmopolitics' best known proponents is Ghanaian-born Harvard philoso-
pher Kwame Anthony Appiah, whose essay 'Cosmopolitan Patriots'
quotes Gertrude Stein most approvingly: 'I am an American and Paris is
my hometown'.[2] This reinforces Appiah's celebration of global mobility as
a freedom to 'elect the local forms of human life within which [you] will
live' (p. 95). This freedom of self-creation, for Appiah, lies at the heart of
cosmopolitanism. And quite tellingly, Appiah suggests that it is the
'modern market economy that has provided the material conditions that
have enabled this exploration for a larger and larger proportion of people'
(p. 98).

The eminent Nigerian writer and critic Chinua Achebe also uses this
same quotation of Gertrude Stein, but to precisely the opposite end, in his
2000 critical study *Home and Exile*. Discussing the contrasting meanings
of travel for First-and Third-World peoples, he suggests that First-World
people of colour are no less globally privileged than white Westerners:

> Even James Baldwin returning to America from France in a casket
> and W.E.B. Du Bois finding a resting place in Ghana … Diverse as
> their individual situations or predicaments were, these children of
> the West roamed the world with the confidence of the authority of
> their homeland behind them. The purchasing power of even very

little real money in their pocket set against the funny money all around them might often be enough to validate their authority without any effort on their part.

The experience of a traveller from the world's poor places is very different, whether he is travelling as a tourist or struggling to settle down as an exile in a wealthy country ... Let me just say of such a traveller that he will not be able to claim a double citizenship like Gertrude Stein when she said: 'I am an American and Paris is my hometown'.[3]

The market economy that makes freedom possible for Appiah's cosmopolitan subject does not empower Achebe's Third-World subject.[4] Indeed, Achebe suggests, hemispheres follow different standards both financially and figuratively. The same market economy that 'frees' Appiah works to 'unfree' non-metropolitan peoples.[5]

I want to suggest that Achebe's *Home and Exile* subtly and powerfully implicates contemporary cosmopolitical thought in the historical violence practised by European colonialism in Africa. Cosmopolitan perspectives, for Achebe, are ultimately present-day expressions of the old 'Pax Britannica': the liberal story that Empire likes to tell about itself. That story Achebe began to explode with his 1958 classic novel *Things Fall Apart*, in which the colonial 'pacification' of the 'tribes' is a exposed as a deadly euphemism; likewise, the 'peace' of Britannica's 'Pax' is revealed as its opposite, war; while the 'justice', 'order' and 'stability' of this new colonial administration is unmasked as mere 'anarchy' which has been 'loosed upon the world'. But if *Things Fall Apart* focused largely on the social consequences of the emergent imperial 'order', *Home and Exile*, as we have already seen, suggests that economics must also be factored in to the analysis of dominatory 'order'. Economic theft, social chaos and physical violence are beautifully condensed in the phrase 'The Killer That Doesn't Pay Back', which Achebe's youthful villagers used to describe the colonial British Post Office. A seemingly benign medium for the creation and furtherment of a global culture, its 'beneficiaries' saw it instead as a 'killer who will not be called to count; in other words, a representative of anarchy in the world' (p.78).[6] Ultimately Achebe suggests contemporary cosmopolitics currently to perform a similar work of political, economic and cultural violence. This chapter focuses on unpacking that postal metaphor, and explaining why it resonates today.

It is no surprise that Achebe should select the institution of the Post Office to launch his attack on imperialism. From *Things Fall Apart* onwards, Achebe has evinced a strong concern with media – in both a broad sense, as a term for the different technologies and agents through which power is channelled – and in a narrow sense of verbal communications. Without the African court messengers in *Things Fall Apart*, the British imperial project could not proceed. As translators, the messengers have extraordinary power over both colonised and coloniser. And as agents of the colonial judiciary – itself, obviously, an imperial *medium* – they have even more power. Achebe's choice of the Post Office as a crucial medium both of letters and of imperial power then is hardly an arbitrary one.

Neither is his description of the two bodies that physically house the postal service. These bodies reek of offensive colonial odour, for those who are careful readers of Achebian metaphor. The fatal Post Office sets up shop in a small, one-room house that 'had been put up in the Native Court premises on the great highway that cut our village in two' (p. 76). Thus the Post Office ominously occupies the same space as the Native Court that worked such harm in *Things Fall Apart*. And this Post Office is situated on a road that literally divides the village in two. And we know the knife metaphor from that same novel: the 'knife' wielded by colonialism there is said to be placed on 'the things that hold us together' and that knife has 'split us apart'.[7] Spatial location is an index of social meaning here: the post office is another aggressive colonial imposition, as integral to its infrastructure as the 'law' and the highway that respectively judge and divide the local community.

If the countertop Post Office is quietly disruptive of precolonial social space and organisation, the truck version is loudly so. The 'killer' sobriquet initially arose from the daily 'majestic arrival of the six-wheeled, blue-painted lorry with the name Royal Mail emblazoned in big, yellow letters on its brow and on each flank' (p. 77). Vehicles are a regular part of Achebe's symbolic repertoire (and for many African writers: recall, for instance, the lorry named 'Progres' with one 's' that Sozaboy learns to drive in Ken Saro-Wiwa's eponymous novel). The thing about Achebe's truck here is that its message is utterly regal, from the majesty of its arrival through to the royalty it advertises on its body. And the early pages of *Home and Exile* pointedly inform us that, to Achebe, Igbo culture is and always has been constitutionally republican, profoundly anti-monarchic in every sense.[8] To describe the truck's demeanour as regal then is to criticise, not to praise it. To emphasise the connection of the postal service to an alien system of undemocratic government is, likewise, to condemn it.

Whether in its stationary or vehicular expression, postal imperial power is essentially destructive of local community, autonomy and culture, a 'killer that doesn't pay back'. As a fixture of the village, it is a visible reminder of autarchic colonial settlement and emblem of African disenfranchisement. And at the same time, as a truck, it expresses the anarchic freedom of a hit-and-run driver, one that doesn't even recognise that a corpse exists to be accounted for. Achebe's account mentions no benefits to local people of their involuntary insertion into a global communication network. As long as the power that controls that global circulation is imposed, alien and unaccountable to local populations, then the circulation itself is unwelcome. People's letters cannot be safe when their courier serves someone else's king (well, any king). Global communication, ultimately, is only liberatory for those sovereigns or states that own the communication structures. For those who do not own them, these international structures simply amplify the depth and range of their unfreedom.

So far I have focused on Achebe's historical account of imperialism through the Royal Mail, his suggestion that its promise of global citizenship is not only false but also fatal. As long as there is an imperial centre to write back to, then there can be no global freedom of exchange. And that metropolitan centre cannot be transformed through physical occupation by Third-World peoples: it is they alone who are transformed by it. It is no accident that the writers who for Achebe do the dirty work of promoting speciously 'global' values all do so while resident in the metropolis. There is most definitely a spatial determinism in Achebe's vision: the Nigerian students who in the 1950s attack the radical literary work of their compatriot Amos Tutuola, or Buchi Emecheta who thirty years later promotes only African writing that can 'pass' as English – they all issue these metropolitan sentiments literally from within the streets and offices of London.

For Achebe, London now fulfils a neo-imperial function that is inseparable from its historical role as imperial throne. Third-World peoples who relocate to it are faced only with different slaveries: ideological or economic. Their mutual entanglement is suggested by Ama Ata Aidoo, whose provocative novel *Our Sister Killjoy* Achebe quotes with approval. Describing African students sent to London to study in the 1970s, she writes (and Achebe quotes):

They work hard for the
Doctorates –
They work too hard,
Giving away
Not only themselves, but
All of us –
The price is high,
My brother,
Otherwise the story is as old as empires.

Oppressed multitudes from the provinces rush to the imperial seat because that is where they know all salvation comes from. But as other imperial subjects in other times and other places have discovered, for the slave there is nothing at the centre but worse slavery. (pp. 94–5)

All of this might suggest that Achebe sees global power and ideology in strictly Manichean terms. And this is, I think, correct: he follows a Fanonian conception of anti-colonial struggle, one which is not diminished by Achebe's decision to make words rather than arms his weapon of choice. And like Fanon his goal is, ultimately, the creation of the conditions for a new and properly global humanity. Cosmopolitics inhibits that creation by masking the inequality that structures contemporary globalisation. Worse, like the original colonial Post Office, cosmopolitics perpetuates irresponsibility of the neo-imperial metropole, a refusal to be accountable for its destructive actions. This refusal stems from the denial that there is indeed anything to account for: the difficulties experienced by formerly colonised countries are entirely of their making. As Achebe observes:

> After a short period of dormancy and a little self-doubt about its erstwhile imperial mission, the West may be ready to resume its old domineering monologue in the world. Certainly there is no lack of zealots urging it to do so. They call it 'taking a hard look' at such issues as the African slave trade and the European colonization of Africa, with the result, generally, of absolving Europe from much of the blame and placing it squarely on African shoulders. (p. 83)

We need only look at the recent advertisement of David Horowitz (aka 10 Big Lies About Slavery!), for corroboration of this phenomenon.[9] What

Achebe does through the historical metaphor of the colonial Post Office
is to connect even the most ostensibly 'liberal' cosmopolitanism with this
reactionary racist hegemony. They all share the refusal to 'pay back'; they
are all, in effect, 'killers'.

Achebe's militance is uncompromising. But it is worth recalling that
throughout this book he talks in terms of dialogue; even the 'killer' sobriquet is, he explains, part of 'the dialogue of dispossession and its rebuttal'
(p. 77). His paradoxical insistence on dialogue with an adversary that can
only monologue, to 'balance' the score of stories, suggests that Achebe is
not about to give up on the possibility of real global communication. The
prerequisite for such communication, however, is physical rootedness and
autonomy – no cult of diasporic freedom and metropolitan self-reinven-
tion, but a reclamation of the very space once physically occupied by the
colonial Post Office. As Achebe pleads to postcolonial writers who want
to 'write back': 'Don't trouble to bring your message in person. Write it
where you are, take it down that little dusty road to the village post office
and send it!' (p. 97) The road is for Achebe 'my link to all the other desti-
nations' and to 'every villager, living and dead, who has ever walked on it'
(p. 91). This reclaimed road is now for pedestrians, not for the Royal Mail
lorry that hits and runs.

Notes

1 See for example Pheng Cheah and Bruce Robbins (eds.), *Cosmopolitics:
Thinking and Feeling beyond the Nation* (Minneapolis: University of
Minnesota Press, 1998), and Bruce Robbins, *Feeling Global: Internationalism
in Distress* (New York: New York University Press, 1999). For a magisterial
discussion of cosmopolitanism see Timothy Brennan, *At Home in the World:
Cosmopolitanism Now* (Cambridge, MA: Harvard University Press, 1997).

2 Quoted in Kwame Anthony Appiah, 'Cosmopolitan Patriots', in Pheng Cheah
and Bruce Robbins (eds.), *Cosmopolitics: Thinking and Feeling beyond the
Nation*, p. 91.

3 Chinua Achebe, 'Today, the Balance of Stories', *Home and Exile* (New York:
Oxford University Press, 2000), pp. 92–3.

4 See Aihwa Ong, 'Flexible Citizenship among Chinese Cosmopolitans', in
Pheng Cheah and Bruce Robbins (eds), *Cosmopolitcs: Thinking and Feeling
Beyond the Nation*, pp. 134–62, for a discussion of the economic advantages
that accrue to 'the emigration of Chinese corporate elites out of Asia' (p. 156).

5 For critical Africanist perspectives on globalisation see Manthia Diawara,
'Toward a Regional Imaginary in Africa', in Fredric Jameson and Masao
Miyoshi (eds.), *The Cultures of Globalization* (Durham: Duke University

Press, 1998), pp. 103–24; Ali A. Mazrui, 'A Tale of Two Continents: Africa, Asia and the Dialectic of Globalization', *Cooperation South*, 2 (1998), pp. 118–33; Nadine Gordimer, 'Cultural Globalization: Living on a Frontierless Land', *Cooperation South*, 2 (1998), pp. 16–21. The literature on globalisation and globalism is vast and expanding. A useful critical discussion is the special issue of *Race and Class: A Journal for Black and Third World Liberation*, 40, pp. 2–3 (1999) on 'The Threat of Globalism'.

6 See James Morris, chapter 3, 'Lifelines', *Pax Britannica: The Climax of an Empire* (Harmondsworth: Penguin, 1968), pp. 51–64, for an account of the British imperial postal service.

7 Chapter 20 of *Things Fall Apart*; Obierika to Okonkwo, p. 125 of the 'Classics in Context' Heinemann edition (London: Heinemann, 1996).

8 See for example: 'The Igbo did not wish to [live under the rule of kings], and made no secret of their disinclination. Sometimes one of them would, believe it or not, actually name his son Ezebuilo: A king is an enemy' (p. 16).

9 Horowitz's controversial and offensive advertisement, 'Ten Reasons Why Reparations for Slavery is a Bad Idea for Blacks – and Racist Too' was placed in student newspapers across US campuses in spring of 2001. Among its 'reasons' against reparations: 'while white Europeans conducted the trans-Atlantic slave trade, Arabs and black Africans were responsible for enslaving the ancestors of African Americans'; the claim that African Americans economically benefited from slavery; the claim that 'there was never an anti-slavery movement until white Anglo-Saxon Christians created one', leading to the conclusion that black Americans 'owe a debt to America' for liberation from oppression. The advertisement and a point-by-point rebuttal by the Department of African American and African Studies, Robert Chrisman and Ernest Allen appear in *The Ohio State Lantern*, 18 April 2001, pp. 6–7. Horowitz's advertisement is reprinted in *The Black Scholar: Journal of Black Studies and Research*, 31, 2 (2001), p. 48. Ernest Allen and Robert Chrisman, 'Ten Reasons: A Response to David Horowitz', appears in *The Black Scholar: Journal of Black Studies and Research*, 31, 2 (2001), pp. 49–55.

11

You *can* get there from here: critique and utopia in Benita Parry's thought

Benita Parry is justly acclaimed as an exemplary demystifier – the thinker who has provided unsurpassed critiques of the neo-colonial elements that lurk in the work of some postcolonial critics and creative writers. Less acclaimed are the affirmative, even utopian elements of Parry's intellectual project. Her writings, from imperialism to postcolonial theory to resistance, articulate optimistic belief in the achievability of political solidarity and common understanding across races, nations and cultures, brought together in the struggle for human freedom. This may sound strange given Parry's renowned emphasis on the Manichean, and her strictures against a postcolonial theory predicated on models of 'negotiation' rather than conflict, intimacy and 'transculturation' rather than violence and domination.[1]

But if we revisit even the most celebrated occasion of Parry's demystificatory practice, her *Oxford Literary Review* discussion of Gayatri Spivak, we find evidence of this affirmative inclination.[2] I am thinking of Parry's account of Jean Rhys's novel *Wide Sargasso Sea*, in particular, her persuasive analysis of the black character Christophine as 'the possessor and practitioner of an alternative tradition challenging imperialism's authorized system of knowledge' (p. 39). In ascribing radical agency to Christophine, Benita Parry also ascribes radical agency to her author. Parry is suggesting, in other words, that texts produced by non-black writers such as Rhys *can* respectfully represent 'alterity', and can recognise racially disenfranchised populations as the creators of different, legitimate knowledge-systems, social structures and aesthetic codes.[3] For Parry, writers who are on the receiving end of imperial privilege are fully capable of interrogating what she nicely terms their 'ethnic solipsism', and they can also go beyond the limits of this internal critique to imagine alternative lifeworlds.[4]

In the case of metropolitan writers who, like Joseph Conrad, ultimately fail to produce a vision beyond imperialism, Parry none the less establishes a utopian dimension to their work, and goes on to distinguish its emancipatory from its dominatory forms. Thus in *Conrad and Imperialism* she sees Conrad's attempt to 'recover the spiritual forces at work ... in imperialism' as halting 'the reappraisal of beliefs demanded by the fiction's arguments and revelations', 'even as it stands as a sign of the principle of hope'.[5] Conrad's 'hope' culminates in his reactionary celebration of European racial solidarity. At the same time, Parry traces another destination for Conrad's utopianism: 'Ironically ... the symbols of anticipation inhere in experiences ... disparaged by the texts – in the many auguries of a fuller and more extensive human condition prefigured in moments of ontological awakening which are formally denigrated' (p. 16). In other words, Conrad's ethnic absolutism, his authorised utopia, is offset by this unofficial version of utopian existential transformation.

Parry's analysis of resistance cultures reveals a similar preoccupation with the meanings, values and modes of utopian drives. The critical procedure she calls for 'retains ... that realm of imaginary freedom which these histories prefigured or configured'; such analysis will 'register decolonising struggle as an emancipatory project despite the egregious failures these brought in their wake.[6] Sartre's work on Lumumba provides, for her, one example of this critical approach: Sartre, she suggests, manages both to 'lament the inevitable failure of a petty-bourgeois leadership to transform the fight for independence into the overthrow of the colonial state' *and* to 'celebrate what an oppressed population, even when handcuffed to a native bourgeoisie, dared to do in the face of international capitalism's remorseless colonialist interventions'.

I want to focus here on the interplay of critique and affirmation in Parry's work, and will start by looking at her analysis of ethnic solipsism in the metropole. From there I will go on to discuss her contribution to the understanding of resistance. If 1987 was the year of Paul Gilroy's famous critique of the white British metropolitan left in *There Ain't No Black in the Union Jack*, it was also the year of Parry's *Oxford Literary Review* article, which gives a pithy reprimand to the same left and for similar reasons. 'Francis Mulhern', writes Parry, 'has proposed that a "socialist politics of literature" be constructed from the writings of western women. This exorbitant demand on the work of first world women to effect the subversion of the west's cultural hegemony ... displays a parochial perspective on the sources of "alternative" literary modes, which is indifferent to the implosions being made ... by postcolonial literary cultures, and suggests an insularity that has no place in radical theory' (p. 51).

Parry's concern with socialist eurovision has intensified since then, as is evident in her forthcoming article 'Liberation Theory: Variations on Themes of Marxism and Modernity'. But if in 1987 she was content merely to identify a problem, now we find she is concerned to *analyse* the problem of the left's non-engagement with colonialism, locating as crucial the 'shift away from the political' in European Marxism that began in the 1930s. However, Parry's politics of hope *and* her analytic rigour prevent her from blanket denunciation. She gets at the problem of European socialist racism by highlighting two major exceptions to it, Sartre and Althusser. By exploring their explicit and theoretical engagement with anti-colonial struggles, Parry shows again how much radical international agency was actually available to the metropole, even if the left chose, for the most part, not to exercise this. The default ethnic solipsism then emerges as another active choice by the left rather than as historically inevitable racial and national baggage. In giving a qualified affirmation of Sartre and Althusser, Parry more powerfully exposes the failure of political imagination at work in the majority of the European left.

Parry's accounts of metropolitan fiction writers demonstrate the same refusal to subscribe to white racial or European continental essentialism. And the same generous willingness to affirm the achievements of those writers who do try to challenge imperialist perspectives. To fully get at Parry's analysis of ethnocentric *and* emancipatory processes, we need to grasp the contrapuntal basis of her work. In 1983, long before Edward Said's *Culture and Imperialism* popularised the phrase 'contrapuntal reading', Parry used the 'contrapuntal' word in her book *Conrad and Imperialism*. She argues Conrad's fiction to display 'disjunctions between established morality and moral principle' in which 'ethical absolutes are revealed to be pragmatic utilities for ensuring social stability and inhibiting dissent'. These innovations ... produce a *contrapuntal discourse*' (p. 2; emphasis added). Edward Said's version of contrapuntal model of writing and reading suggests, at times, the aesthetic harmonisation and displacement of social conflict, the promotion of liberal pluralism over radical struggles for justice. Parry's 'contrapuntal discourse' suggests the opposite: she uses the phrase to designate the fissures produced by what she calls 'Conrad's struggle to escape ideology' (p. 7).

This emphasis recurs in her *Oxford Literary Review* call for critical 'engagement with the manifold and conflicting textual inscriptions – the discontinuities, defensive rhetorical strategies and unorthodox language challenging official thought, the disruptions of structural unity effected by divergent and discordant voices – as the location and source of the text's politics' (p. 49). Contrapuntal critical reading seeks to make these discords audible, not to resolve them. This leads Parry to develop a methodology that is both meticulously political and painstakingly literary. If you look at her analysis of Conrad, or Kipling, or Wells, or Forster, for example, you will find that she approaches each selected text as a complex totality whose political meanings cannot easily be reduced to any one axis or axiom, to use Spivakian terms.[7] The operations of ideology have to be traced as they work across landscape, metaphor, character, rhetoric, action and narrative logic. Most important is the way Parry's contrapuntal reading theorises the notion of the colonised. She apprehends colonised peoples as participants of societies that consist of heterogeneous spheres of social reproduction, including knowledge systems, aesthetic practices and metaphysical traditions. A properly Parryan contrapuntal analysis has then to disaggregate both the metropole and the colony, and explore the metropolitan text's representational politics by foregrounding and differentiating its engagement with epistemology, aesthetics and ontology.

This contrapuntalism impels Parry, in 'Materiality and Mystification in *A Passage to India*', to give an account of Forster's novel that distinguishes between the politics at work in the representation of individual characters and those at work in the representation of the Indian geographical space; this reading technique also differentiates overt contents from symbolic form. She argues that 'the fiction, far from rendering India as epistemologically vacant, reconfigures the sub-continent as a geographical space and social realm abundantly occupied by diverse intellectual modes, cultural forms, and sensibilities' (p. 185) and that 'the novel's dissident place within British writing about India does not reside in its meagre critique of a colonial situation … but in configuring India's natural terrain and cognitive traditions as inimical to the British presence' (p. 180). And Forster's representational politics also lie in his stylistic tentativeness, his intellectual modesty. Even as Forster here affirms India as a complex and oppositional space, he refuses to exercise metropolitan authority. Parry argues that 'the novel approaches Indian forms of knowledge with uncertainty, without asserting the authority of its representations' (p. 184).

I want to spend a little more time on this as I think it gives a useful illustration of Parry's originality as a critic of imperial solipsism, and as a contrapuntal thinker. The contrast between the value she gives to the colonial silence in Forster's text and the colonial silence portrayed in J.M. Coetzee's texts is so acute as to suggest, at first, an active theoretical contradiction.[8] Look here at her discussion of the mute Marabar Caves of *A Passage to India*. She locates the caves as belonging to a Jain tradition, in which 'negation has alternative significations'; Jain belief 'unlike Islam and Hinduism has no sentient protagonists in the book' but through the caves Jain culture 'has written its antique Indian philosophy of renunciation over a material space' that is '*already* in possession of a language without syntax and expressive of abnegation' (p. 186; emphasis added). Forster's text has the decency, she suggests, to admit 'its own incapacity to bring this alien realm into representation' (p. 187).

The silence of the Caves bespeaks both a deliberate narrative non-mastery on Forster's part *and* the positive validation of an autonomous, alternative indigenous tradition that resists European incorporation. The silence of Coetzee's racial 'others' carries an entirely different textual politics: a neo-colonial romanticisation of the dispossessed. For Parry, Coetzee's rendition of silence emerges from 'the cognitive systems of the West' and ultimately serves to ratify those systems and the narrative authority that they assume (p. 150). Furthermore, she suggests, 'the homages to the mystical properties and prestige of muteness undermine the critique of that condition where oppression inflicts and provokes silence' (p. 158). This representation is the result of deliberate authorial exclusion: 'the principles around which novelistic meaning is organized in Coetzee's fictions owe nothing to knowledges which are not of European provenance, but which are amply and variously represented in South Africa' (p. 150). The meanings of Forster's novel, by contrast, are openly and implicitly mediated through non-European knowledges. Again, we see the operations of Parry's optimism here: it is because she thinks it entirely theoretically possible for European writers to recognise and affirm alternative knowledges that she finds Coetzee so lacking here.

There is nothing remotely contradictory about Parry's arguments concerning silence as the expression, respectively, of cultural relativism (in E.M. Forster) and cultural absolutism (in J.M. Coetzee). Whether or not you accept Parry's conclusions, you have to accept the consistency of her reasoning across these texts. I have perhaps risked misrepresenting Parry's work here as that of a romantic who in affirming the legitimacy of non-European cultures and knowledges systems renders the systems static or immutable. Parry's quoted reference to Indian 'cognitive *traditions*' may support this view, as may her previously quoted *Oxford Literary Review* reference to Christophine as 'the possessor and practitioner of an alternative *tradition* challenging imperialism's authorized system of knowledge' (emphasis added). But the 'tradition' word, as Parry uses it here, does not reify so much as it draws the reader's attention to the structural foundations of non-Western practices. In other words, Parry insists here on the systematic, historical character of Indian and Caribbean practices: the metropolitan text is prompted to recognise alternative systems *as* systems, and to address the *langue* as well as the *parole* of its 'others'.

That Parry has anything but a reified conception of non-European traditions is clear from her writings on Fanon, Césaire and other resistance workers. One of her most striking contributions to the study of resistance cultures is her insistence on their constitutively heterogeneous character. This leads her to offer a powerful critique of developmentalist approaches. The hegemonic understanding of resistance is the trajectory 'from protest to challenge', to borrow from Carter and Karis whose multivolumed anthology is organised on the basis of this teleology.[9] A similar developmental telos inheres in Fanon's own 'three stages' theory.[10] And it is also to be found in Said's *Culture and Imperialism* classification of 'decolonising discourses' as a progression from nativist through nationalist to liberationist theory.[11] Rebutting Said, Parry points out that

> Not only are the stages less disjunct than the periodisation suggests – messianic movements and Pan-Africanism were utopian in their goals, Nkrumah's nationalism was not exclusively Africanist, acknowledging as it did the recombinant qualities of a culture which had developed through assimilating Arabic and western features, and so on – but the liberation theory of Fanon and Césaire was more impure than is here indicated, nativism remaining audible despite the strenuous endorsements of a post-European, transnational humanism as the ultimate goal.[12]

As Fanon's nativism – the promotion of black racial unity and pride – continues into his 'final', universal humanist stage, Said's linear historiography is found to be inaccurate.

But nativism is itself, for Parry, far more impure, more composite, than either its detractors or contemporary Afrocentric supporters can allow. Consider Parry's pathbreaking analysis of Negritude (the Caribbean and African formation that argued for a distinctive black

culture and philosophy) in her essay 'Resistance Theory'. This demon-
strates how in Césaire's thought, 'Negritude is not a recovery of a pre-
existent state, but a textually invented history, an identity effected
through figurative operations and a tropological construction of blackness as a sign of the colonised condition and its refusal' (p. 182). This
formulation goes way beyond Spivak's notion of strategic essentialism.
Indeed I read Parry, like Spivak, to emphasise both the utility and con-
structedness of black identity. But to this she adds a profoundly dialectical twist, and this, I want to argue, emerges from her utopian
disposition, something that is altogether lacking in Spivak's work. The
dialectical utopian idea lies in her construction of blackness as a sign
both of colonisation and its refusal. This is a dialectical notion that has
no tendency towards a raceless sublation. The goal of emancipation from
colonialism, or racism, is not, for Parry, tantamount to liberation from
blackness itself. A similarly frozen dialectical argument can be found in
Parry's *Oxford Literary Review* account of Fanon as the articulator of 'a
process of cultural resistance and cultural disruption', in which he writes
'a text that can answer colonialism back, and anticipates another condition beyond imperialism' (p. 44).

If Parry's account of Césaire's Negritude goes beyond the Spivakian
model of strategic essentialism, her account of Fanon's resistant/disrup-
tive text goes beyond the models of 'reverse' or 'derivative' discourse that
we find in a number of contemporary postcolonial theories. For Parry's
models refuse the exclusively reactive basis of these theorisations, and
instead present us with an insurgent agency that is as creative as it is reactive: it is the product of a utopian imagination. Listen again to the passage
I quoted near the start of this chapter, in which Parry refers us to 'that
realm of imaginary freedom which these [resistance] histories prefigured
or configured'.[13] Her equivocation between the verbs 'prefigure' and 'con-
figure' is a different manifestation, I want to suggest, of the utopian force
of her own imagination. She presents the freedom produced by liberation
struggles as both a verifiable historical event and a subjective condition
awaiting future actualisation.

I have been writing about Parry's utopian dimensions as if they have
always taken the same expression in her work. In her resistance writings,
however, we see changes of style that are also, I think, changes in political conceptualisation. Her *Oxford Literary Review* article makes heavy use
of the 'discourse' word, and uses this word interchangeably to designate
aesthetic literature and anti-colonial political thought. By the time of her

'Resistance Theory/Theorising Resistance or Two Cheers for Nativism' article, the discourse word is still a favoured term for the analysis of resistance cultures, but is beginning to be differentiated into its consciously literary and social modes. Parry argues for Césaire's poetry as the most emancipatory instance of this resistance 'discourse', and suggests that the aesthetic medium allows the greatest space for contrapuntal articulations of identity. By the time we get to her forthcoming 'Liberation Theory' article, the discourse word has all but vanished. So has Parry's privileging of the aesthetic medium for the creation of sophisticated political identities and the play of utopian desires. Her focus is now on political movements themselves, rather than literary texts, as the protagonists of utopian imagination. And with this comes an emphasis on the extraordinary range of liberationist thinkers – including Sankara, Cabral, Machel, Nkrumah, Lumumba – who creatively 'co-authored' these movements with the mass of the insurgent populations. This new work gives less centrality to Fanon and Césaire, who, as the most officially sanctioned voices of resistance culture within the metropole, have less urgent need of critical rehabilitation. While I applaud the exploration of political action as imagination (and I certainly applaud the departure of the discourse word) I also want to register Parry's removal of aesthetic culture from her resistance radar as an analytic loss.

I hesitate to bring in a negative dimension to the discussion of Parry's work, though I imagine that she would prefer me to do this rather than deliver an unconditionally glowing account of my fave rave. And we have only to go to the new preface of *Delusions and Discoverie*s to observe Parry's dedication to the socialist tradition of rigorous auto-critique.[14] Taking up her critical cue then I suggest that Parry's relative lack of engagement with the aesthetic accomplishments of anti-colonial and post-colonial cultures is perhaps where her own historical utopian imagination gives way to a critical sensibility nourished by more restrictive metropolitan aesthetic values. She and I have a long-standing disagreement over the literary merits of Olive Schreiner's work, and, more generally, over the aesthetic contributions made by anti-colonial and post-apartheid South African literatures. Parry's own taste tends, I think, towards the modernist, although she has done a great deal, in her work on Forster and Wells, to extend the canon beyond the modernist monopolies presented by Edward Said and Fredric Jameson. Willing as she is to credit metropolitan mimetic modes of the Victorian, Edwardian and modern periods with literary sophistication, she is over-inclined, I think, to disparage the mimeticism of, say, an Alex la Guma, or, indeed, a Nadine Gordimer, as the sign of aesthetic failure. (These two authors receive her critical attention in the *Oxford Literary Review* article.) It falls to other scholars to apply her insights into metropolitan literary-political complexity to the terrain of South African literary production.

I have focused on the utopian rather than the Manichean, the literary rather than the polemical, in Parry's work, for a number of reasons. One is that I feel very acutely, and personally, the need for 'signs of promise', the 'principle of hope', in our contemporary political situation. Parry's work provides a large archive for the student of optimism. But if she eschews the easy comforts of a post-structuralist pessimism premised upon convictions of epistemic violence, the impossibility of 'unlearning privilege' and adequately 'representing alterity'– she also precludes the easy refuge of a postmodern optimism, found, say, in Michael Hardt and Antonio Negri's recent *Empire*.[15] In Parry's work, the utopian drive cannot be realised without extraordinary struggle. Here she concurs with Frederick Douglass in his celebrated West India Emancipation speech, August 4th, 1857, when he argues that

> If there is no struggle there is no progress ... This struggle may be a moral one, or it may be a physical one, and it may be both moral and physical, but it must be a struggle. Power concedes nothing without a demand. It never did and it never will. Find out just what any people will quietly submit to and you have found out the exact measure of injustice and wrong which will be imposed upon them, and these will continue till they are resisted with either words or blows, or with both. The limits of tyrants are prescribed by the endurance of those whom they oppress.[16]

Notes

1 Allison Drew (ed.), *South Africa's Radical Tradition: A Documentary History. Volume One 1907–1950* (Cape Town: Buchu Books, Mayibuye Books and University of Cape Town Press, 1996) supplies historical context for Benita Parry's political origins in Trotskyist South African activism of the 1950s. Useful recent critical discussions of Parry's Manicheanism and the relationship of her thought with that of Gayatri Spivak include Neil Lazarus, *Nationalism and Cultural Practice in the Postcolonial World* (Cambridge: Cambridge University Press, 1999) and Olakunle George, *Relocating Agency: Modernity and African Letters* (Albany: State University of New York Press, forthcoming).

2 Benita Parry, 'Problems in Current Theories of Colonial Discourse', *Oxford Literary Review*, 9, 1–2 (1987), pp. 27–58.

3 See Peter Hulme, 'The Locked Heart: The Creole Family Romance of *Wide Sargasso Sea*', in Francis Barker, Peter Hulme and Margaret Iversen (eds.), *Colonial Discourse/Postcolonial Theory* (Manchester: Manchester University Press, 1994), pp. 72–88, for a probing discussion of the novel. Hulme argues that the 'really troubling figures "in the margins" … are the coloured Cosways, Daniel and Alexander', p. 80.

4 Benita Parry, *Conrad and Imperialism* (London: Macmillan, 1983), p. 4.

5 Ibid.

6 Benita Parry, 'Liberation Theory: Variations on Themes of Marxism and Modernity', in Crystal Bartolovich and Neil Lazarus (eds.), *Marxism and Modernity* (Cambridge: Cambridge University Press, forthcoming).

7 Benita Parry, 'Conrad and England', in Raphael Samuel (ed.), *Patriotism: The Making and Unmaking of British National Identity. Volume 3: National Fictions* (London: Routledge, 1989), pp. 189–98; 'Narrating Imperialism: *Nostromo*'s Dystopia', in Keith Ansell-Pearson, Benita Parry and Judith Squires (eds.), *Cultural Readings of Imperialism: Edward Said and the Gravity of History* (London: Lawrence and Wishart, 1997), pp. 227–46; 'The Content and Discontents of Kipling's Imperialism', *New Formations*, 6 (1988), pp. 84–112; '*Tono-Bungay*: Modernisation, Modernity and Imperialism, or the Failed Electrification of the Empire', *New Formations*, 34 (1998), pp. 91–108; 'Materiality and Mystification in *A Passage to India*', *Novel: A Forum on Fiction*, 31, 2 (1998), pp. 174–94.

8 Benita Parry, 'Speech and Silence in the Fictions of J.M. Coetzee', in Derek Attridge and Rosemary Jolly (eds.), *Writing South Africa: Literature, Apartheid, and Democracy, 1970–1995* (Cambridge: Cambridge University Press, 1998), pp. 149–65.

9 Thomas Karis and Gwendolen Carter (eds.), *From Protest to Challenge: A Documentary History of African Politics in South Africa 1882–1964* (Stanford: Hoover Institution Press, 1972).

10 Frantz Fanon, 'On National Culture', in *The Wretched of the Earth*, trans. Constance Farringdon (1961; Harmondsworth: Penguin, 1971), pp. 166–89.

11 Edward Said, 'Resistance and Opposition', *Culture and Imperialism* (London: Chatto, 1993), pp. 230–340.

12 Benita Parry, 'Resistance Theory/Theorising Resistance or Two Cheers for Nativism', in Francis Barker, Peter Hulme and Margaret Iversen (eds.), *Colonial Discourse/Postcolonial Theory*, p. 180.

13 'Liberation Theory: Variations on Themes of Marxism and Modernity'.

14 Benita Parry, 'Preface', *Delusions and Discoveries: Studies on India in the British Imagination, 1880–1930*, with a foreword by Michael Sprinker (1972; London: Verso, 1998), pp. 1–28.

15 Michael Hardt and Antonio Negri, *Empire* (Cambridge, MA: Harvard University Press, 2000).

16 *Two Speeches by Frederick Douglass: One on West India Emancipation, delivered at Canandaigua, August 4th and the other on the Dred Scott Decision,
   delivered in New York, on the occasion of the anniversary of the American
   Abolition Society, May 1857* (Rochester: C.P. Dewey, 1857), p. 22.

Bibliography

Achebe, Chinua. *Home and Exile*. New York: Oxford University Press, 2000.

Achebe, Chinua. *Things Fall Apart*. 1958; repr. London: Heinemann, 1996.

Agenda: Empowering Women for Gender Equity [Durban, South Africa].

Ahmad, Aijaz. 'The Politics of Literary Postcoloniality'. *Race and Class: A Journal for Black and Third World Liberation* 36, 3 (1995), 1–20.

Ahmad, Aijaz. *In Theory: Classes, Nations, Literatures*. London: Verso, 1992.

Aidoo, Ama Ata. *Our Sister Killjoy*. London: Longman, 1977.

Allen, Ernest and Robert Chrisman. 'Ten Reasons: A Response to David Horowitz'. *The Black Scholar: Journal of Black Studies and Research* 31, 2 (2001), 49–55.

Ansell-Pearson, Keith, Benita Parry and Judith Squires (eds.). *Cultural Readings of Imperialism: Edward Said and the Gravity of History*. London: Lawrence and Wishart, 1997.

Anthias, Floya and Nira Yuval-Davis, with Harriet Cain. *Racialized Boundaries. Race, Nation, Gender, Colour and Class and the Anti-racist Struggle*. London: Routledge, 1992.

Appiah, Kwame. 'Cosmopolitan Patriots'. In Cheah and Robbins, *Cosmopolitics*.

Ashcroft, Bill, Gareth Griffiths, and Helen Tiffin. *The Empire Writes Back: Theory and Practice in Post-colonial Literatures*. London: Methuen, 1989.

Attridge, Derek and Rosemary Jolly (eds.). *Writing South Africa: Literature, Apartheid, and Democracy, 1970–1995*. Cambridge: Cambridge University Press, 1998.

Attwell, David. 'Intimate Enmity in the Journal of Tiyo Soga'. *Critical Inquiry* 23, 3 (1997), 557–77.

Barash, Carol (ed.). *An Olive Schreiner Reader: Writings on Women and South Africa*. London: Pandora, 1987.

Barker, Francis, Peter Hulme and Margaret Iversen (eds.). *Colonial Discourse/ Postcolonial Theory*. Manchester: Manchester University Press, 1994.

Barnett, Clive. 'Constructions of Apartheid in the International Reception of the Novels of J.M. Coetzee'. *Journal of Southern African Studies* 25, 2 (1999), 287–301.

Bartolovich, Crystal. 'Global Capital and Transnationalism'. In Schwarz and Ray, *A Companion to Postcolonial Studies*.

Bartolovich, Crystal and Neil Lazarus (eds.). *Marxism and Modernity*.
    Cambridge: Cambridge University Press, forthcoming.
Baucom, Ian. *Out of Place: Englishness, Empire, and the Locations of Identity*.
    Princeton: Princeton University Press, 1999.
Bennett, Tony. 'Putting Policy into Cultural Studies'. In Grossberg, Nelson and
    Treichler, *Cultural Studies*.
Bhabha, Homi K. 'The Manifesto', *Wasafiri: Caribbean, African, Asian and
    Associated Literatures in English* 29 (1999), 38.
Bhabha, Homi K. *The Location of Culture*. London: Routledge, 1994.
Bhabha, Homi K. 'Signs Taken for Wonders: Questions of Ambivalence and
    Authority under a Tree Outside Delhi, May 1817'. In Gates, Jr *'Race',
    Writing, and Difference*.
Bhabha, Homi K. 'The Other Question …'. *Screen* 24, 6 (1983), 18–36.
Bhabha, Homi K. (ed.). *Nation and Narration*. London: Routledge, 1990.
Bhattacharyya, Gargi. 'Wogs South of Calais: Re-thinking Racial Boundaries for
    Britain in Europe'. *Paragraph: A Journal of Modern Critical Theory* 16, 1
    (1993), 23–33.
Biko, Steve. *I Write What I Like: A Selection of His Writings*, ed. by Aelred
    Stubbs. 1978; repr. Harmondsworth: Penguin, 1988.
Blyden, Edward Wilmot. *Christianity, Islam and the Negro Race*. London: W.B.
    Whittingham, 1887.
Boehmer, Elleke. 'Questions of Neo-Orientalism'. *Interventions: International
    Journal of Postcolonial Studies* 1, 1 (1998), 18–21.
Boehmer, Elleke (ed.). *Empire Writing: An Anthology of Colonial Literature
    1870–1918*. Oxford: Oxford University Press, 1998.
Bourdieu, Pierre. *The Field of Cultural Production: Essays on Art and Literature*,
    ed. and intro. by R. Johnson. New York: Columbia University Press,
    1993.
Braude, Claudia. 'The Archbishop, the Private Detective and the Angel of
    History: The Production of South African Public Memory and the Truth
    and Reconciliation Commission'. *Current Writing. Text and Reception in
    Southern Africa* [Durban, South Africa] 8, 2 (1996), 39–65.
Brennan, Timothy. *At Home in the World: Cosmopolitanism Now*. Cambridge,
    MA: Harvard University Press, 1997.
Brennan, Timothy. 'Black Theorists and Left Antagonists'. *The Minnesota
    Review* 37 (1991), 89–113.
Brennan, Timothy. *Salman Rushdie and the Third World*. London: Macmillan,
    1989.
Bryan, Beverley, Stella Dadzie and Suzanne Scafe. *The Heart of the Race: Black
    Women's Lives in Britain*. London: Virago, 1985.
Bunn, David. 'Embodying Africa: Woman and Romance in Colonial Fiction'.
    English in Africa [Grahamstown, South Africa] 15, 1 (1988), 1–28.

Bush-Slimani, Barbara. 'Hard Labour: Women, Childbirth and Resistance in British Caribbean Slave Societies'. *History Workshop: A Journal of Socialist and Feminist Historians* 36 (1993), 83–99.

Campbell, James T. 'Redeeming the Race: Martin Delany and the Niger Valley Exploring Party, 1859–60'. *New Formations: A Journal of Culture/Theory/Politics* 45 (2001), 125–49.

Campbell, James T. *Songs of Zion. The African Methodist Episcopal Church in the United States and South Africa.* Oxford and New York: Oxford University Press, 1995.

Cantlie, James A. *Degeneration Amongst Londoners.* London: Field & Tuer and The Leadenhall Press, 1885.

Carby, Hazel V. *Race Men.* Cambridge, MA: Harvard University Press, 1998.

Carrington, Ben. 'Fear of a Black Athlete: Masculinity, Politics and the Body'. *New Formations: A Journal of Culture/Theory/Politics* 45 (2001), 91–110.

Caygill, Howard. 'Post-modernism and Judgement'. *Economy and Society* 17, 1 (1988), 1–20.

Césaire, Aimé. *Notebook of a Return to my Native Land* [1956], intro. by Mireille Rosello, tr. by Mireille Rosello with Annie Pritchard. Newcastle-upon-Tyne: Bloodaxe, 1995.

Césaire, Aimé. 'From *Discourse on Colonialism*'. In Williams and Chrisman, *Colonial Discourse and Post-colonial Theory.*

Chaudhuri, Nupur and Margaret Strobel (eds.). *Western Women and Imperialism: Complicity and Resistance.* Bloomington: Indiana University Press, 1992.

Cheah, Pheng and Bruce Robbins (eds.). *Cosmopolitics: Thinking and Feeling beyond the Nation.* Minneapolis: University of Minnesota Press, 1998.

Chen, Kuan-Hsing. 'Cultural Studies and the Politics of Internationalization: An Interview with Stuart Hall'. In Morley and Chen, *Stuart Hall.*

Chrisman, Laura (ed.). Special Issue: '"The Rendez-Vous of Conquest": Rethinking Race and Nation'. *New Formations: A Journal of Culture/Theory/Politics* 45 (2001).

Chrisman, Laura. *Rereading the Imperial Romance: British Imperialism and South African Resistance in Haggard, Schreiner and Plaatje.* Oxford: Clarendon Press, 2000.

Chrisman, Laura. 'Rethinking Black Atlanticism'. *The Black Scholar: Journal of Black Studies and Research* 30, 3–4 (2000), 12–17.

Chrisman, Laura. 'The Transnational Production of Englishness: South Africa in the Postimperial Metropole'. *Scrutiny2: Issues in English Studies in South Africa* [Pretoria, South Africa] 5, 2 (2000), 3–12.

Chrisman, Laura. 'Imperial Space, Imperial Place: Theories of Culture and Empire in Fredric Jameson, Edward Said and Gayatri Spivak'. *New Formations: A Journal of Culture/Theory/Politics* 34 (1998), 53–69.

Chrisman, Laura. 'Local Sentences in the Chapter of the Postcolonial World'.
    Diaspora: Journal of Transnational Studies 7, 1 (1998), 87–112.
Chrisman, Laura. 'Fathering the Black Nation of South Africa: Gender and
    Generation in Sol Plaatje's *Native Life in South Africa* and *Mhudi*'. *Social
    Dynamics* [Cape Town, South Africa] 23, 2 (1997), 57–73.
Chrisman, Laura. 'Gendering Imperial Culture: Problems in Feminist Post-
    colonial Criticism'. In Ansell-Pearson, Parry and Squires, *Cultural Readings
    of Imperialism.*
Chrisman, Laura. 'Journeying to Death: Paul Gilroy's *The Black Atlantic*'. *Race
    and Class: A Journal for Black and Third World Liberation* 39, 2 (1997),
    51–64.
Chrisman, Laura. 'Questioning Robert Young's Postcolonial Criticism', *Textual
    Practice* 11, 1 (1997), 38–45.
Chrisman, Laura. 'Appropriate Appropriations? Developing Cultural Studies in
    South Africa'. In Brenda Cooper and Andrew Steyn (eds.) *Transgressing
    Boundaries: New Directions in the Study of Culture in Africa*. Cape Town:
    University of Cape Town Press, 1996.
Chrisman, Laura. 'Soap. Review of Anne McClintock, *Imperial Leather*'.
    Southern African Review of Books 39–40 (1995).
Chrisman, Laura. 'Inventing Post-colonial Theory: Polemical Observations'.
    Pretexts: Studies in Writing and Culture 5, 1–2 (1995), 205–12.
Chrisman, Laura. 'Theorising "Race", Racism and Culture: Some Pitfalls in
    Idealist Critiques'. *Paragraph: A Journal of Modern Critical Theory* 16, 1
    (1993), 78–90.
Chrisman, Laura. 'The Imperial Unconscious? Representations of Imperial
    Discourse'. *Critical Quarterly* 32, 3 (1990), 38–58.
Chrisman, Laura, Farah Jasmine Griffin and Tukufu Zuberi (eds.). Special
    Issue: 'Transcending Traditions: Afro-American, African Diaspora and
    African Studies'. *The Black Scholar: Journal of Black Studies and Research*
    30, 3–4 (2000).
Chrisman, Laura and Benita Parry (eds.). *Postcolonial Theory and Criticism.*
    Cambridge: D.S. Brewer, 2000.
Chun, Wendy. 'Scenes of Empowerment: Virtual Racial Diversity and Digital
    Divides'. *New Formations: A Journal of Culture/Theory/Politics* 45 (2001),
    169–88.
Cock, Jacklyn. *Maids & Madams: Domestic Workers under Apartheid*. 1980;
    repr. London: The Women's Press, 1989.
Cohen, Phil and Bill Schwarz (eds.). Special Issue: 'Frontlines/Backyards'. *New
    Formations: A Journal of Culture/Theory/Politics* 33 (1998).
Colla, Elliott. 'The Stuff of Egypt: The Nation, the State and Their Proper
    Objects'. *New Formations: A Journal of Culture/Theory/Politics* 45 (2001),
    72–90.

Colleran, Jeanne. 'South African Theatre in the United States: The Allure of the Familiar and of the Exotic'. In Attridge and Jolly, *Writing South Africa*.

Colley, Linda. 'Britishness and Otherness: An Argument'. *Journal of British Studies* 31 (1992), 309–29.

Colls, Robert and Philip Dodd (eds.) *Englishness: Politics and Culture 1880–1930*. London: Croom Helm, 1986.

Conrad, Joseph. 'Letter to Elsie Hueffer, 3 December 1902'. *The Collected Letters of Joseph Conrad, volume 2, 1898–1902*, ed. and intro. by Frederick R. Karl and Laurence Davies. Cambridge: Cambridge University Press, 1982.

Coombes, Annie E. 'The Recalcitrant Object: Culture Contact and the Question of Hybridity'. In Barker, Hulme and Iversen, *Colonial Discourse/Postcolonial Theory*.

Coombes, Annie E. *Reinventing Africa: Museums, Material Culture and Popular Imagination in Late Victorian and Edwardian England*. London: Yale University Press, 1994.

Cooppan, Vilashini. 'W(h)ither Post-colonial Studies? Towards the Transnational Study of Race and Nation'. In Chrisman and Parry, *Postcolonial Theory and Criticism*.

Couzens, Tim. *The New African: A Study of the Life and Work of H.I.E. Dhlomo*. Johannesburg: Ravan Press, 1985.

Cunningham, Hugh. 'The Language of Patriotism'. In Samuel, *Patriotism*.

D'Aguiar, Fred. *Feeding the Ghosts*. New York: HarperCollins, 1998.

David, Deirdre. *Women, Empire, and Victorian Writing*. Ithaca: Cornell University Press, 1995.

Davin, Anna. 'Imperialism and Motherhood'. *History Workshop Journal* 5 (1978), 9–65.

Daymond, Margaret. 'Contexts for "Literature": on "Literary" and "Cultural" Studies in an English Department Syllabus'. *Scrutiny2: Issues in English Studies in Southern Africa* [Pretoria, South Africa] 1, 1–2 (1996), 78–88.

Daymond, Margaret (ed.). Special Issue: Feminism and Writing. *Current Writing: Text and Reception in Southern Africa* [Durban, South Africa] 2, 1 (1990).

Derrida, Jacques. 'Racism's Last Word'. In Gates, Jr *'Race', Writing, and Difference*.

Diawara, Manthia. *In Search of Africa*. London: Harvard University Press, 1998.

Diawara, Manthia. 'Toward a Regional Imaginary in Africa'. In Fredric Jameson and Masao Miyoshi (eds.). *The Cultures of Globalization*. Durham: Duke University Press, 1998.

Dirlik, Arif. 'Bringing History Back In: Of Diasporas, Hybridities, Places, and Histories'. *The Review of Education/Pedagogy/Cultural Studies* 21, 2 (1999), 95–131.

Dirlik, Arif. *The Postcolonial Aura: Third World Criticism in the Age of Global Capitalism*. Boulder, CO: Westview Press, 1997.

Dirlik, Arif. 'The Postcolonial Aura: Third World Criticism in the Age of Global Capitalism'. *Critical Inquiry* 20 (1994), 328–56.

Donald, James and Ali Rattansi (eds.). *'Race', Culture, and Difference*. London: Sage Publications in association with the Open University, 1992.

Douglass, Frederick. *Two Speeches by Frederck Douglass. One on West India Emancipation, delivered at Canandaigua, August 4th and the other on the Dred Scott Decision, delivered in New York, on the occasion of the anniversary of the American Abolition Society, May 1857*. Rochester: C.P. Dewey, 1857.

Doyle, Brian. *English and Englishness*. London: Routledge, 1989.

Drake, St. Clair. *Black Folk Here and There: An Essay in History and Anthropology*. Los Angeles: Center for Afro-American Studies, University of California, 1990.

Drew, Allison (ed.). *South Africa's Radical Tradition: A Documentary History. Volume One 1907–1950*. Cape Town: Buchu Books, Mayibuye Books: and University of Cape Town Press, 1996.

Du Bois, W.E.B. *The Souls of Black Folk* [1903], with an introduction by Donald B. Gibson and with notes by Monica M. Elbert. New York: Penguin Books, 1989.

Du Plessis, Menan. *A State of Fear*. London: Pandora Press, 1987.

Dubey, Madhu. 'Postmodernism as Postnationalism? Racial Representation in US Black Cultural Studies'. *New Formations: A Journal of Culture/Theory/Politics* 45 (2001), 150–68.

Eagleton, Terry. 'In the Gaudy Supermarket: Review of Gayatri Chakavorty Spivak, *A Critique of Postcolonial Reason*'. *London Review of Books* 21, 10 (1999).

Eagleton, Terry (ed.). *Raymond Williams: Critical Perspectives*. Cambridge: Polity Press, 1989.

Easthope, Antony. *Englishness and National Culture*. London: Routledge, 1998.

Edwards, Paul and David Dabydeen (eds.). *Black Writers in Britain, 1760–1890*. Edinburgh: Edinburgh University Press, 1991.

Erlmann, Veit. *Music, Modernity, and the Global Imagination: South Africa and the West*. New York: Oxford University Press, 1999.

Evaristo, Bernardine. *Lara*. London: Angela Royal Publishing, 1997.

Eze, E. Chukwudi (ed.). *Race and the Enlightenment: A Reader*. Oxford: Blackwell, 1997.

Falola, Toyin. *Nationalism and African Intellectuals*. Rochester: University of Rochester Press, 2001.

Fanon, Frantz. *The Wretched of the Earth* [1961], tr. by Constance Farrington. Harmondsworth: Penguin, 1985.

Farred, Grant. 'Unity and Difference in Black South Africa'. *Social Text* 31–2 (1992), 217–34.

Ferguson, Moira. '*Mansfield Park*: Slavery, Colonialism and Gender'. *Oxford Literary Review* 13 (1991), 118–39.

Fincham, Gail and Myrtle Hooper (eds.). *Under Postcolonial Eyes: Joseph Conrad after Empire*. Cape Town: University of Cape Town Press, 1996.

First, Ruth. *117 Days: An Account of Confinement and Interrogation under the South African Ninety-day Detention Law*. 1965; repr. London: Bloomsbury, 1988.

First, Ruth and Ann Scott. *Olive Schreiner: A Biography*. 1980; repr. London: The Women's Press, 1989.

Frankenberg, Ruth and Lata Mani, 'Crosscurrents, Crosstalk: Race, "Postcoloniality" and the Politics of Location'. In Mongia, *Contemporary Postcolonial Theory*.

Fredrickson, George M. *Black Liberation: A Comparative History of Black Ideologies in the United States and South Africa*. Oxford: Oxford University Press, 1996.

Fryer, Peter. *Staying Power: The History of Black People in Britain*. London: Pluto Press, 1984.

Gaines, Kevin K. *Uplifting the Race: Black Leadership, Politics, and Culture in the Twentieth Century*. Chapel Hill: University of North Carolina Press, 1996.

Ganguly, Keya. *States of Exception: Everyday Life and Postcolonial Identity*. Minneapolis: University of Minnesota Press, 2001.

Gates, Henry Louis, Jr (ed.). '*Race*', *Writing, and Difference*. Chicago: University of Chicago Press, 1986.

George, Olakunle. *Relocating Agency: Modernity and African Letters*. Albany: State University of New York Press, forthcoming.

Gershoni, Yekutiel. *Africans on African-Americans: The Creation and Uses of an African-American Myth*. New York: New York University Press, 1997.

Gervais, David. *Literary Englands: Versions of 'Englishness' in Modern Writing*. Cambridge: Cambridge University Press, 1993.

Gikandi, Simon. *Maps of Englishness: Writing Identity in the Culture of Colonialism*. New York: Columbia University Press, 1996.

Gilbert, Sandra M. and Susan Gubar. *No Man's Land. Volume 2: Sexchanges*. New Haven: Yale University Press, 1989.

Giles, Judy and Tim Middleton. *Writing Englishness, 1900–1950: An Introductory Sourcebook on National Identity*. London: Routledge, 1995.

Gilroy, Paul. *Against Race: Imagining Political Culture Beyond the Color Line*. Cambridge, MA: Harvard University Press, 2000.

Gilroy, Paul. *The Black Atlantic: Modernity and Double Consciousness*. London: Verso, 1993.

Gilroy, Paul. *Small Acts: Thoughts on the Politics of Black Cultures*. London: Serpent's Tail, 1993.

Gilroy, Paul. 'The End of Antiracism'. In Donald and Rattansi, '*Race*', *Culture, and Difference*.

Gilroy, Paul. '*There Ain't No Black in the Union Jack*': *The Cultural Politics of Race and Nation*. London: Unwin Hyman, 1987.

Gish, Stephen D. *Alfred B. Xuma: African, American, South African*. New York: New York University Press, 2000.

Goonetilleke, D.C.R.A. 'Appendix D: Major Textual Changes' in Joseph Conrad, *Heart of Darkness*. Peterboro, Ontario: Broadview Press, 1995.

Gordimer, Nadine. 'Cultural Globalization: Living on a Frontierless Land'. *Cooperation South* 2 (1998), 16–21.

Gordimer, Nadine. *The Essential Gesture: Writing, Politics and Places*, ed. and intro. by Stephen Clingman. Harmondsworth: Penguin, 1989.

Gray, Stephen. 'Plaatje's Shakespeare'. *English in Africa* [Grahamstown, South Africa] 4, 1 (1977), 1–6.

Green, Michael. '"Cultural Studies!", Said the Magistrate'. *News from Nowhere: Journal of Cultural Materialism* 8 (1990), 28–37.

Grossberg, Lawrence, Cary Nelson and Paula A. Treichler (eds.). *Cultural Studies*. London: Routledge, 1992.

Gutzmore, Cecil. 'Capital, "Black Youth" and Crime'. *Race and Class: A Journal for Black and Third World Liberation* 25, 2 (1983), 13–30.

Guy, Jeff. *The Destruction of the Zulu Kingdom: The Civil War in Zululand, 1879–1884*. London: Longman, 1979.

Haggard, H. Rider. 'Introductory Address' to T. Adams, *Garden City and Agriculture: How to Solve the Problem of Rural Depopulation*. London: Garden City Press Ltd, 1905.

Haggard, H. Rider. *Rural England*. London: Longmans, Green, and Co., 1902.

Haggard, H. Rider. *The Days of My Life*. London: Longmans, Green, and Co., 1926.

Haggard, H. Rider. *A Farmer's Year*. 1899; repr. London: Longmans, Green, and Co., 1906.

Haggard, H. Rider. 'Preface' to A. Wilmot, *Monomotapa (Rhodesia): Its Monuments, and its History from the Most Ancient Times to the Present Century*. London: T. Fisher Unwin, 1896.

Haggard, H. Rider. *Cetywayo and His White Neighbours. Or, Remarks on Recent Events in Zululand, Natal, and the Transvaal*, London: Truber and Co., 1882, 1888.

Hall, Stuart. 'Aspiration and Attitude … Reflections on Black Britain in the Nineties'. *New Formations: A Journal of Culture/Theory/Politics* 33 (1998), 38–46.

Hall, Stuart. 'The Local and the Global: Globalization and Ethnicity'. In McClintock, Mufti and Shohat, *Dangerous Liaisons*.

Hall, Stuart. 'Gramsci's Relevance for the Study of Race and Ethnicity'. In Morley and Chen, *Stuart Hall*.

Hall, Stuart. 'When Was the "Post-colonial"? Thinking at the Limit'. In Iain Chambers and Lidia Curti (eds.). *The Post-colonial Question: Common Skies, Divided Histories*. London: Routledge, 1996.

Hall, Stuart. 'Cultural Studies and its Theoretical Legacies'. In Grossberg, Nelson and Treichler, *Cultural Studies*.

Hall, Stuart and Martin Jacques (eds.). *New Times*. London: Lawrence and Wishart, 1990.

Hampson, Robert. 'Conrad and the Idea of Empire'. In Fincham and Hooper, *Under Postcolonial Eyes*.

Hanchard, Michael. 'Afro-modernity: Temporality, Politics, and the African Diaspora'. *Public Culture* 27 (1999), 245–68.

Hardt, Michael and Antonio Negri. *Empire*. Cambridge, MA: Harvard University Press, 2000.

Harrow, Kenneth W. (ed.). Special Issue: 'Nationalism'. *Research in African Literatures on Nationalism* 32, 3 (2001).

Hassan, Salah. 'Terminus Nation-state: Palestine and the Critique of Nationalism'. *New Formations: A Journal of Culture/Theory/Politics* 45 (2001), 54–71.

Hayford, Joseph Casely. *Ethiopia Unbound: Studies in Race Emancipation*. London: C. M. Phillips, 1911.

Hemstedt, Geoff. 'George Smiley and Post-imperial Nostalgia'. In Samuel, *Patriotism*.

Henshaw, Peter. 'Enfeebled Lion? How South Africans Viewed Britain, 1945–1961'. Paper presented at New England Workshop on Southern Africa annual meeting, November 2000.

Higgs, Catherine. *The Ghost of Equality: The Public Lives of D.D.T. Jabavu of South Africa, 1885–1959*. Athens: Ohio University Press, 2000.

Hobsbawm, E.J. *The Age of Empire: 1875–1914*. London: Weidenfeld and Nicolson, 1987.

Hochschild, Adam. *King Leopold's Ghost: A Story of Greed, Terror, and Heroism in Colonial Africa*. Boston and New York: Houghton Mifflin, 1998.

Horowitz, David. 'Ten Reasons Why Reparations for Slavery is a Bad Idea for Blacks – and Racist Too'. *The Black Scholar: Journal of Black Studies and Research* 31, 2 (2001), 48.

Horton, James Africanus. *West African Countries and Peoples, British and Native: with the Requirements Necessary for Establishing that Self-government Recommended by the Committee of the House of Commons, 1865; and a Vindication of the African Race*. London: W.J. Johnson, 1868.

Huggan, Graham. *The Post-colonial Exotic: Marketing the Margins*. London: Routledge, 2001.

Huggan, Graham. 'Prizing "Otherness": A Short History of the Booker'. *Studies in the Novel* 29, 3 (1997), 412–33.

Huggan, Graham. 'The Postcolonial Exotic: Rushdie's "Booker of Bookers"'. *Transition* 64 (1994), 22–9.

Hulme, Peter. 'The Locked Heart: The Creole Family Romance of *Wide Sargasso Sea*'. In Barker, Hulme and Iversen, *Colonial Discourse/Postcolonial Theory*.

Hutchinson, Earl Ofari. 'The Continuing Myth of Black Capitalism'. *The Black Scholar: Journal of Black Studies and Research* 23, 1 (1993), 16–21.

James, Tim. 'The Other "Other" in *Heart of Darkness*'. In Fincham and Hooper, *Under Postcolonial Eyes*.

James, Winston. *Holding Aloft the Banner of Ethiopia: Caribbean Radicalism in Early Twentieth-century America*. London: Verso, 1998.

James, Winston and Clive Harris (eds.). *Inside Babylon: The Caribbean Diaspora in Britain*. London: Verso, 1993.

Jameson, Fredric. 'Modernism and Imperialism'. In Seamus Deane (ed.) *Nationalism, Colonialism and Literature*. Minneapolis: University of Minnesota Press, 1990.

Johnson, David. *Shakespeare and South Africa*. Oxford: Clarendon Press, 1996.

Johnson, David. 'Importing Metropolitan Post-colonials'. *Current Writing. Text and Reception in Southern Africa* [Durban, South Africa] 6, 1 (1994), 73–85.

Jolly, Rosemary. 'Rehearsals of Liberation: Contemporary Postcolonial Discourse and the New South Africa'. In Mongia, *Contemporary Postcolonial Theory*.

Jones, Greta. *Social Darwinism and English Thought: The Interaction Between Biology and Social Theory*. Brighton: Harvester Press, 1982.

Joseph, Peniel. 'Where Blackness is Bright? Cuba, Africa, and Black Liberation During the Age of Civil Rights'. *New Formations: A Journal of Culture/ Theory/Politics* 45 (2001), 111–24.

Jusdanis, Gregory. *The Necessary Nation*. Princeton: Princeton University Press, 2001.

Kant, Immanuel. 'Of the Different Human Races' [1775]. In Robert Bernasconi and Tommy L. Lott (eds.). *The Idea of Race*. Indianapolis: Hackett, 2000.

Karis, Thomas and Gwendolen Carter (eds.). *From Protest to Challenge: A Documentary History of African Politics in South Africa 1882–1964*. Stanford: Hoover Institution Press, 1972.

Katz, Tamar. *Impressionist Subjects: Gender, Interiority, and Modernist Fiction in England*. Urbana: University of Illinois Press, 2000.

Kazanjian, David. 'Racial Governmentality: Thomas Jefferson and the African Colonization Movement in the United States'. *Alternation: Journal of the Centre for the Study of Southern African Literature and Languages* [Durban, South Africa] 5, 1 (1998), 39–84.

Keegan, Timothy. *Colonial South Africa and the Origins of the Racial Order.* London: Leicester University Press, 1996.

Kelley, Robin. 'A Poetics of Anticolonialism'. *Monthly Review* 51, 6 (1999), 1–21.

Kelley, Robin. 'How the West Was One: On the Uses and Limitations of Diaspora'. *The Black Scholar: Journal of Black Studies and Research* 30, 3–4 (2000), 31–5.

Kemp, Amanda Denise. *'Up from Slavery' and Other Narratives: Black South African Performances of the American Negro (1920–1943)*. Ph.D. dissertation, Northwestern University, 1997.

Korner, Stephan. *Kant.* Harmondsworth: Penguin, 1990.

Kruger, Loren. 'Apartheid on Display: South Africa Performs for New York'. *Diaspora: A Journal of Transnational Studies* 1, 2 (1991), 191–208.

Kumar, Amitava (ed.). *World Bank Literature.* Minneapolis: University of Minnesota Press, forthcoming.

Kundani, Arun. '"Stumbling On": Race, Class and England'. *Race and Class: A Journal for Black and Third World Liberation* 41, 4 (2000), 1–18.

Kuzwayo, Ellen. *Call Me Woman.* London: The Women's Press, 1985.

Kuzwayo, Ellen. *Sit Down and Listen: Stories from South Africa.* London: The Women's Press, 1990.

Landry, Donna and Gerald MacLean (eds.). *The Spivak Reader.* London: Routledge, 1996.

Lazarus, Neil. *Nationalism and Cultural Practice in the Postcolonial World.* Cambridge: Cambridge University Press, 1999.

Lazarus, Neil. 'Is a Counterculture of Modernity a Theory of Modernity?'. *Diaspora* 4, 3 (1995), 323–40.

Lazarus, Neil. 'Nationalist Consciousness and the Specificity of (Post)colonial Intellectualism'. In Barker, Hulme and Iversen, *Colonial Discourse/Postcolonial Theory.*

Lazarus, Neil. 'Disavowing Decolonization: Fanon, Nationalism, and the Problematic of Representation in Current Theories of Colonial Discourse'. *Research in African Literatures* 24 (1993), 69–98.

Lazarus, Neil. 'Postcolonialism and the Dilemmas of Nationalism: Aijaz Ahmad's Critique of Third-Worldism'. *Diaspora: A Journal of Transnational Studies* 2, 3 (1993), 373–400.

Lazarus, Neil. 'Doubting the New World Order: Marxism and Postmodernist Social Theory'. *Differences: A Journal of Feminist Cultural Studies* 3, 3 (1991), 94–138.

Lazarus, Neil. *Resistance in Postcolonial African Fiction*. New Haven: Yale University Press, 1990.

Lemelle, Sidney and Robin D.G. Kelley (eds.). *Imagining Home. Class, Culture and Nationalism in the African Diaspora*. London: Verso, 1994.

Lewis, David Levering. *W.E.B. Du Bois: Biography of a Race, 1868–1919*. New York: Henry Holt, 1993.

Limb, Peter. 'The "Other" Sol Plaatje: Rethinking Plaatje's Attitudes to Empire, Labour and Gender'. Paper presented at Rand Afrikaans University, Sociology Seminar series, July 2001.

Lloyd, David.'Ethnic Cultures, Minority Discourse and the State'. In Barker, Hulme and Iversen, *Colonial Discourse/Postcolonial Theory*.

Lloyd, David. 'Race under Representation'. *Oxford Literary Review* 13, 1–2 (1991), 62–94.

Loomba, Ania. *Colonialism/Postcolonialism*. London: Routledge, 1998.

Loomba, Ania. 'Overworlding the Third World'. *Oxford Literary Review*, 13 (1991), 164–92.

Louw, P. Eric. 'Rethinking Cultural Studies to Meet the Challenge of the "Information Age" in South Africa'. *Social Dynamics* [Cape Town, South Africa] 21, 1 (1995), 71–8.

Low, Gail. *White Skins, Black Masks: Representation and Colonialism*. London: Routledge, 1996.

Lucas, John. *England and Englishness: Ideas of Nationhood in English Poetry, 1688–1900*. London: Hogarth Press, 1990.

McClintock, Anne, Aamir Mufti and Ella Shohat (eds.). *Dangerous Liaisons: Gender, Nation, and Postcolonial Perspectives*. London: University of Minnesota Press, 1997.

McClintock, Anne. *Imperial Leather: Race, Gender and Sexuality in the Colonial Contest*. London: Routledge, 1995.

McClintock, Anne. 'Maidens, Maps and Mines: *King Solomon's Mines* and the Reinvention of Patriarchy in Colonial South Africa'. In Cheryll Walker (ed.) *Women and Gender in Southern Africa to 1945*. London: James Currey, 1990.

McClure, J.A. *Late Imperial Romance*. London: Verso, 1994.

MacKenzie, John M. *Propaganda and Empire: The Manipulation of British Public Opinion, 1880–1960*. Manchester: Manchester University Press, 1984.

MacKenzie, John M. (ed.), *Imperialism and Popular Culture*. Manchester: Manchester University Press, 1986.

McLeod, John. *Beginning Postcolonialism*. Manchester: Manchester University Press, 2000.

McRobbie, Angela. 'Looking Back at New Times and its Critics'. In Morley and Chen *Stuart Hall*.

Magona, Sindiwe. *To My Children's Children: An Autobiography.* London: The Women's Press, 1991.

Magubane, Bernard. *The Making of a Racist State: British Imperialism and the Union of South Africa, 1875–1910.* Trenton: Africa World Press, 1996.

Malan, Rian. *My Traitor's Heart: Blood and Bad Dreams: A South African Explores the Madness in His Country, His Tribe and Himself.* London: Vintage, 1990.

Mandela, Nelson. *Long Walk to Freedom: The Autobiography of Nelson Mandela.* London: Little, Brown and Company, 1994.

Mandela, Winnie. *Part of My Soul,* ed. by Anne Benjamin and adapted by Mary Benson. Harmondsworth: Penguin, 1985.

Marks, Shula (ed.). *Not Either an Experimental Doll: The Separate Worlds of Three South African Women.* London: The Women's Press, 1987.

Masilela, Ntongela. 'The "Black Atlantic" and African Modernity in South Africa'. *Research in African Literatures* 27 (1997), 88–96.

Matory, J. Lorand. 'Surpassing "Survival": On the Urbanity of "Traditional Religion" in the Afro-Atlantic World'. *The Black Scholar: Journal of Black Studies and Research* 30, 3–4 (2000), 36–43.

Mazrui, Ali A. 'A Tale of Two Continents: Africa, Asia and the Dialectic of Globalization'. *Cooperation South* 2 (1998), 118–33.

Mercer, Kobena. *Welcome to the Jungle: New Positions in Black Cultural Studies.* London: Routledge, 1994.

Midgley, Clare (ed.). *Gender and Imperialism.* Manchester: Manchester University Press, 1998.

Mills, Charles W. *Blackness Visible: Essays on Philosophy and Race.* Ithaca: Cornell University Press, 1998.

Mills, Sara. *Discourses of Difference: An Analysis of Women's Travel Writing and Colonialism.* London: Routledge, 1993.

Mirza, Heidi Safia (ed.). *Black British Feminism: A Reader.* London: Routledge, 1997.

Miyoshi, Masao. 'Sites of Resistance in the Global Economy'. In Ansell-Pearson, Parry and Squires, *Cultural Readings of Imperialism.*

Miyoshi, Masao. 'A Borderless World? From Colonialism to Transnationalism and the Decline of the Nation-State'. *Critical Inquiry* 19 (1993), 726–51.

Mngadi, Sikhumbuzo. 'The Politics of Historical Representation in the Context of Global Capitalism'. In Johannes A. Smit, Johan van Wyk and Jean-Phillipe Wade (eds.) *Rethinking South African Literary History.* Durban: Y Press, 1996.

Molema, S.M. *The Bantu Past and Present: An Ethnographical and Historical Study of the Native Races of South Africa.* Edinburgh: W. Green and Son Ltd., 1920.

Mongia, Padmini (ed.). *Contemporary Postcolonial Theory: A Reader.* London: Arnold, 1996.

Moore-Gilbert, Bart. *Postcolonial Theory: Contexts, Practices, Politics.* London: Verso, 1997.

Morley, David and Kuan-Hsing Chen (eds.). *Stuart Hall: Critical Dialogues in Cultural Studies.* London: Routledge, 1996.

Morris, James. *Pax Britannica:The Climax of an Empire.* Harmondworth: Penguin, 1968.

Moses, Wilson. *The Golden Age of Black Nationalism, 1850–1925.* Oxford: Oxford University Press, 1978.

Mudimbe, V.Y. and Sabine Engel (eds.). Special Issue: 'Diaspora and Immigration'. *South Atlantic Quarterly* 98, 1–2 (1999).

Mudimbe, V.Y. *The Invention of Africa: Gnosis, Philosophy, and the Order of Knowledge.* London: James Currey, 1988.

Mulhern, Francis (ed.). *Contemporary Marxist Literary Criticism.* London: Longman, 1992.

Munshi, Sherally. *Cultural Politics and Arundhati Roy.* Senior Honors Thesis, Brown University, 2000.

Nelson, Jr, William E. *Black Atlantic Politics: Dilemmas of Political Empowerment in Boston and Liverpool.* Albany: State University of New York Press, 2000.

Nichols, Pam. 'A Snowball in Africa with a Chance of Flourishing: Writing Centres as Shifters of Power in a South African University'. *Current Writing. Text and Reception in Southern Africa* [Durban, South Africa] 10, 2 (1998), 84–95.

Nixon, Rob. *Homelands, Harlem, and Hollywood: South African Culture and the World Beyond.* London: Routledge, 1994.

Nkrumah, Kwame. *Neo-colonialism: The Last Stage of Imperialism.* London: Heinemann, 1965.

Nyerere, Julius. *Ujamaa: Essays on Socialism.* Dar es Salaam: Oxford University Press, 1968.

Ong, Aihwa. 'Flexible Citizenship among Chinese Cosmopolitans'. In Cheah and Robbins, *Cosmopolitics.*

Ong, Aihwa. *Flexible Citizenship: The Cultural Logics of Transnationality.* Durham: Duke University Press, 1998.

Orkin, Martin. 'The Politics of Editing the Shakespeare Text in South Africa'. *Current Writing: Text and Reception in Southern Africa* [Durban, South Africa] 5, 1 (1993), 48–59.

Orkin, Martin. *Shakespeare Against Apartheid.* Craighall: Ad. Donker, 1987.

Ousmane, Sembene. *Black Docker,* tr. by Ros Schwartz. 1973; repr. London: Heinemann, 1986.

Padmore, George. *How Britain Rules Africa.* London: Wishart Books, 1936.

Palmer, Colin. 'The African Diaspora'. *The Black Scholar: Journal of Black Studies and Research* 30, 3–4 (2000), 56–9.

Parr, Tony. 'Saving Literature', *Scrutiny2: Issues in English Studies in Southern Africa* [Pretoria, South Africa] 1, 1–2 (1996), 70–7.

Parry, Benita. 'Liberation Theory: Variations on Themes of Marxism and Modernity'. In Bartolovich and Lazarus, *Marxism and Modernity*.

Parry, Benita. *Delusions and Discoveries: Studies on India in the British Imagination, 1880–1930*, with a foreword by Michael Sprinker. 1972; repr. London: Verso, 1998.

Parry, Benita. 'Materiality and Mystification in *A Passage to India*'. *Novel: A Forum on Fiction* 31, 2 (1998), 174–94.

Parry, Benita. 'Speech and Silence in the Fictions of J.M. Coetzee'. In Attridge and Jolly, *Writing South Africa*.

Parry, Benita. '*Tono-Bungay*: Modernisation, Modernity and Imperialism, or the Failed Electrification of the Empire'. *New Formations: A Journal of Culture/Theory/Politics* 34 (1998), 91–108

Parry, Benita. 'Narrating Imperialism: *Nostromo*'s Dystopia'. In Ansell-Pearson, Parry and Squires, *Cultural Readings of Imperialism*.

Parry, Benita. 'Signs of Our Times: Discussion of Homi Bhabha's *The Location of Culture*', *Third Text* 28–9 (1994), 5–24.

Parry, Benita. 'Resistance Theory/Theorising Resistance or Two Cheers for Nativism'. In Barker, Hulme and Iversen, *Colonial Discourse/Postcolonial Theory*.

Parry, Benita. 'Review of Aijaz Ahmad's *In Theory*'. *History Workshop Journal* 36 (1993), 232–41.

Parry, Benita. 'Conrad and England'. In Samuel, *Patriotism*.

Parry, Benita. 'The Content and Discontents of Kipling's Imperialism'. *New Formations: A Journal of Culture/Theory/Politics* 6 (1988), 84–112.

Parry, Benita. 'Problems in Current Theories of Colonial Discourse'. *Oxford Literary Review* 9, 1–2 (1987), 27–58.

Parry, Benita. *Conrad and Imperialism*. London: Macmillan, 1983.

Peach, Linden. 'Yorkshire and the Origins of Cultural Politics'. *Red Letters: A Review of Cultural Politics* 27 (1990), 6.

Pearson, Karl. *National Life from the Standpoint of Science*. London: Adam and Charles Black, 1901.

Pettinger, Alasdair. *Always Elsewhere: Travels of the Black Atlantic*. London: Cassell, 1998.

Phelps, J.M. 'Sol Plaatje's *Mhudi* and Democratic Government'. *English Studies in Africa* [Johannesburg, South Africa] 36, 1 (1993), 47–56.

Phillips, Caryl. *The Atlantic Sound*. New York: Knopf, 2000.

Phillips, Caryl. *Extravagant Strangers*. London: Faber, 1998.

Phillips, Caryl. *The European Tribe*. London: Faber, 1987.

Phillips, Lawrence. 'The Canker of Empire: Colonialism, Autobiography and the Representation of Illness: Jack London and Robert Louis Stevenson in the Marquesas'. In Chrisman and Parry, *Postcolonial Theory and Criticism*.

Phillips, Lawrence. 'Lost in Space: Siting/citing the In-between of Homi K. Bhabha's *The Location of Culture*'. *Scrutiny2: Issues in English Studies in Southern Africa* [Pretoria, South Africa] 3, 1 (1998), 16–25.

Phillips, Mike and Trevor Phillips. *Windrush*. London: HarperCollins, 1999.

Pimomo, Paulus. 'The Centre Writes/Strikes Back?'. *Critical Quarterly* 33, 3 (1991), 43–7.

Plaatje, Solomon T. *Native Life in South Africa Before and Since the European War and the Boer Rebellion* [1916], intro. by Brian Willan, foreword by Bessie Head. Athens: Ohio University Press, 1991.

Porter, Bernard. *Critics of Empire: British Radical Attitudes to Colonialism in Africa, 1895–1914*. London: Macmillan, 1968.

Porter, Dennis. '*Orientalism* and its Problems'. In Williams and Chrisman *Colonial Discourse and Post-colonial Theory*.

Pratt, Mary Louise. *Imperial Eyes: Travel Writing and Transculturation*. London: Routledge, 1992.

Premnath, Gautam. 'Lonely Londoner: V.S. Naipaul and "The God of the City"'. In Pamela Gilbert (ed.) *Imagined Londons*. Albany: State University of New York Press, forthcoming.

Premnath, Gautam. 'Remembering Fanon, Decolonizing Diaspora'. In Chrisman and Parry, *Postcolonial Theory and Criticism*.

Procter, James (ed.). *Writing Black Britain, 1948–98*. Manchester: Manchester University Press, 2000.

Quayson, Ato. *Strategic Transformations in Nigerian Writing: Orality and History in the Work of Reverend Samuel Johnson, Amos Tutuola, Wole Soyinka and Ben Okri*. Bloomington: Indiana University Press, 1997.

Race and Class: A Journal for Black and Third World Liberation 43, 2 (2001). Special issue 'The Three Faces of British Racism'.

Race and Class: A Journal for Black and Third World Liberation 40, 2–3 (1999). Special issue 'The Threat of Globalism'.

Ray, Sangeeta and Henry Schwarz. 'Postcolonial Discourse: The Raw and the Cooked'. *ARIEL: A Review of International English Literature* 26, 1 (1995), 147–66.

Reed, Adolph. *W.E.B. Du Bois and American Political Thought: Fabianism and the Color Line*. Oxford: Oxford University Press, 1997.

Richards, Thomas. *The Commodity Culture of Victorian England: Advertising and Spectacle, 1851–1914*. London: Verso, 1991.

Robbins, Bruce. *Feeling Global: Internationalism in Distress*. New York: New York University Press, 1999.

Robbins, Bruce, Mary-Louise Pratt, Jonathan Arac, R. Radhakrishnan and Edward Said. 'Edward Said's *Culture and Imperialism*: A Symposium'. *Social Text* 40 (1994), 1–38.

Roberts, Richard. 'The Construction of Cultures in Diaspora: African and African New World Experiences'. *South Atlantic Quarterly* 98, 1–2 (1999), 177–90.

Robinson, Cedric. *Black Marxism: The Making of the Black Radical Tradition:* (1983); repr. Chapel Hill: University of North Carolina Press, 2000.

Rosaldo, Renato. 'Imperialist Nostalgia'. *Representations* 26 (1989), 107–21.

Rose, Jacqueline. *States of Fantasy*. Oxford: Clarendon Press, 1996.

Rushdie, Salman. 'Outside the Whale' [1984]. *Imaginary Homelands: Essays and Criticism 1981–1991*. London: Granta, 1991.

Said, Edward. *Culture and Imperialism*. London: Chatto, 1993.

Said, Edward. *Orientalism*. Harmondsworth: Peregrine Books, 1978.

Samuel, Raphael (ed.). *Patriotism: The Making and Unmaking of British National Identity. Volume 3: National Fictions*. London: Routledge, 1989.

San Juan, Jr, E. *Beyond Postcolonial Theory*. New York: St Martin's Press, 1998.

San Juan, Jr, E. 'On the Limits of "Postcolonial" Theory: Trespassing Letters from the "Third World"'. *ARIEL: A Review of International English Literature* 26, 3 (1995), 89–115.

Sandhu, Sukhdev. 'Pop Goes the Centre: Hanif Kureishi's London'. In Chrisman and Parry, *Postcolonial Theory and Criticism*.

Schalkwyk, David. 'Portrait and Proxy: Representing Plaatje and Plaatje Represented'. *Scrutiny 2: Issues in English Studies in Southern Africa* [Pretoria, South Africa] 4, 2 (1999), 14–29.

Schalkwyk, David and Lerothodi Lapula. 'Solomon Plaatje, William Shakespeare, and the Translations of Culture'. *Pretexts: Literary and Cultural Studies* 9, 1 (2000), 9–26.

Schwarz, Bill. 'Black Metropolis, White England'. In Mica Nava and Alan O'Shea (eds.) *Modern Times: Reflections on a Century of English Modernity*. London: Routledge, 1996.

Schwarz, Bill. 'Conquerors of Truth: Reflections on Postcolonial Theory'. In Schwarz, *The Expansion of England*.

Schwarz, Bill (ed.). *The Expansion of England: Race, Ethnicity and Cultural History*. London: Routledge, 1996.

Schwarz, Bill. '"The Only White Man in There": The Re-racialisation of England, 1956–1968'. *Race and Class: A Journal for Black and Third World Liberation* 38, 1 (1996), 65–78.

Schwarz, Henry and Sangeeta Ray (eds.). *A Companion to Postcolonial Studies*. Oxford: Blackwell, 2000.

Semmel, Bernard. *Imperialism and Social Reform: English Social-imperial Thought, 1895–1914*. London: Allen and Unwin, 1960.

Senghor, Leopold Sédar. *On African Socialism*. London: Pall Mall, 1964.

Sharpe, Jenny. *Allegories of Empire: The Figure of Woman in the Colonial Text*. Minneapolis: University of Minnesota Press, 1993.

Showalter, Elaine. *Sexual Anarchy: Gender and Culture at the Fin de Siècle*. London: Bloomsbury, 1991.

Singh, Amritjit and Peter Schmidt (eds.). *Postcolonial Theory and the United States: Race, Ethnicity, and Literature*. Jackson: University Press of Mississippi, 2000.

Sivanandan, A. *Communities of Resistance: Writings on Black Struggles for Socialism*. London: Verso, 1990.

Sivanandan, A. *A Different Hunger: Writings on Black Resistance*. London: Pluto, 1982.

Sole, Kelwyn. 'Writing South Africa'. *Alternation: Journal of the Centre for the Study of Southern African Literature and Languages* [Durban, South Africa] 5, 1 (1998), 256–66.

Sole, Kelwyn. 'South Africa Passes the Posts'. *Alternation: Journal of the Centre for the Study of Southern African Literature and Languages* [Durban, South Africa] 4, 1 (1997), 116–51.

Sole, Kelwyn. 'Democratising Culture and Literature in a "New South Africa": Organisation and Theory'. *Current Writing: Text and Reception in Southern Africa* [Durban, South Africa] 6, 2 (1994), 1–37.

Solomos, John. *Race and Racism in Britain*. New York: St Martin's Press, 1993.

Spivak, Gayatri C. *A Critique of Postcolonial Reason: Toward a History of the Vanishing Present*. Cambridge, MA and London: Harvard University Press, 1999.

Spivak, Gayatri C. 'Subaltern Talk: Interview with the Editors'. In Landry and MacLean, *The Spivak Reader*.

Spivak, Gayatri C. 'Can the Subaltern Speak? Speculations on Widow Sacrifice'. In Williams and Chrisman, *Colonial Discourse and Post-colonial Theory*.

Spivak, Gayatri C. 'Three Women's Texts and a Critique of Imperialism'. In Gates, Jr *'Race', Writing, and Difference*.

Spurr, David. *The Rhetoric of Empire: Colonial Discourse in Journalism, Travel Writing and Imperial Administration*. Durham: Duke University Press, 1993.

Stoler, Ann Laura. 'Making Empire Respectable: The Politics of Race and Sexual Morality in Twentieth-century Colonial Cultures'. In McClintock, Mufti and Shohat, *Dangerous Liaisons*.

Stott, Rebecca. 'The Dark Continent: Africa as Female Body in Haggard's Adventure Fiction'. *Feminist Review* 32 (1989), 69–89.

Stratton, Jon and Ien Ang. 'On the Impossibility of a Global Cultural Studies: "British" Cultural Studies in an "International" Frame'. In Morley and Chen, *Stuart Hall*.

Thomas, Nicholas. *Colonialism's Culture: Anthropology, Travel and Government*. Cambridge: Polity Press, 1994.

Tlali, Miriam. *Soweto Stories*, intro. by Lauretta Ngcobo. London: Pandora Press, 1989.

Tomaselli, Keyan G. 'Reading Stuart Hall in Southern Africa'. In Paul Gilroy, Lawrence Grossberg and Angela McRobbie (eds.) *Without Guarantees: In Honour of Stuart Hall*. London: Verso, 2000.

Tomaselli, Keyan G. 'Cultural Studies and Renaissance in Africa: Recovering Praxis'. *Scrutiny2: Issues in English Studies in Southern Africa* [Pretoria, South Africa] 4, 2 (1999), 43–8.

Torgovnick, Marianna. *Gone Primitive: Savage Intellects, Modern Lives*. Chicago: University of Chicago Press, 1990.

Verwoerd, Wilhelm. 'Continuing the Discussion: Reflections from within the Truth and Reconciliation Commission'. *Current Writing: Text and Reception in Southern Africa* [Durban, South Africa] 8, 2 (1996), 66–85.

Visser, Nick. 'Shakespeare and Hanekom, *King Lear* and Land'. *Textual Practice* 11, 1 (1997), 25–38.

Von Eschen, Penny M. *Race Against Empire: Black Americans and Anticolonialism, 1937–1957*. Ithaca: Cornell University Press, 1997.

Walters, Ronald. *Pan Africanism in the African Diaspora*. Detroit: Wayne State University Press, 1993.

Wamba, Philippe. *Kinship: A Family's Journey in Africa and America*. New York: Penguin, 1999.

Wambu, Onyekachi (ed.). *Empire Windrush: Fifty Years of Writing About Black Britain*. London: Gollancz, 1998.

Ware, Vron. *Beyond the Pale: White Women, Racism and History*. London: Verso, 1992.

Wasafiri: Caribbean, African, Asian and Associated Literatures in English 29 (1999), Special Issue 'Taking the Cake: Black Writing in Britain'.

Watson, Tim. 'Indian and Irish Unrest in Kipling's *Kim*'. In Chrisman and Parry, *Postcolonial Theory and Criticism*.

Weinbaum, Alys Eve. 'Reproducing Racial Globality: W.E.B. du Bois and the Sexual Politics of Black Internationalism'. *Social Text* 67, 19, 2 (2001), 15–41.

Willan, Brian (ed.). *Sol Plaatje: Selected Writings*. Athens: Ohio University Press, 1996.

Willan, Brian. *Sol Plaatje: South African Nationalist, 1876–1932*. London: Heinemann, 1984.

Williams, Eric. *Capitalism and Slavery*. Chapel Hill: University of North Carolina Press, 1944.

Williams, Patrick and Laura Chrisman (eds.). *Colonial Discourse and Postcolonial Theory: A Reader*. Hemel Hempstead: Harvester Wheatsheaf Press, 1993.

Williams, Raymond. *The Politics of Modernism: Against the New Conformists*, ed. and intro. by Tony Pinkney. London: Verso, 1989.

Williams, Raymond. *The Country and the City*. London: Hogarth, 1973.

Wood, Marcus. *Blind Memory: Visual Representations of Slavery in England and America, 1780–1865*. Manchester: Manchester University Press, 2000.

Yegenoglu, Meyda and Mahmut Mutman. 'Mapping the Present: Interview with Gayatri Spivak'. *New Formations: A Journal of Culture/Theory/Politics* 45 (2001), 9–23.

Young, Robert J.C. *Postcolonialism: An Historical Introduction*. Oxford: Blackwell, 2001.

Young, Robert J.C. 'Review of Gayatri Spivak's *Outside in the Teaching Machine*'. *Textual Practice* 10, 1 (1996), 228–38.

Young, Robert J.C. *White Mythologies: Writing History and the West*. London: Routledge 1990.

Zachernuk, Philip. *Colonial Subjects: An African Intelligentsia and Atlantic Ideas*. Charlottesville: University Press of Virginia, 2000.

Zeleza, Paul. *Manufacturing African Studies and Crises*. Dakar: Codesria, 1997.

Index

Note: literary works can be found under authors' names; 'n' after a page reference indicates the number of a note on that page.